Cyclical Time and Ismaili Gnosis

ISLAMIC TEXTS AND CONTEXTS

General Editor
Hermann Landolt
Professor of Islamic Studies, McGill University, Montreal
and The Institute of Ismaili Studies, London

Assistant Editors

Elizabeth Brine
Dr James Morris
The Institute of Ismaili Studies

Cyclical Time and Ismaili Gnosis

Henry Corbin

Routledge
Taylor & Francis Group
LONDON AND NEW YORK

First published in 1983 by
Kegan Paul International

This edition first published in 2010 by
Routledge
2 Park Square, Milton Park, Abingdon, Oxon, OX14 4RN

Simultaneously published in the USA and Canada
by Routledge
711 Third Avenue, New York, NY 10017

Routledge is an imprint of the Taylor & Francis Group, an informa business

Transferred to Digital Printing 2010

British Library Cataloguing in Publication Data
A catalogue record for this book is available from the British Library

ISBN 13: 978-0-415-86165-6 (pbk)
ISBN 13: 978-0-7103-0047-8 (hbk)

The Institute of Ismaili Studies, London

The Institute of Ismaili Studies was established in December 1977 with the object of promoting scholarship and learning in Islam, and a better understanding of other faiths, beliefs and practices.

Its programmes are designed to encourage a balanced study of Islam and the diversity that exists within its fundamental unity. They also deal with the contemporary situation of the Islamic World, focusing on issues that are critical to its well-being.

Since 1980 the Institute has been affiliated to McGill University, Montreal, Canada. It also works in association with other universities.

With the co-operation of McGill University, the Institute runs a Department of Graduate Studies and Research (London and Paris). The series "Islamic Texts and Contexts" is edited by this Department.

The views expressed in this series are those of the respective authors.

Contents

Editorial Note

The three articles contained in this volume, concerning the main themes of early Ismaili thought, were originally presented by Professor Corbin as lectures before learned audiences, the first two at the annual Eranos conferences and the third at a conference given under the auspices of the Accademia Nazionale dei Lincei, Rome. In reprinting them here the assistance of Mme Stella Corbin is gratefully acknowledged.

"Le Temps Cyclique dans le Mazdéisme et dans l'Ismaélisme" was delivered at the Eranos conference of 1951 (general theme: "Man and Time"), and appeared in the *Eranos-Jahrbuch* XX (1951), Zurich, 1952. The English translation by Ralph Manheim, "Cyclical Time in Mazdaism and Ismailism," was first published in *Man and Time: Papers from the Eranos Yearbooks* (Bollingen Series XXX, volume 3), edited by Joseph Campbell, New York, Princeton University Press, and London, Routledge & Kegan Paul, 1957, reprinted by permission of Princeton University Press and Routledge & Kegan Paul Ltd.

"Epiphanie Divine et Naissance Spirituelle dans la Gnose Ismaélienne" was delivered at the Eranos conference in 1954 (general theme: "Man and Transformation"), and was published in the *Eranos-Jahrbuch* XXIII (1954), Zurich, 1955. The English translation by Ralph Manheim, "Divine Epiphany and Spiritual Birth in Ismailian Gnosis," was first published in *Man and Transformation: Papers from the Eranos Yearbooks* (Bollingen Series XXX, volume 5), edited by Joseph Campbell, New York, Princeton University Press and London, Routledge & Kegan Paul, 1964, reprinted by permission of Princeton University Press and Routledge & Kegan Paul Ltd.

EDITORIAL NOTE

"De la gnose antique à la gnose ismaélienne" was the title of a lecture delivered in Rome in 1956, at the XIIth Convegno "Volta": the theme of that conference was "Orient and Occident in the Middle Ages." It was published in the proceedings of that conference, *Oriente e Occidente nel Medioevo*, Rome, Accademia Nazionale dei Lincei, 1957. The English translation, "From the Gnosis of Antiquity to Ismaili Gnosis," was prepared for this volume by James W. Morris.

In accordance with the wishes of the Publishers, the first two articles have been reprinted exactly as they appeared in the original English translations (printing errors excepted). For the third article, a few references have been completed or brought up to date (identified by square brackets), while the transliteration system, following the pattern set in the preceding article, has been slightly adapted to English usage. The indices for this volume were prepared by the Institute's editorial staff.

Books by Henry Corbin available in English translation

Avicenna and the Visionary Recital (Bollingen Series, LXVI), translated by W. R. Trask, New York, 1960; reprinted Spring Books, Dallas, 1980 (paperback edition).

Creative Imagination in the Ṣūfism of Ibn 'Arabī (Bollingen Series, XCI), translated by Ralph Manheim, Princeton University Press, 1969, Routledge & Kegan Paul, 1970.

Spiritual Body and Celestial Earth: From Mazdean Iran to Shī'ite Iran (Bollingen Series, XCI:2), translated by N. Pearson, Princeton University Press, 1977.

The Man of Light in Iranian Sufism, translated by N. Pearson, Shambhala Publications Inc., Boulder and London, 1978.

I

Cyclical Time in Mazdaism and Ismailism

1. Cyclical Time in Mazdaism

THE AGES OF THE WORLD IN ZOROASTRIAN MAZDAISM

A little manual of Mazdean doctrine, written in Pahlavi and dating from the fourth century of our era, contains a number of questions the answers to which everyone over the age of fifteen is supposed to know. The first questions are: "Who am I and to whom do I belong? Whence have I come and whither am I returning? What is my lineage and what is my race? What is my proper calling in earthly existence? . . . Did I come from the celestial world, or is it in the earthly world that I began to be? Do I belong to Ōhrmazd or to Ahriman? To the angels or the demons?"[1]

And here are the answers:

> I came from the celestial world (*mēnōk*), it is not in the terrestrial world (*gētīk*) that I began to be. I was originally manifested in the spiritual state, my original state is not the terrestrial state.[2]

1 *Pand Nāmak i Zartusht* (The Book of Counsels of Zartusht). The short treatise is also entitled *Čītak Handarz i Pōryōtkeshān* (Selected Instructions of the First Doctors of the Faith). Its authorship remains doubtful. One tradition attributes it to the Grand Mōbaδ Āturpat i Mahraspandān, a high dignitary of the Mazdean clergy whom the Sassanid King Shapur II (A.D. 309–79) had empowered to establish the definitive canonical text of the Avesta, divided into twenty-one books or *nask*. A little "book of counsels" by this author has come down to us. It is dedicated to his son Zartusht (so named to assure him of the holy prophet Zarathustra's spiritual sponsorship). But a "book of counsels" is also attributed to his son, who in his turn was Grand Mōbaδ under Ardashir II (A.D. 379–83). A critical edition of our *Pand Nāmak* has been published by H. S. Nyberg in *Hilfsbuch des Pehlevi*, Vol. I (Uppsala, 1928), pp. 17–30, 68–69. Cf. also J. C. Tarapore, *Pahlavi Andarz-Nāmak* (Bombay, 1933). The questions quoted here occur in Strophe 1.

2 On the contrast between the meanings of the verbs *āfrītan* and *būtan*, cf. Nyberg, *Hilfsbuch des Pehlevi*, Vol. II (Uppsala and Leipzig, 1931), Glossary, *s.v.*; and Heinrich Junker, "Über iranische Quellen der hellenistischen Aion-Vorstellung," *Vorträge der Bibliothek Warburg* (Leipzig), I (1923), 133–34.

> I belong to Ōhrmazd (Ahura Mazda, the Lord Wisdom), not to Ahriman (the Spirit of Evil and of Darkness); I belong to the angels, not to the demons. . . . I am the creature of Ōhrmazd, not the creature of Ahriman. I hold my lineage and my race from Gayōmart (primordial Man, Anthropos). My mother is Spandarmat (Angel of the Earth), my father is Ōhrmazd. . . . The accomplishment of my vocation consists in this: to think of Ōhrmazd as present Existence (*hastīh*), which has always existed (*hamē-būtīh*), and will always exist (*hamē-bāvetīh*). To think of him as immortal sovereignty, as Unlimitation and Purity. To think of Ahriman as pure negativity (*nestīh*), exhausting himself in nothingness (*avīn-būtīh*), as the Evil Spirit who formerly did not exist in this Creation, and who one day will cease to exist in Ōhrmazd's Creation and who will collapse at the final time.[3] To consider my true self as belonging to Ōhrmazd and the Archangels (*Amahraspandān*).

These few simple but decisive formulas project the responses simultaneously on a horizon both of pre-existence and of superexistence. They imply that the moment of birth and the moment of death, recorded so carefully in our vital statistics, are neither our absolute beginning nor our absolute end. They imply that time, as we commonly conceive of it, as a line of indeterminate length, losing itself in the mists of the past and the future, has literally no sense, but is simply the absurd. If a modern mathematical philosophy has taught us to conceive of time as a fourth dimension added to the three dimensions of space, we may say that the myth of Mazdean cosmogony reveals to us something in the nature of still another dimension (a fifth dimension?), the one which situates a being's "elevation" of light or depth of darkness.

The terms "elevation," or "height," and "depth" suggest the dimensions of visual space,[4] and the exigencies of language compel the myth to place the power of light and the opposing power of darkness in this sort of spatial relation to one another. Yet any geometrical representation is doomed to failure, since we must conceive of a space both infinite and limited. For in point of fact, the primordial Light and Darkness do not occupy a space

3 Strophes 2, 3. Cf. the somewhat different translation in Junker, p. 133 (*avīn būtīh*, to have become invisible).

4 Or better still, since this light has been announced to us as vibrating eternally with the voice of Ōhrmazd (cf. below), we might evoke the idea of a sonorous space: a being in whom the archetypal dimension that shines through resembles a musical motif which, in marking its own outline, also utters the promise of its metamorphoses. In it the limited and the unlimited coincide.

that is situated and defined in advance; they establish a space that is absolutely peculiar to themselves, that can only be measured in terms of light and darkness. The height or depth of light may be designated as eternal Time, and the space of light, in which awaken the creatures of light, who fulfill the thoughts of this light, is eternally born from this eternal Time.

It is then in this depth of light that originates the personal existence of the being who recognizes himself on earth "as belonging to Ōhrmazd and the Archangels." But the time in which are inscribed the moment of his coming into the earthly form of existence and the moment of his final departure from it is not the eternal Time of this depth of light. It is a time which originated in it, which is in its image, but which is necessitated and limited by the acts of a cosmic drama of which it marks the prelude and whose conclusion will also be its own. Deriving from this eternal Time it returns to its origin,[5] taking with it the beings who intervene as the cast of characters in its cycle, because in this drama each one of them "personifies" a permanent role which was assigned them by another Time. Essentially a "time of return," it has the form of a cycle. The Mazdean cosmogony tells us that time has two essential aspects: the Time without shore, without origin (*Zervān-i akanārak*), eternal Time; and limited time or "the time of long domination" (*Zervān-i deranγ xvatāi*), the Αἰών in the strict sense, although eternal Time also tends to assume this name. Eternal Time is the paradigm, the model of limited time that was made in its image. And that is why our time itself, as a dimension of earthly existence, gives an intimation of a dimension other than its own chronological dimension—a dimension of light which determines its form and meaning. Inversely, the absence or annihilation of this dimension measures the depth of darkness of one who is in this time. Since it discloses this relation with the origin, the dimension of light may be called the archetypal dimension; as such, it characterizes and situates a being of Light, a being of Ohrmazdean essence. Forming a bond between this being and an eternal Time to which the limited time of his actual form of existence carries him back, this archetypal di-

5 Cf. H. S. Nyberg, "Questions de cosmogonie et de cosmologie mazdéennes," *Journal asiatique* (Paris), CCXIV : 2 (Apr.–June, 1929) ["Questions," I], p. 214, li. 9. Note the use of the verb *gumečit* for the return of limited time into unlimited Time; this is the same word which serves to designate the "mixture" (*gumečishn*) of Darkness with Light. Cf. also R. C. Zaehner, "Zurvanica," III, *Bulletin of the School of Oriental Studies* (London), IX (1937–39), *Dēnkart* text 228 on p. 880, and the long extract from *Dēnkart* 282 on pp. 883–84.

mension commands a very specific experience of eternity, or rather the anticipation which makes possible—or which translates—the conception of a cyclical time that is not the Time of an eternal return, but the time of a return to an eternal origin.

The concept of this dimension of light, an archetypal dimension because it grounds every being in another self which keeps eternally ahead of him, can provide us with the key to a celestial world inhabited by figures who are constituted and governed in their being by a law of their own, a law with its very own logic. The responses we have just read refer to the twofold plane or twofold state of being which characterizes Mazdean ontology, and which is designated by the two terms *mēnōk* and *gētīk*. We must take care not to reduce the contrast they express to a Platonic schema pure and simple. We are not dealing precisely with an opposition between idea and matter, or between the universal and the perceptible. *Mēnōk* should, rather, be translated by a celestial, invisible, spiritual, but perfectly concrete state. *Gētīk*[6] designates an earthly visible, material state, but of a matter which is in itself wholly luminous, a matter immaterial in relation to the matter that we actually know.[7] For, and this is the peculiarly Mazdean conception, a transition to the state of *gētīk* means in itself not a fall but rather fulfillment and plenitude. The state of infirmity, of lesser being and darkness represented by the present condition of the material world, results not from its material condition as such but from the fact that it is the zone invaded by the demonic Contrary Powers, the arena of struggle and also the prize. Here the stranger to this creation is not the God of Light but the Principle of Darkness. Redemption will bring the flowering of the *tan i pasen*, the "body to come," the *corpus resurrectionis;* it does not tend to destroy the *gētīk* world, but to restore it to its luminous state, its archetypal dimension.

This dimension of light constitutes every being, every physical or moral entity of the earthly world, as the counterpart of a celestial (or *mēnōk*) reality with which it forms a pair; this *mēnōk* is its spiritual entity, its archetype, its "angel." It is by establishing this dimension that the Mazdean metaphysical imagination attests its characteristic aptitude for configuring hypostases, for making the features of a celestial Person shine through all reality. This representative norm is so fundamental that Time itself, in

6 On these two concepts cf. Nyberg, *Journal asiatique,* CCXIX: 1 (Jul.–Sept., 1931) ["Questions," II], pp. 31–36.

7 Cf. also *Shkand-Gumānīk Vičar* . . ., ed. Jean de Menasce (Fribourg, Switzerland, 1945), Vol. IV, pp. 16–20, and the remarks on "Questions," II, 12–18, on p. 36.

either of its aspects, will be apprehended as a person with definite traits. It is precisely in this personal guise that we mean to consider it, and let us now, for a few moments, reflect on this point.

Logic, if it is not to be discomfited, must conform to the requirements of this norm, for the characteristic of such hypostases is to exist both in themselves and in what they accomplish. What results is not a confusion of the planes of being, but a communicability of names, that sometimes creates difficulties for our thinking—and the worst solution to these difficulties would be to degrade these figures into simple allegories. All our efforts must be directed toward safeguarding and justifying the play of "transparitions" which are made possible in this new dimension of depth in light precisely here and not otherwise or elsewhere. It will become clear to us that if time can be apprehended as a person, it is because, far from being our familiar, abstract notion, it is an archetypal Person—that is to say, this time configures and prefigures the form that a luminous being must take or regain—and because, as time of trial and of combat, it is the mediator of this metamorphosis. Thus is established a homology between the time of action of each personal being and the Time of the total cycle; between fulfilled personal being and the "Person" of eternal Time.

Once these premises have been established, it would seem that by giving our attention to this "person of time" and the variations of its features as manifested to mental vision, we may also distinguish, beneath the variants of the cosmogonic schema, the anthropological differentials characterizing pure Mazdaism on the one hand and the dramaturgy that has been designated as Zervanism on the other, because of the central role played by Zervān in it (and because its schema in turn discloses important variants).

Let us roughly outline the ideal schematization of the possible conceptions. For the pure dualist vision, that of Zoroastrian Mazdaism, the precosmic drama in which the cycle of our "aeon" originated is provoked by the attack and invasion of a Contrary Power, exterior and alien to Ōhrmazd, God of Light. Ahriman, Spirit of Evil, of negation and darkness, rises up from a bottomless abyss of undisclosed origin, existing prior to all cause. For the Zervanist vision, the drama takes place within the very person of Zervān, eternal Time or absolute Time, as the supreme godhead which by itself gives rise both to the principle of light and to the antagonist. Here, it seems to me, we have a much more serious differential than that between two different theological interpretations of an identical situation.[8] Nevertheless, from the standpoint of pure Mazdaism, an attempt at reduction was conceivable; such an attempt results in a schema that might be designated as Mazdeanized Zervanism or as Zervanized Mazdaism.

The schema of integral Zervanism undergoes in turn certain dramaturgical changes: the idea of a mediation appears in the person of the Angel Mithras, who, according to the Zoroastrian theology of our times, shows certain points of resemblance to the Archangel Michael.[9] Finally, the unity that gives rise to the two Contraries is situated no longer at the level of the supreme godhead but at the level of an emanated angelic hypostasis: this hypostasis will assume the role of a Saved Savior, a kind of Archangel Michael who has had to gain his own victory over himself, and the periods of cyclical time must mark this victory in the person of all his followers. This is the form that the drama and the role of the angel of humanity will assume in Ismaili Gnosis.

In the mythohistory of pure Mazdaism, cyclical time is punctuated by three great acts which extend over twelve millennia and constitute the ages of the world. The first of these acts is the primordial Creation (*Bundahishn*), encompassing the prelude of the first three millennia, during which the Creation is established in its *mēnōk*, subtle and celestial, state. In the ensuing period from the fourth to the sixth millennium, the Creation is transferred to the *gētīk*, or earthly, state. Then comes the second act: the catastrophe. The Negator, whose menace had risen up from the abyss at the very outset of the spiritual Creation, succeeds in entering and ravaging material creation. This second act constitutes the period of the "mixture" (*gume-*

8 A. Christensen tends toward a reduction of this sort in *L'Iran sous les Sassanides* (2nd edn., Copenhagen, 1944), p. 154, n. 4; p. 437. Cf. Nyberg, "Questions," II, pp. 81, 82; and *Die Religionen des alten Irans*, German tr. by H. H. Schaeder (Leipzig, 1938), pp. 388ff. (Zervanism as the cosmogonic doctrine of the Median magi before they became Zoroastrians). J. Bidez and F. Cumont, *Les Mages hellénisés* (Paris, 1938), Vol. I, pp. 63ff. E. Benveniste, *The Persian Religion according to the Chief Greek Texts* (Paris, 1929), ch. 4 (Zervanism as the doctrine of the Magi recorded by Plutarch); Cumont's arguments to the contrary—*Les Mages hellénisés*, Vol. I, pp. 65–66, and Vol. II, p. 72, n. 1—are not conclusive. See also Benveniste, pp. 77, 97: Zervān in Soghdian Buddhism and in Manichaeism; here, we may note, the question of the historical existence of a "Zervanite church" does not arise, for we have set out to consider only the pure philosophical schematization of certain concepts and their phenomenological connection with the mode of existence that they indicate.

9 J. J. Modi, "St. Michael of the Christians and Mithra of the Zoroastrians," in *Anthropological Papers*, Part 1 (Bombay, 1911), pp. 173–90; cf. below, nn. 51 and 55, and Part 2, p. 41, n. 47.

čishn), which we are still experiencing.[10] It will end with the act of final "separation" (*vičarishn*), ushered in by the *Saoshyant* or Saviors born from the race of Zarathustra in the course of the three last millennia, and by the "transfiguration" of the world (*frashokart*).[11]

In the Mazdean book of Genesis, the Bundahishn, we read as follows:

> It hath been revealed that during the unlimited Time, Ōhrmazd was in the heights, adorned with omniscience and goodness and surrounded by light. This light is the place and abode of Ōhrmazd. Some call it the infinite Light (*asar roshnīh*). This omniscience and this goodness are the garment of Ōhrmazd. Some call it the Religion (*Dēn*). . . . The Time of the garment is infinite, for the goodness and religion of Ōhrmazd have existed as long as Ōhrmazd himself; they still exist and they will always exist." [12]

Here the unlimited Time is neither a principle superior to Ōhrmazd nor is it his creation; it is an aspect of his illimitableness; it expresses his very being, which is also expressed by his omniscience and by the infinite light in which he resides. However, a play of transparitions, which, as we have said, are possible only in this dimension of thought, ultimately put us in the presence of time as a plastically defined figure. From eternal Time and in the image of eternal Time, Ōhrmazd created the limited Time he required to frustrate the challenge of Ahriman; he was said to have created it "in the form of a youth of fifteen, luminous, clear-eyed, of tall stature, full of a vigor resulting from a perfect endowment and not from a brutal and violent nature." [13] If in this vision of a youth we seem to discern a Mazdean form of the *puer aeternus* motif, we need only recall that the age of fifteen connotes the aspect which our texts give to the "resuscitated ones," [14] in order to realize that the "Person of Time" merely exemplifies the ideal dimension of a being of Light.

But more than this: if we give heed to the equivalences that are sub-

10 On the six millennia as the duration of the actual world, cf. "Apocalypse d'Hystaspe," in Bidez and Cumont, *Les Mages hellénisés*, Vol. II, p. 364.

11 Cf. Nyberg, "Questions," I, pp. 210-11; G. Messina, *Libro apocalittico persiano Āyātkār i Žāmāspīk* (Rome, 1939), pp. 118–20.

12 "Questions," I, pp. 206–7; for a somewhat different translation see Messina, *Žāmāspīk*, p. 85, n. 3; cf. the text of the Zātsparam, ch. 1, in Zaehner, "Zurvanica," II, pp. 576–77; A. V. W. Jackson, *Zoroastrian Studies* (New York, 1928), pp. 114–15; and Junker "Iranische Quellen," pp. 127–28.

13 Cf. Nyberg, "Questions," I, p. 231.

14 *Āyātkār i Žāmāspīk*, ch. 17, verse 16.

stituted for the denomination of Zervān, we shall perceive the intrinsic form of personal experience, the expectation projected in a vision whose "figures" present transparitions of one another. The text cited above has taught us that Religion (*Dēn*), as omniscience and goodness in infinite Time, is the garment of Ōhrmazd, which surrounds and configures his being. Other texts teach us that "what has always been is the voice of Ōhrmazd in the Light," and that from this eternal vibration of the Light, the religion of Ōhrmazd [15] vibrates eternally. This eternal Voice which is the Creative Logos of Ōhrmazd is also designated as the celestial (*mēnōk*) archetype of the Zoroastrian prayer formula par excellence, the formula known from its first words (*yaθa ahu vairyo*) as the *Ahuvar*.[16] But this celestial archetype is also said to be *Dēn*, the eternal Religion. A late Persian translation expressly gives to Ahuvar the name of Zervān.[17] Thus there is an equivalence, a reciprocal transparition, between eternal Time, the celestial archetype of creative prayer, and the eternal Religion.

The substitution of *Dēn* for the celestial archetype of Ahuvar suggests that *Dēn* is precisely the uttering of the eternal Utterance, in which are grounded the melodic themes which state the modality of each being. But the representation of eternal Religion, which is also Omniscience and Goodness as typified in a hypostasis, suffices to orient us toward a whole body of speculations concerning Wisdom, or the divine Sophia. Actually *Dēn* (Religion) does not designate a simple institutional abstraction. The figure of Daēnā (Avestan form of the Pahlavi word *dēn*) is the principle of a whole strictly Mazdean sophiology.[18] Its extreme complexity makes a complete

15 Ibid., ch. 2, verse 2.

16 Cf. the whole of Chapter XIX of the Yasna. Each of the words composing this prayer designates symbolically one of the *nasks* of the Avesta. Held to have existed before the Creation, this prayer is conceived as a hypostasis, a veritable Logos-Sophia (just as Zarathustra's *Gathas* or psalms (cf. Yasna LIV) appear as angelic hypostases; it may be said that to recite them is literally to "recite an angel"). Cf. I. J. S. Taraporevala, *The Holy Word of the Religion of Zarathustra and the Holy Immortals* (Bombay, 1947); J. J. Modi, *The Religious Ceremonies and Customs of the Parsees* (2nd edn., Bombay, 1937), pp. 200–1; Nyberg, *Die Religionen*, pp. 268–69; J. Hertel, *Die Awestischen Herrschafts- und Siegesfeuer* (Leipzig, 1931), p. 58. Unfortunately no two authorities agree about the translation.

17 Cf. in E. B. N. Dhabhar, *The Persian Rivayats of Hormozyar Framarz* (Bombay, 1932), p. 438, the little Persian text in which Zarathustra asks Ōhrmazd: "What was it that already existed when the world became existent?" Answer: "I and Ahunvar (Ahuvar), we both existed." A gloss adds: "Zervān is called 'Ahunvar.'"

18 Cf. W. Bousset, *Die Religion des Judentums im späthellenistischen Zeitalter* (3rd edn., Tübingen, 1926), pp. 37, 344ff., and 520, n. 3 (I expect to come back to this question elsewhere). Cf. also a Mazdean figure of Wisdom in *Mēnōkē Xrat* (the Book of Celestial

exposition difficult; like all the configurations of the Mazdean "imagination," it designates both an angelic hypostasis with personal traits, and its operating counterpart in the earthly being: here it is the visionary soul, the organ of the religious vision of wisdom,[19] in short that attribute of the earthly (*gētīk*) human being which enables him to be coupled with his celestial (*mēnōk*) reality. Let us simply compare two visions: Daēnā-Sophia is the garment and eternal Time of Ōhrmazd. But she is also the feminine Angel who appears after death to the Mazdean soul that has battled faithfully, presenting herself to it as the celestial Self, the light-Self of that soul. Thus the soul incarnated on earth recognizes its celestial partner, or *paredros*, as a figure through which eternal Time is discernible. This comparison grants us a brief glimpse of the dimension of being presupposed by the representation of time in its Sophianic aspect.

Concentrating on the origin, which is also the direction of return, the imagination can face the combat.

"Ahriman rose from his depths," says the Bundahishn,[20] "and arrived at the frontier where the star of Lights (*star-i rōshnān*) is situated." His envious and hateful nature and his bloodthirstiness leap forward, but perceiving "a splendor and an ascendancy superior to his own," he falls back into his darkness to produce his Counter-Creation, the multitude of his demons dedicated to the work of destruction. Ōhrmazd, in his gentleness characteristic of a being of Light (omniscient but not all-powerful), proposes peace to the Antagonist. But is it in his power to convert him into a being of Light? Ahriman replies with a bitter challenge: "I will rise up, I will urge thy creation to fall off from thee and become enamored of me." Ōhrmazd knows that it is not in Ahriman's power to beguile all his creatures. But he also knows that to reduce the Contrary Power of Ahriman to impotence, he will need time, the limited time which he creates in the image of eternal Time; and for the struggle he suggests a period of nine millennia. His Adversary accepts, for his knowledge is of the kind that can only "retard," and he is thus unable to foresee the issue of the cosmic drama whose three great acts we have just mentioned.

Wisdom), Nyberg, "Questions," I, ch. 8, pp. 198–99. For the equivalence of *Dēn* and Sophia in Manichaeism, cf. "Questions," II, pp. 48ff. Cf. also Junker, "Iranische Quellen," p. 164, the end of his n. 50; R. Reitzenstein, *Das Iranische Erlösungsmysterium* (Bonn, 1921), pp. 102ff., 241–42.

19 Cf. Nyberg, *Die Religionen*, pp. 114–20.

20 Cf. Bundahishn, I, in Nyberg, "Questions," I, pp. 208–9.

And in still another grandiose episode the myth suggests that the "cycle of time," the "aeon," is for Ōhrmazd the instrument of his victory over the Antagonist. Taking up Ahriman's challenge, Ōhrmazd inflicts upon him a vision of the future, which Ahriman rejects but which nevertheless overwhelms him: in this vision he beholds the destruction of his demons, the coming of the Resurrection and of the "Future Body" (*tan i pasen*). Then Ōhrmazd sings the *Ahuvar* stanza,[21] the resounding incantation shatters the space intervening between them, and Ahriman falls prostrate to the bottom of Darkness, where he remains for three millennia (the fourth, fifth, and sixth, during which Ōhrmazd aided by the Archangels transfers his Creation from the *mēnōk* to the *gētīk* state). But we have seen that the celestial archetype of the sacred *Ahuvar* stanza is a personification of Ōhrmazd's Time and eternal Wisdom. Thus time is the mediator of Ahriman's defeat.

This episode reveals the hieratic nature of time; and this hieratic nature will give it a privileged position for the unveiling of the world of the archetypes. There is only one sure weapon, the hieratic weapon, the vibration of glorious Light in which Daēnā-Sophia, the wisdom of Ōhrmazd, is eternally embodied. The fact that the sacred stanza of an eternal liturgy within the being of Ōhrmazd is the "person" of time, instrument of the ruin of the demons, also defines the essentially liturgical character of this time. From end to end, the work of Creation and the work of Redemption constitute a cosmic liturgy. It is in celebrating the celestial liturgy (*mēnōk yazishn*) that Ōhrmazd and his Archangels establish all creation, and notably awaken the Fravartis (at once the celestial prototypes and the tutelary angels of men [22]) to the individuality and differentiated consciousness of their enduring Self. And it is by the ultimate celebration of the five liturgies of the *nychthemeron* that the last Saoshyant will accomplish the Resurrection.[23] The total time of the cycle which by the cooperation of all the luminous beings, of all the Fravartis coming to the aid of Ōhrmazd, must ensure the defeat of Ahriman and the subjugation of his demons—this time is a liturgical time.

Of course the fractions of this time (years, months, days, hours) are in turn liturgical moments, homologous to the cycle of the aeon, because they themselves were first created in the celestial (*mēnōk*) state. We have the

21 Ibid., p. 210, li. 18ff.

22 Ibid., p. 236, li. 15ff. (at the hour of the eternal celestial noon); 216, li. 20ff. (from the *Ahuvar* was created the celestial year). See also Junker, pp. 135–36, on time and creation as an epiphany of Ōhrmazd.

23 *Žāmāspīk*, ch. 17, verses 14, 15.

celestial Year, the five celestial sections of the Day, etc. That is why the duration of the millennia cannot be evaluated in the uniform time of our calendars; it is a liturgical time, that is to say, a continuity of liturgical moments.[24] And it is because this is a liturgical time, and because such a time is in essence cyclical, that the time of our cycle is actually conceived in the image of eternal Time. It is the epiphany of eternal Time: the created order as a temporal succession epiphanizes the eternal order which hierarchizes all celestial beings. Carried back to its transcendent origin, the temporal relation exemplifies the multiple organic relations between celestial archetypes; Creation in itself, as an epiphany of the *mēnōk* in the *gētīk*, places the order of succession in limited time.[25] That is why the order of festivals, the entire cycle of the liturgic ceremonial, will be an image, a repetition of the cosmogony: six great solemn festivals (*Gāhambar*) correspond to the six great periods or creations distributed among the six supreme archangels (Ōhrmazd is added to them as a seventh, just as the year encloses the totality of these festivals and with them forms a heptad).[26]

And henceforth, since each of the fractions of time has its celestial archetype and since the liturgical succession of these moments merely exemplifies the relations between these celestial hypostases, their very nomenclature will reveal a communicability of names in conformity with the norm of Mazdean ontology. Each of the twelve months of the year is named after a supreme Archangel (*Amahraspand*, the "Immortal Saints") or after one of the angels (*Yazata*, "venerable"); and so likewise each of the thirty days of the month. Finally, each of the canonical hours is also entrusted to the celestial being or angel who is its archetype, and takes his name;[27] and in its celestial

24 On this concept of hierophanic time cf. Mircea Eliade, *Traité d'histoire des religions* (Paris, 1949), pp. 334–35 (the only possible horizon for an understanding, for example, of the tradition dating the appearance of Zoroaster at 6,000 years before Plato).

25 Cf. Junker, "Iranische Quellen," p. 135, text of the *Dēnkart* in n. 31; on the relation between time and eternity, see Zaehner, "Zurvanica," I, p. 319 (for the quotation from Nāṣir-e Khosraw, cf. H. Corbin and M. Moʿīn eds., *Jāmiʿ al-Ḥikmatain* (Bibliothèque Iranienne, A, 3; Teheran and Paris, 1953), p. 118, li. 8; "Zurvanica," III, p. 885; and de Menasce, *Shkand-Gumānīk Vičar*, pp. 250–51. Limited cosmogonic time is the condition and foundation of Creation; it will be reabsorbed into infinite Time. Not that the world will disappear: "on the contrary, it remains, but transfigured and exempt from the taint of growing old, restored to the transcendent state which was its first state" (p. 251).

26 Cf. Nyberg, "Questions," I, pp. 227–35; Modi, *The Religious Ceremonies*, pp. 419–28.

27 "Questions," I, p. 229 (Bundahishn, end of ch. I and ch. III); on the number of "thirty" *Amahraspands* (or "Archangels") cf. Dhalla (n. 44 below), pp. 357ff. On the canonical hours, see "Questions," I, p. 237 (celestial dawn, celestial noon, celestial sunset, etc.);

(*mēnōk*) entity each of these fractions of time is apprehended as a Person. It is this Person who gives the moments of earthly time their dimension as liturgical moments: one may say that the event of this day *is* this Person, the essence of this day is to be the day of this or that angel after whom it is named (e.g., the day of Ōhrmazd of the month of Farvardīn). This relation to the angel is the archetypal dimension which gives to each fraction of limited time its dimension of height or depth in Light, its dimension of eternal Time. Finally, it is by this same token that the celestial partner of a human being of Light who has completed his cycle of earthly time may be manifested to him as an angelic Form, beneath whose name (Daēnā, Dēn) we have discerned eternal Time. When the angel says to the soul: "I am thy Daēnā," it is tantamount to saying: "I am thine Eternity, thine eternal Time."

To be sure, these notions present difficulties, for here thought operates not with concepts or abstract signs, but with concrete personal figures; their imperative presence fills the individual who, to contemplate them, must reflect them in himself. Then, without confusion of their persons, their reciprocal presence must compose a single whole. Time is not the abstract measure of the succession of days, but a celestial figure in which a creature projects his own totality, anticipates his own eternity, experiences himself in his own archetypal dimension. For although Time reveals itself in two aspects, one of which is an image of the other, it also reveals the disparity, the gap between the celestial Person and the earthly person which strives, or rather fails, to be its image. In view of all this, it is essential to consider how the variable relations between pure Mazdaism and Zervanism and the possible variations within Zervanism itself in regard to the relative degradation or preponderance of the person of time, enable the being who projects his own person into the person of time to anticipate his own eternity.

THE ABSOLUTE TIME OF ZERVANISM

We have characterized these variants as Zervanized Mazdaism and Mazdeanized Zervanism. Both schemas present a kind of attempt at a reduction of integral Zervanism, which affirms the absolute preponderance of Zervān, unlimited Time, over the two principles which, as a superior entity, pregnant

---

Jackson, *Zoroastrian Studies*, p. 129; Modi, *The Religious Ceremonies*, p. 219; F. von Spiegel, *Erânische Alterthumskunde* (3 vols., Leipzig, 1871–78), Vol. II, p. 12.

with both of them, it generates. But Zoroastrian Mazdaism could not compromise in regard to the preponderance of Ōhrmazd over Ahriman and their absolute heterogeneity. In the pure Mazdean vision Zervān, the Unlimited, expresses the very norm of Ōhrmazd's being, which is also expressed by his Wisdom-Daēnā, his omniscience and his infinite Light. But if the figure of Zervān is removed from Ōhrmazd's being and given precedence over it, a first consequence will be that the peculiar dimension which we noted in the beings created by his Light will become accentuated in Ōhrmazd himself. And the second consequence will be that the two antagonistic principles will be reduced to the same inferior level with regard to Zervān. While this second consequence can only meet with absolute rejection on the part of pure Mazdaism, the first did not make a reduction of one schema to the other inconceivable, and perhaps even favored such a reduction.

What we may call Zervanized Mazdaism is attested principally by a Zervanite interpolation in the first chapter of the Bundahishn.[28] Here the subordination of Ōhrmazd is attenuated; that is, it is marked above all by the notion that Ōhrmazd became sovereign only through the Creation, conceived as an act of his thought.[29] This act of his thought first produces Creation in the celestial state and then exerts a kind of dialectic constraint over the ideal world of the Negating Spirit, by compelling it to manifest itself.[30] From the very outset Ōhrmazd embodies movement, restlessness, and struggle, and the Mazdean theosophy endows him with a vision which would be incompatible with a rationalist theology of the pure act.

As for Mazdeanized Zervanism, it clings without hesitation to the preponderance of Zervān but like pure Mazdaism relegates the power of Ahriman to an outer abyss. It accentuates the above-mentioned traits in the person of Ōhrmazd. This schema is attested principally by two texts. In

28 Cf. the penetrating analysis by which Nyberg discovered the exposé of Zervanite cosmology interpolated into ch. I of the Bundahishn, in "Questions," II, pp. 36ff. (text in "Questions," I, p. 212, li. 3ff.). Philosophical schematization here imposes a distinction between Zervanite Mazdaism (integrating the name and concept of Zervān, who is subordinated to Ōhrmazd, his maker) and Mazdeanized Zervanism (which subordinates Ōhrmazd to Zervān but, unlike integral Zervanism, maintains the exteriority of the Antagonist). The premises and consequences of these variations have the broadest implications. On the word *zurvān* or *zervān* cf. "Questions," II, p. 52; Nyberg, *Die Religionen*, pp. 380–88; L. H. Gray, *The Foundations of the Iranian Religions* (Bombay, 1925), pp. 124–29.

29 "Questions," I, p. 212, li. 1–4, 13–17 (creation of unlimited Time and of the Time of Long Domination as an instrument).

30 Ibid., li. 12–24; II, p. 40.

the Book of Celestial Wisdom,[31] Zervān appears as a sovereign of inalienable sovereignty: unaffected by Ahriman's Counter-Creation, he is exempt from old age, pain, and death, and it is with his approval that Ōhrmazd forms his own Light, this Creation, the Archangels, and the celestial Wisdom. And in this book the figure of Destiny—Fatum (*bakhsh*)—shines through the figure of Zervān.[32]

A short Mazdean treatise in Persian, a polemic against the doctors of Islam (whence its title: *'Olamā-ye Islām*[33]), is still more precise, for the author himself seems to profess the Zervanite doctrine. "In the religion of Zarathustra," he writes, "it is revealed that with the exception of Time all the rest is creature, while Time itself is the Creator."[34] It first produced Fire and Water; when they were joined, Ōhrmazd became existent. It is noteworthy that the eternal birth of the personal being of Ōhrmazd results here from the conjunction of those two elements which in Hermeticism are the symbol par excellence of the alchemical operation taken as the generation of divine mankind.[35] Ōhrmazd, wholly luminous, pure and fragrant, perceives his redoutable Adversary in the depths of the abyss. He is filled with surprise and alarm. He ponders how to set in motion forces which may defeat him, and he creates the "time of long duration,"[36] amounting to

31 On this book cf. W. Geiger and E. Kuhn, *Grundriss der Iranischen Philologie* (Strassburg, 1895–1904), Vol. II, pp. 107–8; on the form of the words of the title see Nyberg, "Questions," I, pp. 242–46; cf. principally the text, p. 198. Plastically speaking, Zervān, exempt from old age, imaged in created Time as a youth, resembles the "Ancient of Days" only very remotely.

32 Nyberg, "Questions," II, p. 54.

33 There are two different Persian recensions: cf. Dhabhar, *Rivayats*, pp. 437–57, and Junker, "Iranische Quellen," pp. 143ff.

34 In agreement with Junker, "Iranische Quellen," p. 143, li. 33–34, we must correct the following text (corresponding to *Rivayats*, p. 450, and to the edition, p. 81, li. 8): "There is no one we may call its Creator since it was not made by him who is himself Creation" (and not "because it had not yet made the Creation").

35 The alchemic doctrines of those who have been called the "Hellenized Magi" (Ostanes etc.) are already partially known. But little consideration seems to have been given to the alchemic doctrine implied in Zoroastrian orthodoxy. It is held, for example, that if the Ahrimanian smoke mingled with the Fire, it did not combine with its luminosity, whose antagonist it was (so that pure and purifying Fire could not be the substance of Hell). "Ōhrmazd's creatures (Water and Fire for example) cannot destroy one another." Cf. de Menasce, *Shkand-Gumānīk Vičar*, p. 36. Beings of the same essence form pairs and are complementary, but not so Light and Darkness, which are contradictory. And this is capital. Cf. also Hertel, *Die Awestischen Herrschafts- und Siegesfeuer*, index, *s.v. Gewässer*.

36 As we must read with Dhabhar, *Rivayats*, p. 451. Junker, "Iranische Quellen," pp. 143–44, has unfortunately read the exact opposite, and the schema becomes unintelligible.

twelve millennia, which is manifested in the celestial Sphere, constellated by the twelve signs of the zodiac.[37]

So far the drama has resulted from the clash between the Power of Light (aided by Zervān or subordinated to him) and a Contrary Power which is wholly external, as in pure Mazdaism. But now this clash is conceived as a drama within the supreme deity himself, because in the *person* of Zervān this supreme godhead contains both the elevation of Light and the depth of Darkness. This then is the vision of integral Zervanism. Its schema has been transmitted to us by Christian sources, notably by the Armenian writer Eznik. It need not surprise us that polemical considerations have dispelled every trace of great mythical inspiration and introduced a certain element of the ridiculous.[38]

Before anything existed, the heavens or the earth or any creation—the Magi are made to say in these texts—Zervān existed. And from the outset the name of Zervān holds a twofold meaning: that of Destiny (*bakhsh*) with which we are already familiar, and that other meaning, no less fraught with consequences, of celestial Glory or Light (*xvarr*), the keystone of Mazdean theosophy. It is further related that for one millennium Zervān performed sacrifices in order that a son might be born to him, a son who

37 Dhabhar, *Rivayats*, p. 451. Cf. *Mēnōkē Xrat* in "Questions," I, p. 198 (two last paragraphs); p. 214 (last four lines). I disregard the question as to which of the two figures, nine or twelve millennia, is of Zervanite rather than Mazdean origin. Concerning the difficulty created by the recognized Ahrimanian nature (in *Mēnōkē Xrat*) of the "seven" planets (thus including the sun and the moon, though they belong to Ōhrmazd's initial Creation), cf. Nyberg, "Questions," II, pp. 62–65, and the sketch on Iranian astrology given by de Menasce, *Shkand-Gumānīk Vičar*, pp. 45–49. The usual type of explanation with which too many students content themselves (degradation of gods as a result of the political circumstances attendant on an encounter between two religions) really misses the essential point, as Hans Jonas remarked in *Gnosis und spätantiker Geist* (Göttingen, 1934), Vol. I, pp. 29–31. As for the twelve signs of the zodiac considered as twelve generals (Pahlavi *spāhbat*) on the side of Ōhrmazd (and the seven planets as seven generals on the side of Ahriman), it should be noted that in the Ismailian Nāṣir-e Khosraw the seven Enunciatory Prophets, respectively inaugurating each of the seven periods of a cycle, are also "generals" commissioned by the prime Intelligence (*Jāmi' al-Ḥikmatain*, p. 121).

38 Cf. the texts in Nyberg, "Questions," II, pp. 71ff.; Bidez and Cumont, *Les Mages hellénisés*, Vol. II, pp. 88ff.; the text of the Nestorian monk Iohannan bar Penkayē, ed. de Menasce, "Autour d'un texte syriaque inédit de la religion des Mages," *Bulletin of The School of Oriental Studies*, IX (1937–39), 537–61. Cf. also Junker, pp. 142–43. This myth has been called puerile mythology, a gross and primitive myth. Whatever may be the responsibility of Eznik and the other Christian writers, one thing is certain: it is impossible to see why "spiritualization" must necessarily set in at the end of a long "evolution," and why an "evolution" might not equally well bring about the degradation of a so-called "primitive" spirituality.

would be called Ōhrmazd and who would be the Creator of the Heavens and the earth. But then a doubt arose in Zervān's mind: is this solitary liturgy not in vain? Is it effective? Would Ōhrmazd, the child of his thought and his desire, really be born? And then, from this thought *and* this doubt, two beings were conceived: one was Ōhrmazd, child of his liturgical act, the other Ahriman, the child of the Shadow, of the Darkness of his doubt. But at first Zervān knew only that they were two and vowed that he would bestow the sacerdotal kingdom upon the first one to appear.

This vow was known to Ōhrmazd; with the loyalty and simplicity of a being of Light, he informed Ahriman, who by himself, with his "retarded knowledge," would have known nothing. No sooner did he learn this than he found a way of being born prematurely, as it were, and appeared before his father (who was also his mother).[39] Zervān asked him: "Who art thou?" "I am thy son." And the enraged Zervān replied: "My son is fragrant and luminous, thou art dark and foul-smelling." And now Ōhrmazd, born in due time, presented himself luminous and fragrant to Zervān, who realized at once that this was his son, for whom he had performed long liturgical rites. He wished to invest him with the royal priesthood and gave him his blessing. But Ahriman intervened and reminded Zervān of his vow. In order not to break the vow, Zervān resolved on a compromise: "O false, maleficent one, to thee will be given a reign of 9,000 years, and Ōhrmazd will be sovereign over thee.[40] After 9,000 years, Ōhrmazd will reign, and all that he desires to do, that he will do."

Thus the dominant theme of Zervanism imposes a thesis which would be intolerable to pure Zoroastrian Mazdaism: the primogeniture of Ahriman. Still more serious, Ahriman is the prince of this world and his reign is legitimate, since Zervān, to avoid breaking his vow, was himself compelled to confer the kingship upon him. Ōhrmazd is sovereign, to be sure, but he does not reign; he will reign only at the end of this aeon, at the end of the 9,000 years. The cycle of the millennia is not even imposed by Ōhrmazd himself as in the Mazdean dramaturgy. It is decided upon by Zervān as a

39 The Bundahishn also declares that Ōhrmazd "acquired the position of father and mother of Creation" ("Questions," I, p. 221). Another opinion, however, attributes to Ōhrmazd and Ahriman a celestial mother named Xvashīzag (an affectionate diminutive, signifying roughly "she who is wholly beautiful"), a kind of Iranian Venus Urania, as Nyberg says: "Questions," II, p. 83.

40 Concerning this translation, cf. the important note in Nyberg, "Questions," II, p. 73, n. 1.

compromise, because, to eliminate the Shadow, the Darkness engendered by his doubt, he must agree to limit himself: limited time, our aeon, the time of our world, is the repentance of Zervān the Eternal.

The dialectic of Yes and No thus introduced into the godhead brings forth a cosmogony comparable to that which Schelling set out to develop speculatively in his sketch on the Ages of the World.[41] Here likewise the contradiction of Yes and No, introduced into eternity itself, shatters eternity and sets a series of eternities or aeons in place of a single one. Eternity resolves into time.[42] It is in this contradiction that the succession of the "Ages of the world" originates. The cycle of Ahriman will be followed by a new aeon, that of Ōhrmazd. Similarly in the Ismailian theosophy it is the two phases, the Light and Darkness of the Angel who is the demiurge of our cosmos, which will motivate the alternation of cycles of epiphany and occultation.[43] The eschatological resolution of the present aeon, it is true, is similar in Zervanism and in pure Mazdaism; it is the elimination of the Power of Darkness. But infinite Time, detached from Ōhrmazd and rising above him on the horizon of all the creatures of Light, is also a whole new archetypal zone, which now, together with this Infinite, stretches out immeasurably.

We have already mentioned the Mazdean concept of the Fravartis (*fravashi, farvahar, ferouër*), celestial archetypes of the creatures of Light,[44] acting as the tutelary angels of earthly creatures. Ōhrmazd revealed to his prophet that without their aid and support he would be unable to defend his Creation against Ahriman's assault.[45] Now the episode of a pre-existential choice is at the root of the whole Mazdean anthropology and assuredly provides the clearest motive for the naming of these feminine archetypal

41 Schelling, *The Ages of the World*, tr. F. de W. Bolman, jr. (New York, 1942). In this work the religion of the Magi is referred to (pp. 102, 159, 173).

42 Ibid., p. 137. It must be noted that Mazdaism aspires not to a new beginning but to a restoration of all things, a return to the original state, an ἀποκατάστασις. But we also find (cf. below in the myth developed by Dion), tied up with the religion of the Magi, explicit mention of the idea of an indefinite succession of cycles (cf. below in Ismailism the succession of the cycles tending toward the final restoration, the Grand Resurrection).

43 With this difference, that the first cycle is a cycle of Light, not a cycle of Ahrimanian domination. Even though Darkness here has its origin in a being of Light, this being is no longer the supreme godhead. Cf. below, pp. 20ff., and Part 2.

44 Cf. a summary account in M. N. Dhalla, *History of Zoroastrianism* (New York, 1938), pp. 232–43, 375–78.

45 Ibid., p. 238, and Yasht, XIII, 12, 13, 28, 76, etc. H. W. Bailey, *Zoroastrian Problems in the Ninth-Century Books* (Oxford, 1943), p. 143.

entities as "those who have chosen." [46] In the prologue of the millennia belonging to the period of Mixture, Ōhrmazd confronted the Fravartis of human beings with a free choice, which is at the origin of their *destiny*, that is to say, their Time, their Aeon: either they might dwell in heaven, safe from the ravages of Ahriman, or they might descend and be incarnated in material bodies in order to combat Ahriman in the earthly world.[47] The Fravartis elect to join battle on earth. And now a kind of duplication occurs. In the end the incarnated Fravarti is identified with the soul; but this soul does not cease to possess an archetypal dimension, since its celestial condition was to *be* an archetype. It is in point of fact only the "person" and earthly part of a Whole, of a syzygy, completed by a celestial Person, another "self" which is its Destiny, the Angel-Soul, the celestial Self, which comes to meet it after death on the road to the Činvat Bridge, which is accordingly referred to in the texts as "the Soul on the road,"[48] and which calls itself Daēnā.

A whole chivalric ethic hangs from this conception.[49] To lose this archetypal dimension is literally to cease to have an angel, it is to die as a soul can die: to cease to answer for one's celestial partner, which can then no longer answer for its earthly soul. Ōhrmazd is not an all-powerful god imposing a Law, imposing trials and sufferings to which one submits without understanding. He is one whose companions share his combat, whose suffering they assume, and whom they do not betray. In the Zervanite ethics the Fravartis are no longer merely the knights of Ōhrmazd but are his suffering members, those in whom "he endures affliction,"[50] because here Ōhrmazd assumes the features of the active and suffering God, foreshadowing the primordial Man of Manichaeism.

But beyond this there is a surprising feature—to which philosophical reflection, which ought to draw its consequences, seems to have devoted little attention. The Mazdean ontology of the celestial archetypes accords

46 Cf. other etymologies, in Bailey, pp. 107ff.

47 Text of the Bundahishn, Bailey, p. 108; and "Questions," I, pp. 236–37.

48 Cf. Dhabhar, *Rivayats*, p. 511 (*Saddar Bundehesh*, ch. X, verse 9; *ravān-e rāh*). Cf. Bailey, p. 115 (*dēn* = *ruvān ī rās*). I shall have more to say of this central question later.

49 As Eugenio d'Ors says in commenting on the Avestan idea of the angel, "the Zoroastrian religion is translated into a sort of order of chivalry." *Introducción a la vida angélica* (Buenos Aires, 1941), p. 111.

50 "*anākīh . . . dīt.*" Cf. the just remarks of Nyberg, "Questions," II, pp. 80, 81. Ōhrmazd's creatures (and the same is true of Ahriman and his counter-creatures) are his "members"; they stand in a kind of *unio mystica* with him who has formed them, but the essence of Ōhrmazd as such is inaccessible to evil.

to each of them a Fravarti: the Archangels (Amerta Spanta), the Angels (Yazata, Izad) have each their Fravarti. More important still, Ōhrmazd himself has his Fravarti.[51] But this "Angel of Ōhrmazd" cannot then be like the Angel of Yahweh who stands before His Face and manifests Him to His creatures. Rather, it is the Angel who goes ahead of him because he reveals him to himself and manifests to him the horizon, the eternal advent of unlimited Zervān. Thus the archetypes have in turn their Angels, and Ōhrmazd himself, who conceived them as conscious and active Powers, also has his own archetypal Archangel—but this extraordinary intuition projecting the archetypes into a new archetypal dimension is intelligible only if this dimension opens up a *distance* and a distention within eternity itself. Then Ōhrmazd's being must not be an immutable and immobile existence, the pure act of the rational theodicies, but must be projected into the dimension of an eternal future. His Angel stands in the same relation to Ōhrmazd as Daēnā (the aeon) to the human being (the incarnate Fravarti), who—eschatologically speaking—attains to his angel only to be drawn with him into a new height, as though a new archetypal Archangel forever preceded their syzygy. Ōhrmazd and all the beings of the celestial universe are drawn into the ascending movement of limitless eternities toward horizons and toward creative acts of thought belonging to universes still informulable. Here then we may speak of a "Gothic style" of cosmology. In this sense the Zervanite horizon, that of absolute Time without shore, without origin, and without end, would truly be in keeping with the Mazdean universe of those archetypal Archangels who, far from being "fixed," multiply beyond themselves, always sending out another Angel ahead of themselves.

Still there remains something in the schema of integral Zervanism that cannot be reduced to the needs of uncompromising Mazdaism. In the Zer-

51 On the Fravartis of the Archangels cf. Yasht, XIII, 82–84; in Vendidād, XIX, 46–48, Zarathustra is enjoined to invoke the Fravarti of Ahura Mazda (cf. Yasht, XIII, 80). Unfortunately Dhalla's article "Ahura Mazda's Fravashi" (Fravarti) in *Indo-Iranian Studies in Honour of Darab Sanjana* (London, 1925), pp. 115–16, does not go to the bottom of the question. Here we are approaching an archetypal structure. The Parsee theologian J. J. Modi, referring to a vision of Catherine Emmerich, makes an allusion to what he calls Christ's "Fravarti"—cf. his *Dante Papers* (Bombay, 1914), 7: "Angelology," pp. 157–58. On the other hand we know the close relations in the ancient Church between Angelos Christos and the Archangel Michael. Cf. Hans Söderberg, *La Religion des Cathares* (Uppsala, 1949), pp. 77ff. (cf. also n. 9, above; and below, n. 55, and Part 2, p. 41, n. 47).

vanite dramaturgy there remains an ambiguity capable of compromising that prodigious infinite *élan*, an ambiguity capable of beguiling the incarnated Fravartis into a betrayal that will deprive them of their dimension of Light. For Ahriman is the legitimate prince of this world; moreover, although he is a Power of Darkness, this Darkness is an aspect of the supreme godhead itself. To affirm this world is assuredly to serve the Power of Darkness, but is it not also to serve the godhead which itself gave birth to this Darkness and made of this time the time of its wrath, of its renunciation of being itself? And such indeed seems to be the secret of the nocturnal cult which, according to Plutarch, certain Magi devoted to Ahriman. Thus the effort to surmount radical dualism ends by establishing the Darkness as the norm of the Day; what was the "Day of the Angel" is inverted into the "Day of Ahriman." In order that the dawn of Resurrection may shine upon the night of this false day, in order that the day which will be the negation of this negation may grow, the Zervanite schema must undergo certain dramaturgical alterations. Unlike Zervanized Mazdaism or Mazdeanized Zervanism, integral Zervanism may be preserved in an aspect of its essential idea, the idea of a unity mediating between the duality of Light and Darkness; but on condition that this unity shall cease to be at the level of the supreme godhead and regress to an ontologically subsequent rank.

DRAMATURGICAL ALTERATIONS

Here unfortunately we can speak of these dramaturgical changes only briefly, to the degree in which they prepare us for the periods and cycles of the Ismaili mythohistory.

The alterations of the Zervanite dramaturgy are attested by Greek and Islamic sources. In his thirty-sixth oration, Dion of Prusa has transmitted the famous myth of the chariot of the Magi, which seems to have come from a psalter belonging to Magi celebrating the mysteries of Mithras, and which might be compared to the famous vision of Ezekiel. The chariot is harnessed to four chargers typifying the elements, consecrated to the four gods which they respectively represent. One of them is endowed with wings and is of a beauty and splendor surpassing the apparent animal nature of its myth; it is the soul of the invisible guide, and it is forever in movement through all the periods that follow one upon another unceasingly throughout the eternities. In it we may recognize Ōhrmazd as the soul of Zervān (as he will be in Manichaeism), and here again Zervān is expressly identified with eternal Wisdom.[52]

In mentioning the astonishing Magian rite to which we shall refer below, Plutarch introduces a new figure among the *dramatis personae:* Mithras the mediator. Here a new Zervanite tetrad is presupposed: Zervān, Ōhrmazd, Ahriman, Mithras.[53]

It is precisely this idea of a mediator that is emphasized in the account of Zervanism given us by Shahrastānī (12th century), the estimable Persian historian of religions. It is this idea which radically alters the schema of integral Zervanism and puts an end to all ambiguity in its anthropology and ethics. Darkness and Light do not confront each other from the very origin in an irreducible dualism, but are born from the same being, who makes Time "temporalize" itself—an eminently Zervanite idea. Yet this being, the superior and mediating unity in which the contraries originate, is no longer the absolute original godhead. Zervān is one of the beings of Light, the greatest among the angels; thus there is a shift, a regression of the level at which duality—and with it cyclic time—bursts forth. The object of Zervān's doubt is expressed in more metaphysical terms than in Eznik's myth: "Perhaps this universe is nothing," or than in the words of those whom Shahrastānī calls the Gayōmartians (from Gayōmart, the primordial Anthropos): "If I had an adversary, what would he be like?" [54] Here we

52 Cf. Nyberg, "Questions," II, pp. 91–99 (recalling *Phaedrus* 246D–249D, the winged chariots of Zeus and the gods, the race of the souls); Bidez and Cumont, *Les Mages hellénisés*, Vol. I, pp. 91ff., and Vol. II, pp. 142ff.; F. Cumont, *Textes et monuments figurés relatifs aux mystères de Mithra* (Brussels, 1899), Vol. II, pp. 60–64 (cf. another exemplification of the myth of the chariot applied to the Angel Sraosha, in Yasna, LVI, 27–29). The chariot of the Magi has inspired comparisons with the celebrated vision of Ezekiel, which is the origin of the Jewish mysticism of the Merkabah; cf. Bousset, *Die Religion des Judentums*, pp. 355–57; Reitzenstein, *Das Iranische Erlösungsmysterium*, pp. 246ff.

53 *De Iside et Osiride*, 46–47. Cf. Benveniste, *The Persian Religion*, ch. 4 (above, n. 8), especially pp. 89ff.; Nyberg, *Die Religionen*, pp. 392ff. On the Zervanite tetrads see "Questions," II, pp. 108ff.

54 Shahrastānī, *Kitāb al-milal* (lithographed, Teheran, 1288 A.H.), pp. 113–14. I do not believe that we should go too far in denying the historical reality of this sect (R. Reitzenstein and H. Schaeder, *Studien zum antiken Synkretismus aus Iran und Griechentland* (Leipzig, 1926), pp. 236–39). True, the sect of the Gayōmartians is attested only by Shahrastānī, but nothing proves to us that he did not possess data which are no longer at our disposal. Though his effort at systematization is indeed discernible, his exegesis is itself a historical fact. Among the Gayōmartians the Angel Zervān al-kabīr (Zervān the Great) of Shahrastānī's Zervanites does not appear. It is Ōhrmazd himself (Yazdān) who by his doubt engenders his Antagonist. The mediating role of the angels is similar among the Zervanites and the Gayōmartians (note

have the fascination of the void, and the thought of the Other, a thought which as such engenders that Other, so unleashing a combat in heaven which will endure for three millennia. It is, then, the angels as a whole who here fulfill the function of Mithras or of the Archangel Michael, and their mediating role permits us to recognize also their features in those of the Angel Metatron, who dominates so great a part of the mystical literature of the Jews.[55] In the account of Shahrastānī, the angels decree for Ahriman a time of seven millennia, during which the world will be given over to him, but at the end of which he will be compelled to return it to the Light.[56]

We shall see that in the Ismaili schema of mythohistory the angel corresponding to the Angel Zervān not only is the mediator who gives rise to Light and Darkness as well as their respective cycles, but also is the mediator of the victory over Darkness, the mediator of his own victory over himself. To this victory all his companions, made in his image, must contribute, his companions whose archetype he is; this they must do by undertaking in turns a combat punctuated by heptads of millennia. In concluding his account of the angelic mediation, Shahrastānī recalls the fundamental episode of the Fravartis' choice and of their descent to earth. Here the combat of the Archangel Michael has its parallel not in the idea of a "fall of the angels" (never, in Mazdean terms, can an angel, *Izad*, *fereshta*, be "evil"), but in a voluntary descent, a voluntary renunciation of the Abode of Light, in favor of the perilous combat on earth. And a similar angelological structure will be formulated in the Ismaili anthropology.

TIME AS A PERSONAL ARCHETYPE

The episode of the descent of man's Fravartis to earth is thus both the consequence and the signal of the *shift* of eternal Time into limited time. Very opportunely Shahrastānī mentions this at the end of his account of modified Zervanism. And I believe that it is by concentrating our attention

---

that among the latter the motif of the descent of the Fravartis appears explicitly).

55 Cf. H. Odeberg, *3 Enoch or the Hebrew Book of Enoch* (Cambridge, 1928), pp. 131–33 (cf. above, n. 9, n. 51). It is not so much the historical derivations that are to be sought here; there will never be a decisive solution. To explore the meaning of an archetype's recurrence is in itself a sufficient and satisfying task.

56 I do not believe that the figure of seven millennia (instead of nine or twelve) is due to a copyist's error. It is no accident that this figure accords precisely with the Ismaili schema and the astrological correspondences of the Great Cycle.

upon this motif that we in turn shall best be able to gain an intimation of how eternal Time can be apprehended as a celestial Person, and what experience of time in its twofold aspect is expressed in this personalization. Let us briefly recall certain of our initial findings: every creature is composed of his earthly part and of his celestial counterpart, his archetype or angel. Hence through every reality it is possible to discern a person—that is, to grasp this reality *as* or *in* its celestial person. The fractions of time (months, days, hours) may themselves be visualized as persons (angels and archangels whose names they bear and who are their *event*). This relation to their angel constitutes precisely their archetypal dimension; it is this relation that makes it possible to apprehend them as a complete Whole and thereby to apprehend them as Persons. This norm applies *a fortiori* to the Fravarti incarnated as an earthly human soul whose celestial counterpart is the Soul of Light or Angel which it encounters "on the way" to the Činvat Bridge, which separates the two universes. Thus the visualization not only of all reality as a person but also of that person as transcendent and celestial depends essentially on the archetypal dimension constituted by the relation with the angel, a new "dimension of Light" which determines the entire structure of the Mazdean ontology.

Let us keep in mind this fundamental norm in seeking to follow the chain of relations that confronts us here. Not only do the fractions of time appear as celestial Persons—that is to say, as eternal individuations—but absolute Time itself, eternal Time, appears in multiple personal Figures: Zervān, eternal Time, is a sovereign; he is Wisdom-Daēnā; Zervān is Destiny; Zervān is Light and Glory, as we learn in the myth recorded by Eznik. Moreover, the Greek equivalents of these Iranian notions tend to fix the play of transparitions upon the vision of a determinate figure, namely that of the *Agathos Daimōn*—that is to say, upon a figure which in every case becomes the tutelary angel or celestial *paredros*. The transparition corresponds to that which in Zervān gives us an intimation of Daēnā, and in Daēnā of the celestial Self. And it is precisely this insistent and precise transparition which should enable us to ask with some hope of an answer: what mode of existence and experience is presupposed by the apparition (the phenomenon) of eternal Time as a personal figure, tending to become fixated in the form of the angel which is the celestial *paredros* and as such the archetype, the guide, and the destiny of life? This form of angel-*paredros* also signifies a totality that is consummated only by the conjunction of the earthly person and of the celestial Self which is its superior existence. Until the incarnated Fravarti is joined, upon her return, with the Angel who comes to meet her "on the road" to the Činvat Bridge—up to this moment the earthly soul is lacking, it lags behind itself—that is, behind the totality of its being. In short, we are led to this conclusion: the visualization of eternal Time as of a person identifying himself with the archetypal Person of every earthly individual signifies literally that in compensation limited earthly time, the time Ōhrmazd needs in order to expel Ahriman from his Creation, in short the time that we ourselves are in (for us earthly creatures "time" pure and simple)—this time is *retarded eternity*.[57] That is why in the Angel's annunciation after death—"I am thy Daēnā"—we were able to perceive the equivalent of "I am thine Eternity."

At this point let us consolidate our general statements and illustrate them by examples. There are numerous texts that might enlighten us. But I shall be brief, condensing the themes as much as possible.

1. A first series of examples tends to show the epiphany of eternal Time as essentially multiform—that is to say, it shows the Αἰών as *παντόμορφος θεός*.[58] Not only does this modality provide a foundation for its numerous epiphanies; it also makes possible the exegetic transition leading the being from the hypostasis as such to the being in its function. It is thanks to this multiformity that eternal Time can in each instance manifest itself as an archetypal Figure, for this precisely is what assures its presence in that "instance." The idea of a unity which is the unity of each member of a Whole and also that of their totality may also be verified in connection with the archangelical heptad in Mazdaism, and in the earliest Christianity as well.[59] This idea makes possible a simultaneity of divine unity and divine plurality which avoids the simplest dilemma between monotheism and poly-

57 The term is that of Nédoncelle.

58 Cf. Reitzenstein, *Das Iranische Erlösungsmysterium*, pp. 172ff.

59 On the origins of this Iranian method of enumeration (which always considers the totality as a new unity added to the number of members composing it) cf. Reitzenstein, *Das Iranische Erlösungsmysterium*, pp. 154ff., and Nyberg, "Questions," II, pp. 54ff. This is by no means a naïve logic; cf. the remarks of Junker, "Iranische Quellen," pp. 160–61. Cf. also the Christian inscription at Miletus, where each of the seven archangel aeons is *also* the Whole (Deissmann in Reitzenstein, p. 175, n. 2; ibid., Christ as *auriga cherubim;* and cf. above, n. 52, the myth of the chariot). Also see Reitzenstein, "Eine frühchristliche Schrift von den dreierlei Früchten des christlichen Lebens," in *Zeitschrift für die neutestamentliche Wissenschaft* (Giessen), XV (1914), in which Christ is at the same time the sum of the seven Angels and one of them (pp. 67–68, 82).

theism. This might be an occasion to redefine the old term of "kathenotheism" as the hierophantic category of "every instance."[60] This means that given the figure in which the transparitions of the aeon tend to become fixated, the mode of existence of the soul for which eternal Time is epiphanized as a figure that is its archetypal dimension culminates neither in the void of its own isolation nor in a uniformly nameable divine presence, but in a rigorous and irreplaceable individuation (καθ' ἕνα, *singulatim*) of that divine presence.

The epiphanies of the aeon assume this aspect of an eternal individuation which is always a totality. We might conceive a predetermined number of such epiphanies, but each is multiplied in turn. There are, for example, the celestial archetypes or personal figures of the divisions of the Mazdean year, typifying personal creative powers. We find examples of a similar mental iconography in the Gnostic, Nosayrī, and Ismaili calendars;[61] in Manichaeism; and finally, we have the twelve maidens, Virtues, or "Majesties" —the "twelve glorious maidens of Zervān"—a mystery which in the twelve hours of Light leads the soul from earth to perfect Light. But in addition Time itself as an eternal totality is epiphanized in individuated figures, whose play of reciprocal transparitions are fixated in a figure which may enable us to define the mode of existence for which eternal Time announces itself in this manner.[62]

Zervān is eternal Wisdom: Zervān is Destiny (*bakhsh*) as an elected and imparted finality, leading back to itself (personal destiny or finality which is something other than what is popularly called fatalism). In his capacity of Destiny and personal Destiny, Zervān also appears as *xvarr* (Avestan *xvarenah*)—that is to say, as the celestial Light of Glory, the "fire of vic-

60 Cf. Betty Heimann, *Indian and Western Philosophy, a Study in Contrasts* (London, 1937), pp. 37ff. And this is not a problem peculiar to India.

61 Cf. R. Reitzenstein, *Poimandres* (Leipzig, 1904), p. 270, and our study, "Rituel sabéen et exégèse ismaélienne," *EJ 1950*, pp. 235ff.

62 Cf. E. Waldschmidt and W. Lentz, *Die Stellung Jesu im Manichäismus* (Berlin, 1926), p. 127; Reitzenstein, *Das Iranische Erlösungsmysterium*, pp. 154–59; de Menasce, p. 255. On the three greatest periods of cosmic Time represented in three figures forming a unity we may compare (for the archetype) Gayōmart, Zarathustra, Saoshyant (Reitzenstein, pp. 99, 242); Nuriel, Enoch, Metatron (Odeberg, *3 Enoch*, p. 124); primordial Man, Archangel Michael, and Christ (Söderberg, *La Religion des Cathares*, p. 78). In the Ismaili theosophy the seven Imāms of the seven periods of a cycle epiphanize the essence of a unique and eternal Imām (cf., in Manichaeism, Adam, Seth, Enoch, Buddha, Zoroaster, Jesus, and Mani).

tory" which is primarily the property of the celestial Yazatas.[63] This Glory was visibly manifested as a nimbus and flame forming haloes round the heads of the princes of dynasties consecrated prior to our chronologies; it still retains this visibility in the stylized nimbus which accompanies it from the figure of the Mazdean Saoshyant to the Western representations of Christ, to the Eastern figures of Buddhas and Bodhisattvas. But it is not only the royal and sacerdotal charisma; it is the power which constitutes and knits together the existence of a being of Light. In this sense, this "Glory" signifies the soul itself insofar as it exists before the body.[64] Henceforth, if this Light of Glory, figure of eternal Time, is imparted to every being of Light as its very soul, we shall be justified in calling it the Destiny and Eternity of that being.

It should be mentioned that these alternating denominations in which we glimpse the Figure of Zervān in the myth recorded by Eznik were given precise Greek equivalents: Δόξα and Τύχη.[65] And the fact that this Light of Glory, which is also Destiny, was represented by the term Τύχη is of the greatest importance. For in the same context the figure Τύχη (fate, destiny) was identified with the figure which dominates the Hermetic horizon, *Agathos Daimōn*, who appears simultaneously as a Hermetic divinity and as the personal "good daemon," the δαίμων πάρεδρος, the celestial *paredros* or partner—that is to say, the helping, tutelary angel—a gratuitous gift obtained by prayer.[66]

In whatever sense we consider it, we perceive a figure with increasingly precise traits. On the one hand, Daēnā is Zervān and she is also the Angel-Self, the celestial archetype coming to meet the soul. In the *Corpus hermeticum* Sophia is the aeon; she is the mother of Anthropos—that is to say,

63 Cf. Gray, *Foundations*, pp. 120–23; Spiegel, *Erânische Alterthumskunde*, Vol. II, pp. 42–44; Hertel, *Die Awestischen Herrschafts- und Siegesfeuer*, pp. VIII, XIff., 12, 76.

64 Cf. Reitzenstein and Schaeder, *Studien*, p. 230, n. 2; pp. 17, 321; p. 320 (Iranian *xvarenah* and Hebrew *shekhina*).

65 Cumont, *Textes et monuments*, Vol. I, pp. 284–85; Bidez and Cumont, *Les Mages hellénisés*, Vol. I, pp. 68ff.; Vol. II, pp. 52, n. 5; 87; 89; 92, n. 2; Nyberg, "Questions," II, p. 71, and ch. 5, pp. 66–67. In the Pahlavi script, *xvarr* (glory) is represented by the Aramaic ideogram *gaddeh* (fortune, luck): Gray, *Foundations*, pp. 121, 128; it reappears in Ismailism under the Arabic form of *jadd* (= Persian *bakht* in Abū Yaʿqūb Sejestānī (*Mawāzīn*, XII, and below, Part 2, p. 36, n. 27) characterizing the angel identified with Gabriel, who would correspond topologically to Zervān.

66 Cf. Reitzenstein, *Das Iranische Erlösungsmysterium*, pp. 192–93 (also p. 191, n. 1; and *Poimandres*, p. 18, n. 8; Agathoel, angel of victory and of rejoicing); *Corpus hermeticum*, text established by A. D. Nock and tr. A.-J. Festugière (Paris, 1945–54; 4 vols.), Vol. I, Treatise X, 22–23, and n. 78.

of the regenerated *mystes*, for she has given birth to his immortal body, *ἀθάνατον σῶμα*.[67] But in addition, the assurance of immortality is bound up with the attainment of the *daimōn paredros*, the celestial angel or partner. At the same time, Zervān is Τύχη, Personal Destiny; Τύχη is *Agathos Daimōn*, who is a divine figure as such and also a *daimōn paredros*, the personal angel of each soul.[68]

2. Now it is by this figure of the *daimōn paredros* that we may finally understand the characteristic mode of being of a soul for which time is epiphanized as a person. If all the transparitions or hierophanies of eternal Time tend to be fixated in this person, it is because the soul for which it is thus modalized has taken cognizance of its archetypal dimension and knows that the totality of its being can be fulfilled only in conjunction with its celestial *paredros*. But at the same time we perceive the "transitive" way in which a godhead, without ceasing to be in itself a hypostasis, can exist totally in each of its individuations; this is the case with the figures of the Mazdean angelology, such as the *agathos daimōn*, which is also a *daimōn paredros*, etc.

To this structure corresponds exactly that of the soul which exemplifies it, the being whose archetype this godhead is. So it is that the same name will designate the angelic hypostasis in itself and its presence in its earthly counterpart considered as a part or potency of it and revealing precisely its dual structure, its reference to the angel or celestial archetype. In Mazdaism, for example, *fravarti* (*farvahar*) and *daēnā* (*dēn*) are celestial entities and human potencies or faculties as well; more precisely they are that part of human beings which enables them to be coupled with these celestial entities. Similarly in Hermeticism the *Nous* is at once a god, the faculty of intuitive knowledge in man, and his tutelary angel (as *Agathos Daimōn*).[69] Here we do not have two inconsistent theories, but the dimension of an anthropology which is already an angelology: "the man without *Nous*" means the man deprived of that faculty of knowledge and precisely the "man without an angel," in short something which is no longer a human being.[70] But, on the other hand, to attain to the *angelos paredros* is to gain immortality,[71] to become aeon; and similarly the meeting with Daēnā "on

67 Ibid., XI, 3; Vol. II, XIII, 2. Cf. n. 2 of Vol. II, p. 268. Reitzenstein, *Poimandres*, p. 44; *Das Iranische Erlösungsmysterium*, p. 44. Junker, "Iranische Quellen," p. 164.

68 Reitzenstein, *Poimandres*, pp. 153; 156, n. 2; 365.

69 *Corpus hermeticum*, Vol. I, p. 134, n. 73, and p. 139.

70 Ibid., X, 24, and p. 139 (bottom).

71 Cf. above, n. 68.

the road" to the Činvat Bridge signifies the shift of limited time to eternal Time; the attainment of Destiny itself and the plenitude of the Light of Glory or *xvarenah.*

Thus it is only by anticipation that the soul can now be granted a vision of its eternal Time in the form of its Angel-Archetype; and this prevision, by showing the soul what it is *not yet* but has still to be, reveals to it its own being as "retarded eternity." In consequence, anticipation is the vital law of an existence which, by thus understanding itself, must tend toward its superexistence on pain of being *eternally retarded* over against itself This anticipation is manifested in rites and injunctions, in the enchantments of a mental iconography or of ecstatic visions.

The symbolism of the *kosti* has rightly been interpreted in this sense.[72] The *kosti* is the sacred cord, woven of lamb's wool, which the Zoroastrians wear as a girdle and which is venerated as their distinctive religious sign. The cord is passed three times around the waist and knotted four times, twice in front and twice behind. The symbolic significance traditionally attached to these four knots makes it possible to identify them as a Zervanite tetrad to which, as in the myth of the "chariot of the Magi," is added a fifth member which fastens together and totalizes the tetrad; but here precisely Zervān or Wisdom, the invisible *auriga* of the chariot, is represented by the very person of the Mazdean believer. In this sense the symbolism of the *kosti* approaches the symbolism of the robe in which the *mystes* was clad: the *stola olympiaca* of which Apuleius speaks,[73] or the heavenly robe constellated with the signs of the zodiac, mentioned in the mysteries of Mithras, which was such that when the *mystes* donned it he in person became the god passing through the constellations.[74]

It is likewise as an injunction to abolish the delay, to convert retarded eternity into anticipated eternity that we may understand the solemn announcement of the *Nous* to Hermes: "If you do not make yourself like

72 Cf. Junker, "Iranische Quellen," pp. 136, and 160, n. 36; Modi, *Religious Ceremonies,* pp. 178–79. It should also be noted that the third knot itself refers to the sacrosanct Zoroastrian trilogy: "Good thought, good word, good action," projected spatially as forming the three levels of paradise: *Humat, Hūxt, Huvarsht* (*Mēnōkē Xrat,* II, 145; LVII, 13).

73 Reitzenstein, *Das Iranische Erlösungsmysterium,* p. 167.

74 Ibid., pp. 168, 239. Cf. also the motif of the heavenly girdle brocaded on the robe donned by the *mystes,* in Junker, "Iranische Quellen," p. 162: the *kosti* makes the Zoroastrian believer a symbol or exemplification of the aeon, an Anthropos, one reborn, a son of God like the "All in All, composed of all the powers" (*Corpus hermeticum,* Vol. II, XIII, 2).

unto God, you can not understand God, for the like is intelligible only to the like. Make yourself grow until you correspond to greatness without measure, by a leap that will free you from all body; raise yourself above all time, become aeon (become eternity); then will you understand God." [75]

There is, finally, a mental iconography that anticipates the supreme hierophany. Here the perpetual recurrence of one and the same figure, whose soul takes delight in foreseeing the encounter, might well form the basis of a comparative study. It is eminently in Mazdaism that we encounter the apparition of Daēnā at the entrance to the Činvat Bridge, under the aspect of a heavenly Maiden whose beauty surpasses all imagination.[76] But the same vision occurs in Manichaeism [77] and in Sufism as well.[78] We find its equivalent in the Buddhism of the Pure Land.[79] And the Liturgy of Mithras contains an ecstatic anticipation of this eschatological vision when the *mystes*, having become aeon, sees the gates open before him, and the world of the gods and the angels becomes visible to him; when his soul, beside itself with joy, comes face to face with "the god of glittering presence, the god of the golden ringlets, in the flower of his youth, clad in a robe of splendor, crowned with a golden diadem." [80]

Ismaili gnosis will characterize this attainment of transcendence as a passage from the "angel *in potentia*" to the "angel *in actu*." Here we shall find the significance of angelology not only for a certain form of mystical experience but also for an entire anthropology, for a philosophy of the person and the personality. But precisely this philosophy is bound up with a cosmology in which cyclic time has its origin in a *retard*, a *passing beyond*, a relegation to the past. This origin is the drama that befell one of the angels of the pleroma, who will here play the role of the Angel Zervān in the schema of Shahrastānī; and the entire anthropocosmic dramaturgy

75 *Corpus hermeticum*, XI, 20.

76 *Hādoxt Nask*, II, 1–15 (= Yasht, XXII, 1–15); Vendidād, XIX, 98–104; *Mēnōkē Xrat*, II, 123–39 (cf. below, Part 2, p. 57, n. 102).

77 Cf. our "Récit d'initiation," *EJ 1949*, pp. 183–84.

78 'Abdolkarīm Gīlānī, in R. A. Nicholson, *Studies in Islamic Mysticism* (Cambridge, 1921), p. 117; and cf. Suhrawardī's hymn to Perfect Nature in our "Récit d'initiation," p. 160.

79 For the motif of the descent of Amida (Amitābha), cf. H. Minamoto, "L'Iconographie de la 'descente d'Amida,'" in *Etudes d'orientalisme* published by the Musée Guimet in memory of Raymonde Linossier (Paris, 1932), Vol. I, pp. 99–129.

80 Junker, "Iranische Quellen," p. 152; Reitzenstein, *Das Iranische Erlösungsmysterium*, pp. 238–40; G. R. S. Mead, *A Mithraic Ritual* (London and Benares, 1907), pp. 32, 61, 63.

will be carried toward its final act by the torment of a "retarded eternity." This will be the theme of our next discussion.

2. *Cyclical Time in Ismailism*

ABSOLUTE TIME AND LIMITED TIME IN THE ISMAILI COSMOLOGY

It was in the course of the tenth and eleventh centuries of our era (fourth and fifth centuries after the Hegira) that the Ismaili theosophy took form in great systematic works, chiefly under the influence of several great Iranian thinkers.[1] One of these thinkers, Abū Ḥātim Rāzī, whose work, like so many others, still exists only in manuscript, was a Fatimid dignitary (dā'ī) in the Dailam (region to the southwest of the Caspian Sea). He was a contemporary of the celebrated Moḥammad ibn Zakarīyā Rāzī (the Rhazes of the Latin writers of the Middle Ages, d. *ca.* 923–32), a physician and alchemist suspected of crypto-Manichaeism, whose philosophical work has today been in large part lost.[2] As their name indicates, both men have a bond with Rhages (the city mentioned in the book of Tobit, the Ragha of the Avesta, today Rayy, several kilometers south of Teheran). It is fortunate for philosophy that these two eminent contemporaries should have met and known each other and that, moreover, since Zakarīyā Rāzī was (even posthumously) the object of Ismaili attacks,[3] these two fine minds should have clashed in controversies which were no less intense for all their courtesy.

In one of his books Abū Ḥātim Rāzī left us a record of one of these discussions.[4] His adversary set his name to a cosmology in which he restored—or perhaps actually founded—an ideal Sabaean philosophy. This cosmology asserted the existence of five eternal principles: Demiurge, Soul, Matter, Space, and Time.[5] Here we shall be concerned solely with the passage regarding the eternity of Time.[6]

1 Abū Ya'qūb Sejestānī, Mo'ayyad Shīrāzī, Ḥamīdaddīn Kermānī, Nāṣir-e Khosraw, etc.

2 On Abū Ḥātim Rāzī, cf. W. Ivanow, *A Guide to Ismaili Literature* (London, 1933), p. 32, VIII; *Studies in Early Persian Ismailism* (Leiden, 1948), p. 37 and passim; S. Pines, *Beiträge zur islamischen Atomenlehre* (Berlin, 1936), pp. 35ff. On Moḥammad ibn Zakarīyā Rāzī cf. Pines, pp. 35, 69, and passim. The remains of his philosophical work have been collected by Paul Kraus, *Razis Opera philosophica fragmentaque quae supersunt*, Vol. I (Cairo, 1939).

3 Notably on the part of Nāṣir-e Khosraw.

4 In the *Kitāb A'lām al-Nobowwat* (Ivanow, *Guide*, n. 19).

5 Cf. our "Rituel sabéen."

6 Cf. Kraus, *Razis Opera*, p. 304; Pines, *Beiträge*, p. 53.

The bout opens with a loyal challenge:

> You have said then that the five principles are eternal (*qadīm*) and alone eternal? Well then, time is constituted by the motion of the spheres, the passage of days and nights, the number of years and months; are all these co-eternal with time, or are they produced in time?—The defender seeks to draw the assailant into a terrain where his weapons will be ineffectual. True, measured by the movement of the Heavens, all the things he has just named are produced in time. But in so arguing he is merely upholding the thesis of Aristotle. Who will venture to say that it has never been disproved? Moḥammad ben Zakarīyā Rāzī—but at this point let us give him back his old name of Rhazes to simplify matters and distinguish him from his homonym—Rhazes, then, who will end by invoking Plato, begins by stating his own thesis in simple terms: "For my part, I profess this: Time implies an absolute Time (*Zamān muṭlaq*) and a limited time (*Zamān maḥṣūr*). Absolute Time is eternal Duration (*mudda, dahr*); this is the time that is eternally in movement and never halts. Limited time is that which exists through the movements of the celestial spheres, the course of the sun and the heavenly bodies.

But Abū Ḥātim asks skeptically what substantial reality (*ḥaqīqa*) one can represent under the concept of this absolute Time. It is not so simple; his adversary asks him to compare the time of this world which is moving toward exhaustion and completion, with the absolute Time that can neither be completed nor destroyed.

What interests us here is neither the details nor the development of the discussion but essentially the statement of Rhazes' thesis. Here we have no wish to debate the question of a historical filiation running from the philosophemes of Mazdaism to those of Ismailism, nor to determine the "influences." [7] But we may say this much: in its terminology, Rhazes' distinction between an absolute Time and a limited time presents a direct and lateral correspondence with the two fundamental aspects of time in the Mazdean cosmogony.[8] The relation seems to have been suggested as early as the

7 This is a problem which in any case cannot be elucidated by the current methods of purely static and analytical exegesis, by a historicism limited to an essentially causal type of explanation which reads causality into things. With regard to the extreme complexity of the data and the seriousness of the irreparable gaps in our sources, cf. e.g. G. H. Sadighi, *Les Mouvements religieux iraniens au IIème et au IIIème siècle de l'Hégire* (Paris, 1938).

8 *Zamān* (= *Zervān*) *i akanārak* and *Zamān i kanārakomand* or *Zamān i derangxvatāi* have been studied in our first lecture.

eleventh century by Ibn Ḥazm, the celebrated Andalusian Arabic writer, in his critical history of religions.[9] On the other hand, as the historian Bīrūnī remarked, the doctrine of Rhazes borrowed from Neoplatonism [10] in so far as it distinguished between (1) the Time (*Zamān*, χρόνος) with which number is concerned and which corresponds to the definition of Aristotle; (2) Duration (*Mudda*), analogous to διάστασις τῆς ζωῆς, the distance that dis-tends the life of the soul (for the soul which is not attached as such to the movement and number of the Heavens is that which numbers this number); [11] and finally (3), the aeon (*dahr*), the time of the eternal intelligible world. Actually, the last two aspects tend to fuse into one, and in this respect the entire distinction of Rhazes' doctrine might be attributed to his master Irānshahrī, an Iranian philosopher who lived in the ninth century and who seems to have been a highly original thinker, but whose work is known to us only from a few quotations. Irānshahrī regarded the terms "time," "duration," and "eternity" as one and the same thing considered under two aspects: unmeasured Time (independent of the movements of the Heavens and even of the soul, since it refers to a plane of the intelligible universe that is superior to the soul) and Time measured by the movement of the heavens. Thus, since eternal Duration and Time are only two aspects of the same essence, the distinction made by Rhazes between absolute Time and limited time would correspond to that between separated time and unseparated Time: χώριστος χρόνος and ἀχώριστος χρόνος in the terminology of Proclus.[12]

Now the Ismaili theosophy of mythohistory presupposes precisely the representation of an eternal Time—whose eternity, however, erupts in cycles of successive times whose rotation carries them back to their origin. What, then, we cannot help wondering at this point, was the reason for the per-

9 *Kitāb al-Fiṣal* (Cairo, 1348), Vol. I, p. 35.

10 Cf. Bīrūnī's text in Pines, pp. 49–52.

11 Ibid., p. 50, n. 2: the interpretations of Simplicius and Alexander of Aphrodisias. Cf. Nāṣir-e Khosraw, *Jāmi' al-Ḥikmatain*, ed. Corbin and Moīn, ch. 9, pp. 117–20, §§ 114–15; and ch. 17 (cf. below).

12 Cf. Pines, pp. 51–52; 41, n. 2; and 85, n. 4. The problem also attracted the attention of the philosophers of the Safawid period, Mīr Dāmād and Ṣadrā Shīrāzī. Cf. also Proclus, *The Elements of Theology*, ed. E. R. Dodds (Oxford, 1933), p. 228 (Αἰών-Zervān as hypostasis); and E. Zeller, *Die Philosophie der Griechen* (3rd edn., Leipzig, 1903–22), Vol. III, Part 2, p. 707 (Iamblichus). The powerful personality of Irānshahrī is indicated by the tradition according to which he rejected all religions and created one of his own. Do the words of sympathy and praise with which Nāṣir-e Khosraw refers to him suggest that this personal position was not without its affinity to Ismailism?

sistent attacks on Rhazes? Essentially he was attacked as the "Sabaean philosopher," the negator of Prophecy; not that Ismailism upheld the prophetology of official and orthodox Islam, but its entire technique of interior or spiritual exegesis (*ta'wīl*) presupposes the text transmitted by the Prophets (*Nāṭiq*). Similarly, the correspondence between celestial hierarchy and earthly hierarchy presupposes that the "mediators" of salvation are not merely the spiritual angels of ideal Sabaeanism.[13] Even when Rhazes sets out to describe absolute Time, the Ismaili thinker, under the stress of polemical considerations, seems to suppose that he is still speaking of the time of sensuous things, of the time that "is nothing other than the changing states of that which is body." [14] And there will be all the more indignation when Rhazes, positing Time as one of the five eternal principles, seems to make a thing, a substance, of it.[15] But once polemical ardors have abated, the motif of the twofold aspect of Time as a *single* essence will reappear with an imperious necessity.[16] This will be the case with the great Iranian Ismaili philosopher, Nāṣir-e Khosraw (eleventh century).

In a closely reasoned chapter of a work which is a synthesis of Greek and Ismaili philosophy,[17] Nāṣir compares the notions of eternity (*dahr*) and of time (*zamān*),[18] and sets forth this proposition: "Time is eternity measured by the movements of the heavens, whose name is day, night, month, year. Eternity is Time not measured, having neither beginning nor end." "It is the Time of Duration without end, absolute Duration." [19] The cause of this eternal Duration is the first divine Emanation, the first primordial Intelligence or Archangel: eternity is in the horizon (or in the sphere) of this Intelligence. The cause of time is the Soul of the World; but the Soul is itself in the horizon of the Archangel; it is not in time, for time is in the horizon of the Soul as its instrument, as the duration of the living mortal who is "the shadow of the Soul," while eternity is the duration of the living immortal—that is to say, of the Intelligence and of the Soul.[20]

13 Cf. our "Rituel sabéen," pp. 195ff.
14 Nāṣir-e Khosraw does this in *Kitāb Zād al-Mosāfirīn*, ed. Kaviānī (Berlin, n.d.), p. 111.
15 Ibid., pp. 112–13.
16 Ibid., p. 110. On the importance of Nāṣir-e Khosraw (d. *ca.* 481 A.H./A.D. 1088), who organized the Ismaili community of Badakhshan, the Oxus region at the eastern end of the Iranian world, cf. W. Ivanow's recent study, *Nāṣir-i Khusraw and Ismailism* (The Ismaili Society, series B, V, Leiden and Bombay, 1948).
17 This is the work cited above, n. 11, which is a synthesis of Greek and Ismaili philosophy.
18 Ibid., p. 118, li. 6, 7. Cf. § 109 and *Zād*, pp. 117–18, 364–65.
19 Ibid., p. 118, li. 8.
20 Ibid., p. 113, § 109; p. 117, § 114; cf. p. 188, § 192.

In declaring, "The Intelligence is one with eternal Time," Nāṣir-e Khosraw is also stating the secret of the speculative Ismaili cosmology: the eternal birth of the pleroma from the *Ibdāʿ* (eternal Existentiation), formed of archangelical hypostases originating in the first among them. This world is not of an immutability and immobility presenting a simple contrast to the perishability of sensuous things; there are Events in Heaven, archetypal Events preceding the Creation of things, and these Events are the very genesis of being. This ontological mystery is circumscribed by Nāṣir in three words (*azal, azalīyat, azalī*) the nuances of which we should have some difficulty in translating if the author, even though writing in Persian, did not relate them to Arabic paradigms. Thus we have an eternally-being (*azal*) as *nomen agentis* (present participle *fāʿil*); an eternal actuation of being (*azalīyat*) as *nomen verbi* (noun of action, *fiʿl*); an eternally being made-to-be (*azalī*) as *nomen patientis* (past participle, *mafʿūl*).[21] The text is marvelously abstruse, but it discloses the following: by being eternally, the eternally-being (*azal*) actuates precisely its own being-that-has-become, its being which has eternally been—that is to say, which is eternally made-to-be by its own act of being. We must bear in mind that in terms of Ismaili philosophy the eternally-being constitutes the supreme godhead, absolutely unknowable and unpredicable.[22] But what this godhead is eternally in actuating its being, in revealing it, is the first archangelical hypostasis (*al-mobdaʿ al-awwal*),[23] its eternal Personification, its very Ipseity, the Only One forever being revealed. This Archangel is the *Deus determinatus* (*al-Lāh*) to such a point that all the predicates which the exoteric religions would focus on the supreme godhead should actually be applied to this divine Epiphany within the first Intelligence (*ʿAql awwal*).

Here Nāṣir explicitly calls our attention to an ontological aspect with which the "speculative grammar" of our Middle Ages was very much concerned and which was designated as the *significatio passiva*. Here it is the aspect which action assumes in its end, in that wherein it is accomplished (*nomen patientis*), at the very point where action in being fulfilled is no longer distinguished from *passio*, since *passio* is its outcome (as, for example, writing and the thing written, *scriptio* and *scriptum*). As Nāṣir said: "The *significatio passiva* of the *nomen patientis* (*mafʿūlī-e mafʿūl*) consists in the

21 Ibid., ch. 17, pp. 187–89, §§ 191–93, much more precise than *Zād*, p. 195.

22 "He who cannot be attained by the boldness of thought." Cf. R. Strothmann, *Gnosis-Texte der Ismailiten* (Göttingen, 1943), p. 55.

23 Cf. *Jāmiʿ al-Ḥikmatain*, p. 188, li. 9.

very action of the agent, which is accomplished in him." In this sense the Archangel of the primordial theophany considered as the end in which is accomplished the ontomorphosis of the eternal Being appears as eternal Action or divine Energy and as eternal, divine Passion (or divine "pathetism"). As eternally made-to-be, the Archangel is the eternal, divine Past. Since by this very token he is in his person Action-made-to-be, this active aspect of his eternal being summons to being, actuates the procession of archangelical entities that follow him; and the same duality of *actio* and *passio* is repeated at every degree, producing the eternal birth of a new Archangel.

In their very nature these premises are difficult to understand. But without them it is impossible to grasp the principle of the Ismaili cosmic dramaturgy, to understand why the consequence of the error of the angel which will take the role of the Angel Zervān (in the schema of Shahrastānī) will be described as a "retard"—the regression of a rank (that of the Angel) which lets itself be surpassed, put behind (*ta'akhkhor, takhallof*). Actually if this is true, the eternal Existentiation (*Ibdā'*) of the primordial Archangel, which is at the origin of the pleroma, is not only eternal actuation of being but also eternally to come, eternal advent. The eternal Past *is* eternally actuated; it does not *become* a past, it is not *thrust into* the past, it does not sink into a past that is more and more past, as we say that the past sinks into time. But then the intoxication that will seize the Angel in the illusion that he himself is the actuation of his being—precisely this intoxication will remove him from eternal actuation, from the eternal advent of being. His doubt stops him to himself, thrusts him into the past, and by this fall into the past his own rank is *surpassed* (here again space is born from time).[24] At this moment "temporal (or limited) Time" is born, a time in which there is a remoteness, a past that is no longer eternal, a past that is no longer.

Nevertheless, the Ismaili vision contains a repentance, a *conversion* already accomplished by the Angel; and through this conversion the temporal time originating in his fault has also *shifted back.* That is why this Time has the form of a cycle; it is not a rectilinear time indefinitely accumulating a past and leading nowhere, but a time leading back to the origin. There is redemption from the past: the angelic rank is surpassed, it falls into the

24 Or again visual space is only one aspect of space, perhaps a symbol of true space, just as the time of our chronologies is only an aspect or a symbol of Time; there is no opposition between Time and Eternity, there are only two aspects of Time as such, Αἰών and Αἰῶνες.

past, and then again becomes future. To lead back to the origin: this is the exact meaning of the word which designates esoteric spiritual exegesis (*ta'wīl*), the central operation of Ismaili thought, of which the alchemical operation is only a special case.[25] Thus cyclical Time leading back to the origin becomes itself an exegesis, the total exegesis of mankind, the archetype of all exegesis.

This generation of Time and this redemption by Time may be viewed differently according to the diversity of our sources: Iranian sources of the Fatimid period, Iranian sources of Persian Neo-Ismailism of the Alamūt tradition, Arabian Fatimid sources, or Yemenite sources in the Fatimid tradition.[26] In any event these schemata put forward a representation of Time as an instrument, making it possible to overcome a retard, a being-passed-by. But according to the greater or lesser amplitude seen in the archangelical pleroma, the generation of Time occurs peacefully, as it were, under the pressure of a sense of ontological imperfection—or else it occurs through a catastrophe ushering in a dramaturgy analogous to that of the Mazdean cosmology.

The first schema is drawn from Iranian sources, particularly Nāṣir-e Khosraw. He describes the procession of the five primordial archangelical hypostases, the first two of which are the Intelligence (*'Aql*) and the Soul (*Nafs*).[27] This eternal motion which moves the being of the first Intelligence or Archangel is an eternal movement of adoration of the Principle, which eternally actuates it toward being. From this eternal movement of adoration, from this cosmic liturgy, the Soul of the World eternally takes its birth.[28] This Soul is a second Archangel which is like the first in that it is

25 Cf. our study "Le Livre du Glorieux de Jābir ibn Ḥayyān," *EJ 1950*.

26 It is not possible to discuss the periods of Ismailism here in detail. For an orientation cf. L. Massignon's article "Karmates" in the *Encyclopédie de l'Islam;* W. Ivanow, "Ismā'īlīya" (ibid., *Supplément*), and the introduction to his *Guide;* Strothmann, *Texte*, pp. 1–8. The sources to which I have been constrained to limit myself here are essentially: for Fatimid Ismailism, Nāṣir-e Khosraw (Persian)—cf. above, n. 16; for the post-Fatimid Yemenite (Arabic) tradition, Sayyid-nā Idrīs 'Imādaddīn, 19th Yemenite dā'ī (d. 872/1462, cf. the *Guide*, LV, p. 62); for the Persian tradition of Alamūt, the *Rawḍatu't-Taslīm* (Persian) attributed to Naṣīraddīn Ṭūsī (d. 672/1274).

27 The three others being *Jadd* (= Persian *bakht*—cf. above, Part 1, p. 26, n. 65), *Fatḥ*, and *Khayāl*, identified with the Archangels Gabriel, Michael, and Seraphiel, according to Abū Ya'qūb Sejestānī, *Kitāb al-Mawāzīn* (The Book of Balances, unpublished MS), ch. 12.

28 Cf. Nāṣir-e Khosraw, *Six Chapters or Shish Fasl also called Rawshana'i-nama*, Persian text ed. and tr. into English by W. Ivanow (The Ismaili Society, series B, VI, Leiden, 1949), p. 42 (pp. 13, 14 in the pagination of the Persian text).

perfect (*in potentia*) but unlike it in that it is imperfect (*in actu*), since its being proceeds from the principle only through the intermediary of the first Archangel. Just as this Soul *is* the adoration of the primordial Archangel, so the Cosmos *is* in turn the adoration of the Soul—with this difference, that the Soul cannot complete its work, cannot make good the margin of imperfection and incompleteness that comes to it solely from Time.[29] That is why it starts the movement of the Cosmos; it tends toward its perfection through the great souls which appear from epoch to epoch in this world, not only the Prophets but in general all the members of the esoteric Church, up to the coming of the *Qā'im*, the Resurrector.[30] Here then the cycle of Time is measured by the Soul's effort to make good its own ontological imperfection.

Another schema develops the procession of ten archangelical hypostases.[31] With one of them, the third, a crisis occurs which shakes the celestial pleroma. This is the drama in Heaven, which is the origin of the drama on Earth; the earthly persons exemplify the eternal *dramatis personae* through the periods of an indefinite succession of cycles. This is the dramaturgy that we shall consider here.

THE PERIODS AND CYCLES OF MYTHOHISTORY

1. *The drama in heaven.* We have already stressed the idea that in eternal Time the eternal divine Past *is* eternally actuated and does not fall into the past as a time which "is no longer." Thus the procession of archangelical hypostases, which are the events of this past eternally in the present, is manifested to us as the harmony of a perfect hierarchy; there is no retard, no surpassing of one by the other.[32] If such a surpassing does occur, it will bring about a rupture of this eternal Presence in the present; there will be a sort of fraction of pure ether that has become impermeable to the Light. And it is always through the idea of surpassing and obfuscation, of

29 Ibid., pp. 50, 51, 66 of the translation. Cf. the fine ch. 54 of the *Khwān al-Ikhwān* (Table of the Brothers) of Nāṣir-e Khosraw, ed. Y. al-Khachab (Khashshāb) (Cairo, 1940), pp. 137–39, on the cosmic liturgy of the universal Intelligence or primordial Archangel.

30 Ibid., p. 49.

31 Described, notably, in a voluminous work by Ḥamīd Kermānī (*Rāḥat al-'Aql*) consecrated to the correspondences between the hierarchies of the celestial and earthly universes. Cf. below, n. 96.

32 Idrīs 'Imādaddīn (cf. above, n. 26), *Zahr al-Ma'ānī* (unpublished MS), ch. 4.

regression and opacity that our Ismaili theosophists describe the catastrophe that befell one of the Angels of the pleroma of the *Ibdāʿ*.

Thus the temporal dimension expressed as retard (we have just spoken of "retarded eternity") introduces into the pure Light an alien dimension which is translated as opacity and so alters a relation that could be measured and spatialized only in the dimension of pure Light. For a being of Light this temporal dimension is a falling off from himself, and that is why it is defined as the radical Evil.[33] Here lies the source of the entire Ismaili ethic, which enjoins upon man an unremitting effort to tear himself away from this heaviness, which in every surpassed excellence (*mafḍūl*) finds a reason for striving toward a higher excellence (*afḍal*), and which thus from step to step accomplishes in the mythical hierarchy a repetition of resurrections (*qiyāmāt*) whereby the mystic rises unremittingly above himself.

But how did the rupture take place? In contemplating itself, the prime Intelligence recognizes the mystery of its being; the act of eternally-being which actuates it constitutes it eternally in being; this is the act of which it is the *significatio passiva*, the *mafʿūl*, and which in itself, as something eternally made-to-be, it is not.[34] This recognition is its eternal adoration (its *tawḥīd*), which actuates the Angel who issues from it and who is the Soul of the World; it is the cosmic liturgy which is eternally celebrated by the Archangel[35] and in which beings of every form have their source. The mystery of its being, according to the Yemenite theologian Idrīs ʿImādaddīn (fifteenth century), is like the light (here *perfectio prima*) which, in penetrating the absolutely limpid ether, makes it Light (*significatio passiva*) and thus constitutes it in its own perfection of Light (*perfectio secunda*). And that is why the prime Intelligence is at the same time the veil (*ḥijāb*) and the supreme Name (*Ism aʿẓam*) of the eternally-Being.[36]

At once act and passion, at once the Veil that conceals and the Name that names and reveals, at once adoring (in respect to the Principle that actuates it) and adored (by those to whom it reveals the Principle), the

33 Ibid.

34 Here one must bear in mind the dialectic of the *mafʿūl* mentioned above (nn. 21, 23). The prime Intelligence is the *Mobdaʿ* of the *Ibdāʿ* of the *Mobdiʿ*. Now the *Mobdaʿīya* (=*mafʿūlīya*) of the *Mobdaʿ* (= *mafʿūl*) is only the passive aspect, the *significatio passiva* of the active *Ibdāʿ* (eternal existentiation).

35 Cf. above, n. 29.

36 The prime *ʿAql* is the Angel brought closer (*malak moqarrab*), the sacrosanct (*moqaddas*) Angel, the Lotus of the Limit, etc. Cf. Idrīs, *Zahr*, chs. 6, 7; Strothmann, *Texte*, III, 4–6.

prime Intelligence is constituted in its being by a simultaneity which conditions both its transparency and the potency by virtue of which all the beings of Light, the archangelical hypostases, emanate from its being. The second of these hypostases (called Enclosure of the Sacrosanct, Paradise of the Refuge, Universal Soul [37]) stands in the same relation to the prime Intelligence as the prime Intelligence to the Principle; in it is repeated the same simultaneity of obedience and prerogative. It is the first to hear the appeal of the prime Intelligence [38] (the *da'wat,* and this is the very word which denotes the esoteric *mission* of the Ismaili Church on earth), an appeal summoning all the other Intelligences to celebrate the same liturgy as itself. This appeal has been heard by innumerable worlds (*'awālim*) of angels, forming ten great divisions, each of which is peopled with innumerable angels and has an angel-prince at its head.[39]

Yet this obedience implied an exception, a transgression against it, and this was the prologue of the cosmic dramaturgy. From the dyad of the first and second Archangel, Intelligence and Soul of the World, issues a third Archangel,[40] who is called *Adam Rūḥānī,* the spiritual Adam; this is the Angel of mankind, demiurge of our world. He appears as a hypostasis of Arabo-Persian Neoplatonism, but also shows certain traits of the Manichaean and Gnostic Anthropos. Still more precisely, his role corresponds to that of the Angel Zervān. Let us recall this Angel's doubt as set forth in Shahrastānī: "If the entire universe were nothing . . ." (Ibn Ḥazm speaks of an excess of melancholy, a prostration).[41] But what universe could have been nothing? Zervān was an Angel of the pleroma existing before the physical universe. And Ismaili Gnosis states exactly what it was that the Angel's error placed in doubt: the eternal ontological anteriority of the two Archangels who mediate between the Principle and the third Archangel.

37 *Zahr,* ch. 7. It is by his adoration mingled with an eternal rejoicing that the first Angel (*Sābiq*) gives existence to the following Angel (*Tālī*), who is then actually the first Emanation (*Inbi'āth*), since the first is not *monba'ith* but *mobda'.* The *tawḥīd* of the second Angel consists in recognizing his ontological rank in the *Ibdā',* his *maf'ūlī* (*significatio passiva*) with regard to the first Angel. Thus we have the original dyad or syzygy, the pair *Sābiq-Tālī.*

38 Ibid., ch. 8.

39 Here I cannot develop the interesting comparisons that might be drawn with the angelological schemata of *3 Enoch,* ed. Odeberg. Cf. also G. Scholem, *Major Trends in Jewish Mysticism* (3rd edn., New York, 1954), pp. 68ff.

40 And second Emanation (*al-Inbi'āth al-thānī*). On this angel's relation to the Angel Gabriel in the philosophy of Suhrawardī, cf. our "Récit d'initiation," *EJ 1950.*

41 *Istawḥasha.* Not so much a sin of "pride" as an attack of melancholy in forsakenness and solitude.

Is he not their equal? Does he not even precede them? Is he not first and alone, originating in himself? Hence his refusal to recognize their precedence, to hear the appeal, to testify to the Oneness (*tawḥīd*).[42]

Thus the third Angel stops at himself: he remains motionless in a stupor which gives rise to a gap, a distance between himself and the world of eternal Existentiation from which he cuts himself off. There comes to be a "Time which passes" and creates a remoteness. The transgression becomes a regression: this is the rupture of the eternal Future (*abad*) which eternally actuates the eternal Past (*azal*) in the Present. When the Angel tears himself free from this stupor, he sees himself "retarded," surpassed (*ta'akhkhor, takhallof*), fallen behind himself. From third he has become tenth. To the Time of his stupor that he must redeem corresponds the emanation of the seven other Intelligences which are called the seven Cherubim or the seven Divine Words.[43] Similarly seven periods will punctuate each of the cycles of cosmic Time. Because this drama of the Angel forms the prologue in Heaven of the drama of mankind whose Angel he is, writers have been pleased to find in his deed the archetype of Adam's transgression (his paradise was the world of the *Ibdāʿ;* the tree which he was not to touch was the rank of the Archangel preceding him, who is the mediator of his being, etc.). Moreover, as we have said, the retard, as a temporal dimension, introduces an opacity in the dimension of pure Light. Here, as in the Angel Zervān, the Imagination of the Angel who goes astray manifests his Darkness, his Ahriman, his Iblis.[44]

But here precisely we perceive the difference of which we have spoken. If this Iblis-Satan is born within the angelic being as Ahriman taking birth in Zervān, a no less decisive change occurs in the Zervanite dramaturgy. Externalized as Ahriman outside of Zervān, Iblis is not invested with any legitimacy whatsoever. No ambiguity remains. He is expelled from the Angel and becomes as radically alien from him as Ahriman to Ōhrmazd. More precisely, the Angel, freeing himself from his stupor, tears Iblis out of himself, like an Archangel Michael achieving his own victory over himself.[45]

42 Cf. Idrīs, *Zahr*, ch. 9, and the text of Sayyid-nā Ḥosain ibn 'Alī, eighth Yemenite dāʿī (d. 667 A.H./A.D. 1268: Ivanow, *Guide*, XLIX, p. 60), ed. Bernard Lewis, "An Ismaili Interpretation of the Fall of Adam," *Bulletin of the School of Oriental Studies*, IX (1937–39), 702. It should also be recalled that this drama in heaven derives from our sources of Fatimid or Western Ismaili tradition (the old *daʿwat*).

43 Cf. Strothmann, *Texte*, XIII, 1.

44 Cf. Lewis, "Ismaili Interpretation"; Idrīs, *Zahr*, ch. 13.

45 Lewis, p. 703; and Idrīs, *Zahr*, ch. 9.

Iblis is hurled to earth and his form subsists as the purely Demonic. Thus the being of the third Angel is the mediator, the medium through which Darkness is born, but through which it is also vanquished.

At the same time he is the Angel-prince of an entire universe of Angels who are formed in his image (*ṣuwaruhum ʿan ṣūratihi*); they follow his destiny and he is responsible for them. He has thus immobilized them by his own stupor; it is their entire universe that is *surpassed,* that is retarded. Thus the Angel's movement of *conversion* is accompanied by the appeal (*daʿwat*) which he finally transmits to them from the prime Intelligence (appeal to the esoteric *tawḥīd*), and which is also a calling to accomplish in themselves, in their being which is in his image, this conversion and victory of their Angel. Some hear the appeal, others persist in negation and denial. The former, who show a striking resemblance to the Mazdean Fravartis, are the celestial archetypes of the earthly heralds and proclaimers of the mystical *daʿwat;* they are the posterity of the spiritual Adam. The others are the posterity of Iblis, the implacable adversaries, demons with human faces, who appear from cycle to cycle until the form of Iblis-Ahriman is extinguished.[46]

The profound metaphysical idea that this temporal distance or dimension engenders space is here applied to the generation of the Cosmos. As our Yemenite theologian points out, the retard brought upon the Angels themselves by the fault of their Archangel places them in a situation where a threefold mental movement lends their being a tridimensionality adapted to an existence in the dense and opaque world of material nature. Not only because he is compassionate and merciful,[47] but also because he himself suffers in these Angels who are his members, their Archangel (far from being the wicked Archon of certain Gnostic systems) creates for them a cosmos which is the instrument of their purification and the scene of the combat which is at once theirs and his.[48]

46 Lewis, p. 703; Idrīs, *Zahr*, chs. 9, 10; Strothmann, *Texte*, XII, 38.

47 Cf. the nature of the Archangel Michael in I Enoch 40:9, in *The Book of Enoch*, tr. R. H. Charles (Oxford, 1912), p. 73; and *3 Enoch*, ed. Odeberg, intro., p. 98, n. 1 (Metatron). Cf. above, Part 1, nn. 9, 51, 55.

48 Idrīs, *Zahr*, ch. 10. The idea that in and through their existence and his metamorphoses all his fellow Angels are the time and place of the Angel's battle—and that their existence is equally a battle *for* the Angel—belongs to a chapter of mystical experience to which we are planning to devote a comparative study. Cf. e.g. the case of Johann Georg Gichtel of the school of Jacob Boehme: ch. 5, "Vom Streit Michaels und des Drachens" in *Eine kurze Eröffnung und Anweisung der dreyen Principien*

Here we have a magnificent symbol. The repentance and nostalgia of the Angel are conceived as an energy penetrating the entire universe: the spheres, the elements, and the adepts—that is to say, the human beings of the posterity of the spiritual Adam. This energy is the leaven of the original Existentiation (*al-khamīrat al-ibdā*ʿ*īya*); it is the eternal Eve of the Angel of mankind. It is at the same time his nostalgia and his return to Paradise; it is this energy which from cycle to cycle engenders all his fellows in the angelical state, and finally engenders the *Imām* of Resurrection, the *Qā'im* or Resurrector.[49] This nostalgia then presupposes a past time, something which is relegated to the past in time. But it is also the expectation of something to come. And this something to come is precisely what the fault, the retard of the Angel, has put into the past: the paradisiacal state of pure Light. The nostalgia and expectation lead back to this past, they are a conversion *toward* it. Here, then, the phenomenon of cyclical Time is the reverse of our linear time which accumulates the past. In its passing, cyclical Time abolishes the past, changes it into the future that approaches increasingly. It does not remove us from the source, but leads us back to it; in the being whose form it is and who is *converted* back to his origin, cyclical Time presupposes that special dimension which we have called archetypal and which has its original form in the primitive universe of the Angel.

This form of cyclical Time is subject to developments. The simplest primitive schema would seem to have been a single cycle, punctuated by seven periods or millennia, each ushered in by an Enunciator prophet (*Nāṭiq*) of a new Revelation, assisted by a spiritual legate (*Waṣī*) who is the foundation (*Asās*) of the Imamate and who throughout his period transmits the secret or esoteric meaning of the doctrine to the Seven Imāms who are descended from him.[50] Later, astronomical and astrological speculations made it possible to conceive of a Grand Cycle (*kawr a*ʿ*ẓam*) composed of cycles each governed by a planet and divided into seven periods of seven

---

und Welten im Menschen . . . durch Johann Georg Grabern . . . Johann Georg Gichtel (new edn., Berlin and Leipzig, 1779), pp. 91–98.

49 Idrīs, *Zahr*, ch. 10; and cf. Naṣīraddīn Ṭūsī, *The "Rawdatu't-Taslim" commonly called Taṣawwurāt*, Persian text ed. and tr. into English by W. Ivanow (The Ismaili Society Series, A, 4, Leiden and Bombay, 1950), p. 70 of the tr.

50 It has already been observed that the fundamental doctrines professed by various Islamic and Christian Gnostic sects have certain elements in common. In regard to this periodicity of Revelation cf. the Clementine Homilies quoted in W. Ivanow, *The Alleged Founder of Ismailism* (The Ismaili Society Series, A, 1, Bombay, 1946), p. 131, No. 2. Cf. also below, n. 74.

millennia, the whole to be concluded by the Grand Resurrection.[51] The resulting figures are truly "astronomical" [52] (a Grand Cycle of 360,000 years; some of the sayings of the Imāms reckon the time past at 400,000 Grand Cycles, each including 400,000 periods). Furthermore, the cycles of Time were held to reflect the drama that they exemplified: just as the aeon of Ahriman was expected to be followed by the aeon of Ōhrmazd, so cycles of Epiphany or Unveiling (*dawr al-kashf*) were conceived as alternating with cycles of Occultation (*dawr al-satr*).

But here we discern the consequences of the alteration of the Zervanite dramaturgy. Iblis-Ahriman is never invested with a legitimate sovereignty, he is the Adversary pure and simple. During the cycles of Epiphany, the form of Iblis (*al-ṣūrat al-iblīsīya*) is held prisoner in the "world of the mothers," that is to say, in the world of the simple elements.[53] And because the Angel had defeated his Iblis, the Grand Cycle began with a cycle of Epiphany and not with a cycle of Occultation and Darkness. It was ushered in by the appearance of the earthly Anthropos, the universal Adam (on the island of Ceylon) in the sixth millennium (governed by Mercury-Hermes) of the first period of the first cycle (both governed by Saturn).[54] On earth this universal Adam typifies the spiritual Adam and is the prototype of the Adam of the Bible and the Koran. The cycle of Unveiling which he inaugurates is a beatific cycle in which the true Gnosis is openly preached, in which men are exempt from bodily infirmity and ugliness of soul.[55] It endured until the approach of the first cycle of Occultation, when the form of Iblis reappeared and the drama on earth actually began.

2. *The drama on earth.* But how many cycles, each inaugurated by a "partial Adam" (*Adam juz'ī*), alternated prior to the cycle of Occultation whose rigors we are now experiencing? The Ismaili mythohistory does not record

51 *Qiyāmat al-Qiyāmāt* (literally the Resurrection of Resurrections). On the connections with Babylonian astrology (Planets, Metals, and Ages of the World) cf. W. Bousset, "Die Himmelsreise der Seele," *Archiv für Religionswissenschaft*, III (1900), 243–44.

52 Idrīs, *Zahr*, ch. 11; *Texte*, I, 8 (p. 12 of the text); II, 1 (p. 19), IV, 20 (p. 53); Naṣīr Ṭūsī, *Taṣawwurāt* (above, n. 49), pp. LXXV–LXXVI, and pp. 67–68 of the translation; *Kalāmi Pīr*, ed. and tr. W. Ivanow (Bombay, 1935), p. XXXV, and p. 19 of the text.

53 Cf. Strothmann, *Texte*, I, 6; IV, 2.

54 The πανάνθρωπος as substitute for the tenth Angel (cf. *Texte*, p. 56): *Ādam al-awwal al-kollī*, cf. Idrīs, *Zahr*, ch. 12. This is the primordial Imām, repository and foundation of the Imamate, the institution which by preserving the esoteric meaning of all the Revelations gives mankind the possibility of mystical salvation.

55 Cf. Strothmann, *Texte*, I, 5.

the exact number, but only the vastness of the perspective.[56] It merely registers the veiled memory of nameless upheavals and crimes which preceded the history of present mankind. No archive records them, but their trace has been found in every epoch by the activity of the metaphysical Imagination—from the ecstatic books of Enoch down to Franz von Baader.

The postulates of the Ismaili theosophy might here be amplified in the light of a comparative research.[57] First of all they present a decisive contrast to the idea of "primitive man" accepted by our human sciences. Present mankind is regarded not as a summit of progress but as descended from a superior mankind through a catastrophe of whose mystery we can gain only a distant intimation. It does not issue from the gloom of savagery, from a void and an absence of humanity; the most ancient monuments bear witness not to a babbling, nor even to a dawn, but rather to a twilight.[58] When the speculative Imagination encounters the proposition of vulgar exoteric theology "that there was a time when the world did not exist," it is fitting, declares Naṣīraddīn Ṭūsī (Iranian theologian of the thirteenth century) to remind these theologians that they have remained on a plane of fictitious representation, that in the sense in which they take the words *time* and *world* "there never was a time when this world did not exist." [59] Or rather, this proposition is intelligible only if we have in mind the universe constituted by 18,000 worlds—that is to say, successive cycles each of which is actually one world.[60] These worlds result not from a historical causality but from a homology between cycles exemplifying the same archetypes. In short, there was a race of human beings superior to ours, who were the educators of our race; to this race belonged the Adam of the Bible and Koran. Far from having been the first man on earth, Adam was one of the last survivors of the cycle of Epiphany preceding our cycle of Occultation.[61]

The idea of this *exegesis* from one cycle to another inspires all Ismaili exegesis of the Koran. At the approach of the cycle of Occultation, the form

56 Cf. ibid., B, 1 (pp. 142–43 of the Arabic text).
57 Cf. above, n. 47.
58 Cf. Schelling, *Essais*, tr. into French by S. Jankélévitch (Paris, 1946), pp. 213–15.
59 *Taṣawwurāt*, p. 48 of the text and pp. 65 and 67 of the translation. It should be noted that we also find this figure of 18,000 worlds in *3 Enoch* 24 : 17. Cf. also Hans Bietenhard, *Die himmlische Welt im Urchristentum und Spätjudentum* (Tübingen, 1951), pp. 72–73.
60 Ibid., pp. 65, 66–67.
61 One might well amplify this cyclical conception of history in which the idea of an intercyclical homology contrasts sharply with an evolutionist conception of rectilinear "progress." One cannot help thinking of Spengler's ideas.

of Iblis is liberated and is manifested by grave symptoms which disturb the state of harmony and innocence characterizing the angelical mankind of the ending cycle.[62] These disturbances oblige the dignitaries to restore the discipline of the arcanum at the threshold of a world and a mankind which the direct vision of the celestial figures would only incite to destructive fury. But those who had been the "Angels" of the cycle of Unveiling—that is to say, those initiated into the Gnosis of Resurrection (*da'wat-e Qiyāmat*) —cannot bear the prospect of renouncing the state of freedom and innocence, of direct intuition of all truth; they cannot defer to the demands of the new esotericism. Their horror at the strictures of a religious Law gives way, however, in the course of a dialogue full of prescience and sadness. In the literal Koran text the dialogue takes place between God and his Angels; the Ismaili *ta'wīl* transposes it by one octave: here it is the last Imām of the cycle who gravely declares to his earthly angels: "I know what you do not know" (Koran 2 : 28). One of them, the young Adam, is invested as Proclaimer (*Nāṭiq*) of the new religious Law.[63] Now begins a drama which must be understood as an imitation and exemplification of the drama in Heaven. It consists of two episodes: the revolt of Iblis and the vengeance of Iblis, having as corollary what may be called "the error of the hierophant."

At the beginning of the new cycle the form of Iblis was incarnated in one of the dignitaries named Ḥārith ibn Murra, one of those whose office it had been to initiate the earthly angels of the cycle of Unveiling in the Gnosis of Resurrection. His refusal to recognize the new religious Law is implacable: is he to begin the arduous pilgrimage of the degrees of initiation all over again? Was he not created of fire, whereas the young Adam, restricted to the science of symbols, is made only of clay? Why then should he and the other earthly angels bow down before Adam? [64] When the Angel tears his Iblis from within him and hurls it to earth, all the ambiguity that is still possible in Zervanism has ceased: Ḥārith incarnates an Iblis-Ahriman in the pure state, the No without the Yes, the contrary power of the Adversary.[65]

The temptation to which Iblis incarnated as Ḥārith ibn Murra subjects

62 Cf. Idrīs, *Zahr*, ch. 12, and Naṣīr Ṭūsī, *Taṣawwurāt*, ch. 16, p. 49 of the text. Here the versions of the two great Ismaili traditions are in agreement.

63 Cf. Koran 2:35. On the father of Adam, on Ḥonaid, his Imām *mostawda'* and their Ismaili descendants, cf. Strothmann, *Texte*, X, 26.

64 "They all bowed down except for Iblis, who was one of the genii" (Koran 18 : 48). Cf. the order to worship Adam in "Vita Adae et Evae," quoted in Wilhelm Lueken, *Michael* (Göttingen, 1898), p. 29.

65 Cf. *Taṣawwurāt*, pp. 68–69.

Adam, and through which he takes his vengeance, consists in persuading Adam that since the perfect science of Resurrection was revealed by the last Imām (Qā'im) of the preceding cycle to which they both belonged, and since the blissful men of that cycle owed their state of innocence and freedom to this gnosis, the men of the new cycle should not be deprived of it.[66] In his inexperience, the young Adam lets himself be convinced and commits the supreme "error of the hierophant": he reveals the secret to men who are unfit to receive it, betrays the symbols to the unworthy. And now the drama which befell the Angel of Mankind in heaven finds its earthly exemplification,[67] and here it is shared by two persons. Now Iblis represents only the Angel's *past*, which the Angel by his victory has cut off from himself and which Time, from cycle to cycle, carries toward its annulment. And Adam, having approached the forbidden tree—that is to say, the Gnosis of Resurrection (the divulging of which was reserved for the last Imām)—"escaped through the wide-open door of Mercy." Like the Angel readmitted to the pleroma, Adam by his repentance returns with his posterity to the "paradise *in potentia*" [68]—that is, the *da'wat*, the esoteric Ismaili Church on earth. Its members are the "Angels *in potentia*," like the incarnated Fravartis of Mazdaism, carrying on the battle against the demons with human faces, who are the posterity of Iblis-Ahriman.

And just as the repentance of the Angel, the spiritual Adam, was the eternal Eve, his nostalgia and return to Paradise, so, Naṣīr Ṭūsī declares, Eve, wife of the earthly Adam, is the spiritual and secret meaning of the positive religion (its *bāṭin*), for she had knowledge of the esoteric laws and hidden meanings (the *ta'wīl*).[69] Thus it is through the mystery of Adam-Eve—two beings in one, the text of the religious law *and* the esoteric exegesis

66 Cf. our "Rituel sabéen," pp. 204ff.

67 Cf. Idrīs, *Zahr*, ch. 13; the article of Lewis in *Bulletin of the School of Oriental Studies* (n. 42 above), pp. 702–3; *Taṣawwurāt*, p. 70. The texts of the Yemenite tradition relate Adam's error and repentance to those of the Angel; the prohibitions enjoined upon Adam are compared to the situation of the third Angel; the tree he was not to approach was the ontological rank of the *Tālī*, the second Angel who *follows* the first but who stands in the relation of *Sābiq* (of him who *precedes*) to the third, etc.

68 And on these ideas of "paradise *in potentia*" and "Angels *in potentia*" rest the entire Ismaili anthropology and ethic (cf. *Zahr*, ch. 12; *Jāmi' al-Ḥikmatain*, ch. 13; *Taṣawwurāt*, pp. 59–60, 93–94). Cf. below and our "Rituel sabéen," pp. 199–200, 243–44.

69 *Taṣawwurāt*, p. 70. Cf. the *Jāmi' al-Ḥikmatain* of Nāṣir-e Khosraw (ch. 19, § 226, p. 209): the *waṣī*, the repository of the esoteric sense of the symbols, is regarded as the spiritual mother of the adept, while the Prophet, proclaimer of the letter, is his father.

that transcends it, the Prophet *and* the Imām, the Proclaimer (*Nāṭiq*) *and* the Silent One (*Ṣāmit*)—that the fruit of the positive religion, and the final Resurrection (*qiyāmat*), can spring forth. It is worth noting that Ismaili esotericism here configures its supreme symbol as the conjunction of the masculine and the feminine, which was also the great symbol of Hermeticism. The consummation of this mystery will mark the completion of the Grand Cycle, when the last Imām will proclaim and accomplish the Grand Resurrection. All the adepts, distributed through all the ranks of the esoteric hierarchy, compose the mystical Body, the Temple of Light of this Imām-Resurrector.[70] It is the horizon of Resurrection which for each adept gives its meaning to the Time of combat; here too "the history of the universe is that of the kingdom of the Spirits." [71]

RESURRECTION AS THE HORIZON OF THE TIME OF "COMBAT FOR THE ANGEL"

It is evident that this conception of the Imām as lord of Resurrection, summit of the eternal Imāmate in which culminates the Ismaili vision of the aeon, is far above the political ideology of a final successor who will be a legitimate descendant of the Alids.[72] This political ideology was effaced by the Gnostic idea of the Imām as Anthropos or as the Perfect Child (*al-walad al-tāmm*) who engenders himself in the secret of the cycles of the aeon, and who, in his eschatological Epiphany, is expected to be the ultimate "exegete" of mankind, a member of the true posterity of Adam,[73]

70 Cf. Strothmann, *Texte*, I, 1; VI, 3; XIII, 2; *Taṣawwurāt*, pp. 149–54; *Jāmiʿ al-Ḥikmatain*, ch. 9, § 117, p. 121.

71 Schelling, *Essais*, p. 215.

72 With the transformation of the concept of the Imām, Persian Ismailism becomes eminently a religion of personal salvation, taken as a religion of Resurrection. Cf. the interesting remarks of W. Ivanow on the aspect of docetic Christology assumed by the doctrine of the Imām as divine epiphany, *Taṣawwurāt*, p. LXXVIII (cf. also below, n. 100). Here a vast field of inquiry opens. Unfortunately what one might call the "secret of Alamūt" still eludes us—that is to say, we do not know the reasons why August 8, 1164, was chosen as the date for the Grand Resurrection, for the advent of the Religion of Absolute Truth; cf. ibid., pp. LXXVI and LXXX, LXXVII, and LXXIX, and *Kalāmi Pīr*, p. XXXV. And perhaps there is a hopeless paradox, if not a *desperatio fiducialis*, in proclaiming the divulging of the esoteric meaning: in so becoming exoteric, will it not in turn necessitate a new *ta'wīl?* The danger of this *regressio ad infinitum* seems to have been discerned by the commentator on Avicenna's mystical tale entitled "Ḥayy ibn Yaqẓān" (cf. the translation following our study, *Avicenne et le Récit visionnaire* (Teheran and Paris, 1954).

73 This posterity, it should be recalled, does not include *all* human beings (for mankind also embraces the posterity of Iblis), but only those "whose Angel" by associating him-

which he will lead back (*ta'wīl*) to the celestial archetype in which it originated. Just as the universal primordial Adam is the first earthly manifestation of the spiritual Adam or Angel of mankind, exemplified in the partial Adam of each cycle, so the Imām Resurrector, blossom of the eternal Imāmate, will be its final *parousia*, as the ultimate primordial, earthly substitute for the Angel to whom he leads back. Among the spiritual Adam, the primordial earthly Adam, and the Resurrector (*Qā'im*), there is the same relation as among Gayōmart, Zarathustra, and the Saoshyant to come, who will be *Zarathustra redivivus*. Similarly each of the Imām's manifestations, the Imām of each period, is only the manifestation of a unique and eternal [74] Imām who, in the person of the last among them, will consummate the totality of the Aeon or Grand Cycle.

By projecting itself on the horizon of the Imām Resurrector, the expectation now commands a process of resurrection which shakes the entire esoteric sodality by a movement that is communicated from degree to degree: each adept must "resuscitate" (or "suscitate") an adept like himself—that is, by rising from degree to degree cause another at every step to rise to his own former rank.[75] The mystical Body, the Temple of Light (*haykal al-nūr*) of the Imāmate is thus constituted by the totality of adepts; *each one* reflects it in himself, just as the pupil of the eye can contain the highest mountain.[76] And precisely this comparison gives us an idea of the experience of eternity that is offered the adept: to reflect the whole of the Temple of the Imāmate is to become in his own person an exemplification of the aeon; it is for each adept to attain to his own eternal person—that is to say, to angelicity *in actu;* it is, by a series of resurrections (*qiyāmāt*), to induce in himself the flowering of the Grand Resurrection (corresponding to the final Transfiguration, which in Mazdean Pehlevi is called *Frashokart*, *Restakhīz*).

This ethic of resurrection, to which we have already referred (as an ethic of struggle against a retard, against a being-surpassed), shows us each adept supporting the responsibility of the whole Temple of the Imāmate. By

---

self with the repentance of the third Angel at the time of the drama in Heaven, connects them archetypally with his battle against the posterity of Iblis.

74 *Taṣawwurāt*, p. LXXVI and p. 138; Strothmann, *Texte*, II, 5; cf. above, n. 50. Here one might compare the sequences: Gayōmart, Zarathustra, Saoshyant (= *Zarathustra redivivus*). Spiritual Adam (the third Angel), earthly Adam (universal and partial), the Imām *Qā'im* (the "Perfect Child," herald, or "Angel" of Resurrection). Nuriel, Enoch, Metatron. Cf. also below, n. 101 and above, Part 1, p. 26, n. 63.

75 Cf. Strothmann, *Texte*, I, 1; VIII, 3; XIII, 2.

76 Ibid., I, 1.

virtue of this responsibility the adept does not merely live *in* a fragment of measurable and measured Time. He is himself the total Time of his own measure, and that is why the entire combat constituting the essence of cyclical Time is carried on in the cycle of his own life. Since this Time is a retard, the gap between the fall and the reconquest of angelic rank is the Time of the combat for the Angel.[77] This expression (which results from our situation and reverses the famous image of the "combat *with* the Angel") is to be understood in a twofold sense. It is a combat *for* the person of the Angel of mankind (the third Angel who has become tenth), for the Angel does not carry on alone the combat which is to lead to the final reabsorption of Iblis-Ahriman, whose form reappears throughout the cycles of Occultation. But, since they have assumed his repentance and his nostalgia, his fellows, made in his image, become responsible in their own person for the combat that they wage *for him*. It is their own Iblis that they must hurl into the abyss, and in so doing they battle for the Angel who is in them *in potentia*. To reflect in oneself the Temple of the eternal Imāmate is to anticipate the consummation of the aeon; it is here "to become aeon," to produce in oneself the mutation of cyclical or measured Time, and for each adept this consists in assuming in his person an increasing exemplification of the Angel's being. This implies that what occurs in and by the person of each adept also affects the being of the Angel who is their archetype and who finds his exemplification in them.

Thus we are confronted with situations which reflect one another. The experience of Time lived as a totality here presents a character similar to that which we analyzed at the end of Part 1; here speculative foundation and spiritual experience meet. The Figures shine through one another and exemplify one another. The tenth Angel shines through the person of the

77 Unfortunately I cannot here discuss at any length the highly original aspect which the idea of this combat of and for the Angel assumes in the *Taṣawwurāt (jihād-e rūḥānī, ʿaqlānī, ḥaqīqī)*, where it is related to the triple auto-intellection by which, according to the schema of Avicenna, each *ʿAql* or Angel, by understanding his own being, confers existence on three things: another Angel, a Heaven, and the Soul which is the mover of this Heaven. Ch. 14 (on good and evil) opens with a brief recollection of Zoroastrian dualism, which is rejected, it goes without saying, but reintroduced a few pages further on, where the primordial Inscience (*Jahl-e awwal*) is opposed to the primordial Intelligence (*ʿAql-e awwal*), and "a substance exhausting itself in nothingness" is opposed to a "true substance" these being the source respectively of evil and good creatures. The Ismaili *daʿwat* "separates" the antitheses (cf. the Mazdean *vičarishn*). It acts upon the primordial Intelligence and the true substance like the elixir of alchemy; upon their opposites it has no effect.

primordial Adam, through that of each partial Adam, and finally through the person of the Imām Resurrector; and similarly the Imām Resurrector is already manifested and announced in the person of every Imām of every period. One and the same archetypal Figure, the eternal Imām recurs in multiple exemplifications, just as all the adepts have their celestial archetype in the Angels who followed the tenth Angel in his repentance. This exemplification gives them their archetypal dimension and constitutes them as the cast of characters in a cyclical drama whose prologue was played in Heaven and whose antagonists meet again in every period, in every generation.[78]

The special and characteristic nature of the situation is shown in this process of *exemplification*, which constitutes the individual person and raises him to the dimension of an archetypal Person. Essentially, the perception of all reality becomes the perception, or visualization, of a concrete person. This situation creates the schema of a fundamental angelology, which is essentially the mode of self-understanding of an existence which undergoes what we may now call an *angelomorphosis*—that is to say, the passage from "angelicity *in potentia*" to "angelicity *in actu*," which is the positive culmination of the Ismaili anthropology.[79] On the other hand, this exemplification which personifies all reality in a concrete person presupposes both coincidence *and* distance, identity *and* difference, and for this reason the totality must also be present in the "every instance." This recurrence is the foundation of the *homology* between the total cycle of the aeon and the cycle of resurrections which in the life of the adept constitutes his ascension from one esoteric degree to another. In the Ismaili theosophy the idea of an exemplification of archetypal persons and the idea of a homology between the cycles define the religion of Resurrection (*da'wat-e qiyāmat*) as an angelomorphosis.

1. *Archetypal Persons.* How is exemplification possible? It is to Naṣīraddīn Ṭūsī that we owe the elements of a brief and profound analysis. It seems to postulate that the aspect of action which we state in the infinitive, or the aspect of the event which we denote by an abstract noun, are by no means the true aspect of their reality, and that in the last analysis they refer back to the person of the *agent* who enacts the action or the event as the true reality of both. For all mental or ideal reality, every concept (*ma'nā*) in the

78 Cf. our study, "Le Livre du Glorieux," pp. 61–65.
79 Cf. "Rituel sabéen."

world of the universal has its counterpart in the world of the individual: a concrete person (*shakhṣ-e ʿaynī*) outside of which this ideal or mental reality remains virtuality and pure abstraction.[80] Everything takes place as though the question "Who is it?" were substituted for the question "What is it?"—as though to name the *person* were to define its *essence;* and it is to this person and not to the abstract, universal concept that the *ta'wīl* or internal exegesis leads back.[81] We gain this impression by juxtaposing propositions such as these: "Paradise is a *person* (or a human being)."[82] "Every thought, every word, every action *is* a person."[83] And finally: "Every true thought, every true word, every good action *has* an Angel."[84]

Around these propositions Naṣīr Ṭūsī develops an analysis which may well be called phenomenological. To be in Paradise, or to come into this world, designates above all different modes of being and understanding.[85] It means either to exist in true Reality (*ḥaqīqat*), or, on the contrary, to "come into this world"—that is to say, to pass into the plane of an existence which in relation to that other is merely a metaphoric existence (*majāz*). Measured time, too, is only a metaphor for absolute Time. Thus coming into this world has meaning only with a view to leading that which is metaphoric back to true being, and the external (exoteric, *ẓāhir*) back to the internal (esoteric, *bāṭin*), by means of an exegesis (*ta'wīl*) which is also an exodus from existence. Here, then, we have a mode of understanding (*modus intelligendi*) in which a mode of being (*modus essendi*) is expressed. Even while one is materially present in this world, there is a mode of being in Paradise;[86] but it goes without saying that this *mode of being*, Paradise, can be realized, can exist "in the true sense," only in a person who precisely

80 *Taṣawwurāt*, p. 62 (p. 46 of the Persian text).

81 Cf. "Rituel sabéen," p. 230.

82 *Taṣawwurāt*, pp. 39–60; and "Rituel sabéen," pp. 241–42.

83 *Taṣawwurāt*, p. 60.

84 Ibid.

85 Ibid., p. 91 (p. 63 of the text). This whole passage is of the greatest importance.

86 Such is the meaning of the "person of the (= that which is the) *sirāṭ mostaqīm*" (which corresponds eschatologically to the Činvat Bridge of Mazdaism); cf. *Taṣawwurāt*, pp. 62–63 (45–46 of the text). "The man whose head is raised toward the heavenly periphery (*moḥīṭ*), even while his feet are in the earthly center. Although in relation to the Angel he has not yet arrived at the World of absolute freedom, compared to the animal, he has already attained to it." The person who exemplifies this archetype of the "strait way" is the person who lives in the world beyond as though this beyond were already his present existence, and who carries all the aspects of this present existence back to something unique. This is the internal metamorphosis, the state of discerning lucidity accomplished by the secret of the *ta'wīl* (*bāṭin-e ta'wīl*), and such precisely is the Angel's (*fereshta*) mode of existence in contrast to that of the jinni (*perī*) or demon (*dīv*). Cf. ibid., pp. 64 (47 of the text), 81–82 (57–58 of the text).

is this Paradise—that is to say, who always personifies this mode of being. It is clear that because personification corresponds to an archetype, it is here the exact opposite of allegory.

Fundamentally we may say that since the reality of the act, of the event, is thus reduced to the person who enacts it and understood as that person's mode of existence, every *verb* is mentally conjugated in the middle voice (e.g., the *ἀποφαινεῖσθαι* of the phenomenology which shows *itself* the *phainomenon*). Or else we find a circuit of thought similar to that which in the Archangel's eternally actuated being (*azalī*) seizes upon the very act of eternally being (*azal*), which by eternally actuating his being (*azalīyat*) becomes personified in the Archangel.[87] Here action, thought, or word have their term in the agent: they are reflected and personified in him, by making him to be what they are. They are his modes of being; they are in "every instance" *this* person. In this light, the person in whom his own action is incarnated is the *significatio passiva* of his action—that is to say, he is what his action *makes him be.*

But that implies that this person is an *agent* only in a superficial and metaphoric sense. More active than the person himself is the thought that is thought through him, the word that is spoken by him (and personified in him). And this thought of his thought is precisely what Naṣīr Ṭūsī calls the Angel of this thought (or of this word or action).[88] This Angel endows the soul with the aptitude for thinking it and rising by it; he is the Archetype, the finality without which a cause would never be a cause. He is the "destiny" of that soul. The subjective case becomes an instrumental. The act of thinking is simultaneously a being-thought (*cogitor*) by the Angel,[89]

87 This is the "hermeneutic circuit" (cf. above, Part 2, sec. 1), the phenomenological rotation of which presents the action as a *fi'l* whose *maf'ūl* refers *to* the agent—that is to say, is done and concluded *in* and *for* the agent. The *intention* of the "middle voice" leads one to consider in the *maf'ūl* of every action the modification of the agent's mode of being, his event. It leads one to discover the transcendent subject, which is here the angel. The problem of the *intellectus agens* and the *intellectus patiens* in Arabo-Persian Neoplatonism might be considered in this connection. We shall return to it elsewhere.

88 *Taṣawwurāt*, p. 60 (p. 44 of the text, last par.): "Every true thought, every truthful word, every good action has a spiritual (*rūḥānīya*) entity—that is to say, the Angel (*fereshta*) who endows the soul, in its progressive rise, with the ability to pass easily through the successive degrees of perfection and return to its original source. Then this soul becomes a magnificent Angel (*fereshta-ye karīm*), and the Angels of its thought, speech, and action become integral parts of it, setting their imprint upon it."

89 In thinking this thought the person who thinks it is thought by the Angel, or on the contrary by a demon, for the alternative can only be the person "without an Angel." Cf. ibid.

causing the soul to be what he himself is. The ethic is posited not in terms of values but in terms of the Angel's modes of being. The propositions stated above (every thought *is* a person . . . every true thought *has* an Angel) describe a hermeneutic circle which fuses the schema of *angelology* with the process of *angelomorphosis*, and it is in this fusion that the possibility of exemplification resides.

The soul performs its action and understands it only beginning with the act which actuates the soul itself. It can become a magnificent Angel (*fereshta-ye karīm*) or an accursed demon,[90] deciding its eschatology through the very thing that it exemplifies. For its action is then its own form, which it sends out in advance of itself as its herald, and which is in the image of the Angel—or of the demon—who comes to meet it after death, announcing: "I am thyself." The burgeoning and growth in the soul of the angelical or demoniacal virtuality is the measure of its ascent (*miʿrāj*), or of its fall into the abyss. In the first case, as our author says: "Its thought becomes an Angel issuing from the original world; its word becomes a *spirit* issuing from that Angel; its action becomes a *body* issuing from this spirit." [91]

2. *The homology of the cycles of Resurrection* (*Qiyāmāt*). At the end of this ascension, the adept has completed the Time of his "combat for the Angel." The increasing exemplification of the angelical form which is potentially in the soul leads the soul back to its origin. It is the elimination of its own Iblis: as such, the individual existence of the adept forms a cycle homologous to the Grand Cycle by which the tenth Angel progressively annuls the form of Iblis which he tore out of himself at the time of the "drama in heaven." These are two aspects of one and the same combat, the combat which the heavenly Angel and the virtual or earthly Angels carry on together. Between the two there prevails the same homology as between all the degrees of being through which—by virtue of the Great Return, the *ta'wīl* that is the

90 To be made the "person of the Angel," or the "person of Salmān," to become the "Salmān of the microcosm," etc. Cf. our "Rituel sabéen," pp. 242ff., and "Le Livre du Glorieux," § 6.

91 *Taṣawwurāt*, p. 102 (70 of the text). Moreover, his "homogeneity with divine Reality implies that his *anima* (*nafs*) is conjoined with the light of the religion of the True Absolute (*daʿwat-e ḥaqq*) and that through the energy of the Angel (*rūḥānīya*) of this religion, an Angel (*fereshta*) is appointed to guard over his thought, in which he preserves forever the ornament of the divine truth." Ibid. And man's angelomorphosis is correlative to an anthropomorphosis of the celestial universe, since the glorified human form is its form of light and that of all the other beings of Light. Cf. also Strothmann, *Texte*, I, 1; *Jāmiʿ al-Ḥikmatain*, last paragraph of ch. 11; Idrīs, *Zahr*, ch. 12 and above, n. 86.

cycle of combat for the Angel—the past is abolished and metamorphosed into the future of Resurrection (*Qiyāmat*).

In a stirring vision Naṣīr Ṭūsī describes the contiguity of all the series of beings, each communicating by its highest degree with the lowest degree of the series immediately above it. Thus the worlds of minerals, plants, and animals, the world of man, and the world of the Angel are graduated. And always the higher degree resembles Paradise for the degree below it. The same is true of the phases of a single being. The condition in which an infant cannot yet open his eyes in the sunlight is like his Hell in relation to the condition in which he can face the light, and the latter condition is then like his Paradise. But it is his Hell in relation to the condition in which he can walk and talk. Hell, again, is the condition in which the adult cannot yet attain to knowledge of the spiritual world through that of his own spirit and in which he is unable to experience the meaning of the adage: "He who knows himself (*nafsahu*, his *anima*), knows his Lord." When he attains to it, this state becomes his Paradise.[92] In this vision of an incessant rising from Hells, we see an *alchemy of Resurrection* operating from cycle to cycle. It offers a series of unfoldings, of divestments and revestments, to which one must consent on pain of falling backward, beneath oneself.

Here we may also speak of a "continual exaltation"[93] a cosmology "in Gothic style," or of a pursuit of "retarded eternity." Just as their Fravartis sustain the gods themselves (including Ōhrmazd and his Archangels) in this state of ascension, and just as the Fravartis incarnated on earth must there propagate this effort toward superexistence, so likewise, in the Ismaili schematization of the world,[94] the sum of the degrees of the esoteric hierarchy appears to the adept as a cycle of *resurrections*, each one of which must be transcended, as a succession of Paradises which must be surmounted on pain of falling back into a Hell. Each rank or spiritual degree is a resurrection (*qiyāmat*) whereby the adept becomes conjoined with new immaterial forms which appear on his horizon.[95]

And just as each of the periods of our cycle is concluded by an Imām-

92 *Taṣawwurāt*, pp. 58–59 (43 of the text, bottom).

93 Cf. above, Part 1, end of sec. 2. Schelling, *The Ages of the World*, tr. Bolman, p. 149. Rudolf Otto, *Mysticism East and West*, tr. B. L. Bracey and R. C. Payne (New York, 1932), pp. 184ff.

94 One should also remember the constantly affirmed homology among the mesocosmos (*'ālam-e Dīn*, the initiatic cosmos), the world of nature, and the celestial world.

95 Cf. Strothmann, *Texte*, IX, 5; Idāḥ 11 and Ism 2–3; Idrīs, *Zahr*, quoted in Ivanow, *The Rise of the Fatimids* (Bombay, 1942), p. 243 (54–55 of the Arabic text).

Qā'im, so likewise each of the adepts occupying an esoteric rank is a Qā'im, a Resurrector, in respect to the adept of the next lower rank: by a simultaneity of *action* and of *passion* he must "resuscitate" the following (*tālī*) adept to the rank which he himself had hitherto occupied, while he himself must "be resuscitated" to the next higher rank. The movement of perpetual elevation is propagated from the summit to the base of the mystical hierarchy. Finally, just as the seven periods of a cycle are closed by a Grand Resurrection (*Qiyāmat-e-Qiyāmāt*), instituted by the Qā'im par excellence, the "Perfect Child" who leads back (*ta'wīl*) to the Angel all those in the cycle who have belonged to his posterity—that is, who have borne his image and fought his battle—so, likewise, at the end of the cycle of his individual life, at the seventh degree of his ascension, the adept finds himself on the threshold of the perfect angelicity (*fereshtagī*) of the tenth Intelligence.[96] This is the dawn of his Grand Resurrection. Thus his own initiate's life reproduces the whole cycle or aeon whose totality the Imām Resurrector will complete in his person when limited time *reverts* to absolute Time. By this homology the adept also anticipates his eternity.

In the end the vision embraces all the universes and draws the physical universe of material bodies toward Resurrection.[97] When the highest degree of potency which consolidates the mineral universe is conjoined with the first degree of vegetal potency, the resurrection of mineral nature occurs. In a similar way, plants and animals are resurrected in the next higher order. And finally the angelical potency is the Resurrection of the human potency carried to its highest perfection. Just as the vital soul is like a *body* in relation to the imaginative soul; so the latter in turn is like a body in relation to the thinking human soul; and the latter, finally, is like a body in relation to the angel (the angelic Intelligence, *'aql*). When each of these souls is existentiated in the form immediately above it, this is the corporal resurrection (*ḥashr-e jasadānī*).[98]

96 The decade is completed by three superior esoteric ranks corresponding respectively to the third Angel, to the *Tālī*, and to the *Sābiq* (*Nafs* and *'Aql*, second and first Angels), the primordial pair from which issued the third Angel (become tenth after his error) and the Seven Cherubim Angels, or Words, of the pleroma of the *Ibdā'*. Cf. Ḥamīd Kermānī, above, n. 31.

97 Cf. *Taṣawwurāt*, pp. 93–94 (64–65 of the Persian text).

98 The text of the *Taṣawwurāt* recalls one of the doctrines which Shahrastānī attributes to Empedocles (*Kitāb al-milal*, lith., Teheran, 1288 A.H., p. 165, li. 11), though here *jasad*, body, is replaced by *qishr*, shell, rind, also garment. On this point P. Duhem pointed to the kinship in language and conception between this doctrine and that of the *Zohar;* cf. *Le Système du monde . . . de Platon à Copernic* (Paris, 1917), Vol. V, pp. 121–22.

At the end of our study we perceive a common typology in the horizons of Resurrection set forth in the Mazdean and Ismaili visions. In neither vision is Resurrection an event that simply occurs one fine day. In Ismailism it is accomplished in the person of all those who are "resuscitated" up to its triumphant unfolding in the person of the last Imām, the *parousia* of the tenth Angel. It is the work of each one of the adepts; its time is brought about by the involution of the time of each individual. Similarly in Mazdaism the Fravartis incarnated on earth to fight the combat of Ōhrmazd begin in their own person and action the event of the final Transfiguration. This is the sentiment expressed in the often repeated Zoroastrian prayer: "May we be those who bring about the Transfiguration of the world." [99]

In both doctrines we find a chivalrous ethic inspired by the feeling that evil and suffering are not inflicted by a divine being who consents to them while remaining aloof from them. This suffering is in the divine being himself since it is in his creatures; and by rejecting and combating it, all his followers make a rampart of their souls for him.[100] In both cases, the great moments of the cosmic drama are announced and "dated" in the homologous periods of the cycles by the apparition of figures which are conceived

Naṣīr Ṭūsī speaks of a kind of perpetual alchemy, a formation and unfolding of the spiritual Body. Here we can only mention in passing the fine texts in which Schelling speaks of the "general ability of matter to be raised again to spiritual properties" (*Ages of the World*, p. 173). "Thus man does not pass into the world of spirits with only his spirit in the restricted sense of the word, but also with that which in his body was himself, with what was spiritual in this body" (*Essais*, tr., pp. 357–58). *Reductio ad essentiam:* it is the task of soul to guide its corporeal senses to their perfection. Thus the soul resuscitates through the body, just as the body resuscitates through the soul. In the end, as Naṣīr Ṭūsī says, the spiritual and the corporeal will be one, and it is precisely because of this that "the Angel can become visible after death" (below, n. 102).

99 Yasna, XXX, 9.

100 The Persian word *Javānmard*, which recurs frequently in Shiite Sufism, is best translated by "spiritual knight." It corresponds to the piety and passionate devotion which the idea of the Imām, of the eternal Imām, inspires in the Friend of God exposed on earth to the implacable contradiction of men. Between the two branches of Ismailism, and even more so between them and Duodeciman Shiism, there are, to be sure, nuances and changes which profoundly modify the spiritual physiognomy. A proto-Ismailian treatise such as the *Omm al-Kitāb* (The Mother of the Book) abounds in precise Manichaean reminiscences and features borrowed from the apocryphal books of the Bible. On the other hand, as we have pointed out above (n. 72), the concept and the figure of the Imām led to a recurrence of the problems encountered in Christology. Indeed, all the positions from Arianism to the theology of St. Athanasius recur in speculative Imāmology. Cf. R. Strothmann, *Die Zwölfer-Schī'a* (Leipzig, 1926), pp. 79ff., 155ff.

as the recurrence of one and the same eternal Figure.[101] Finally, in both Mazdaism and Ismailism we have the same denouement of the individual eschatology: the face-to-face encounter between the human I and the celestial I, because the soul finally sees its "self." The episode of the feminine angel Daēnā in Mazdaism has its exact counterpart in Naṣīraddīn Ṭūsī's angel of the amiable and beautiful form, who becomes the companion of the soul for all the eternities.[102] It is the vision of the I knowing itself and finding itself in a transcendent I (a *paredros*), which is both the same and different, as in one same essence without confusion of persons, since a dialogue at once confirms the authenticity of the vision. But this celestial dimension of the Soul of the Perfect One is confirmed and visualized only after the cycle of his resurrections has been completed (after Time has ceased to "retard" over against Eternity); in both doctrines it completes the cycle of the Return, the combat "for the angel."

To the triple question of the little Mazdean catechism cited at the beginning of this study corresponds a situation which, as I have said, Naṣīr Ṭūsī analyzes with the sure hand of the phenomenologist. Here is its conclusion: "To come into this world" and into the time of this world, should not be confused with corporeal presence in the world of existence: it is above all a mode of understanding this existence. To come into this world, as we said a moment ago, can have no significance other than to convert its metaphoric reality (*majāz*) into its True Reality (*ḥaqīqat*).[103] Our author makes it clear that there can be beings who, although they have in appearance come into this world, since they are *there*, have in fact never come into it.[104] Inversely—and here the analysis becomes most striking—there are men whom we can visually discern to have left this world. They are dead, they are no longer there. We say: "They have departed." No,

101 Cf. *Taṣawwurāt*, p. 138 (94 of the text). G. Messina, *I Magi a Betlemme* (Rome, 1934), pp. 59ff.; it is curious to note that the term *al-monba'ith al-thālith* (= the Qā'im, *Texte*, IV, 3) is a literal parallel to the Tertius Legatus of the Manichaean soteriology. Cf. n. 74, above.

102 *Taṣawwurāt*, p. 94 (65 of the text). Cf. n. 98 above and nn. 76–80 of Part 1. Cf. also the motif of the celestial *houris* in Naṣīr Ṭūsī, *Āghāz o Anjām* (lith., Teheran, 1320 A.H.), p. 24. There are abundant exemplifications of the archetype; cf. the motif of the robe in *Acta Thomae*, etc.

103 *Taṣawwurāt*, pp. 91–92 (63 of the text). It is to accomplish (and undergo) the metamorphosis of the *ta'wīl;* cf. above, n. 86, and Nāṣir-e Khosraw, *Jāmi' al-Ḥikmatain*, ch. 14, pp. 163, 166 (to be on the Earth of Tomorrow, which it is said will be illumined by the Light of its Lord, whereas today this Earth still holds us shrouded in Night).

104 *Taṣawwurāt*, p. 91.

actually they have never left this world and they will never leave it. For to leave this world it does not suffice to die. One can die and remain in it for ever. One must be living to leave it. Or rather, to be living is just this.[105] Can we distinguish in the winter, as Nāṣir-e Khosraw says, between a living tree and a dead tree? Both, it is true, are materially there. But in one the sap flows secretly. In the other the sap does not flow, because its roots are dead. When the spring comes—that is, the Imām of Resurrection—only the first will be covered with flowers and savorous fruits at his call.[106] It is no indulgence in a mere literary reminiscence if the image of the Iranian philosopher suggests this thought of Balzac: "Resurrection is accomplished by the wind of heaven that sweeps the worlds. The Angel carried by the wind does not say: Arise ye dead! He says: Let the living arise!" [107]

105 Ibid., p. 92 (63 of the text, end).
106 In *Six Chapters*, ed. Ivanow, pp. 85–86 of the translation.
107 In *Louis Lambert* (Paris, 1902), p. 151.

2

Divine Epiphany and Spiritual Birth in Ismailian Gnosis

1. The Metamorphoses of Theophanic Visions

In the Acts of Peter, a book belonging to those so-called "apocryphal" collections which were particularly esteemed and meditated upon in Gnostic and Manichaean circles, we read a narrative that provides an exemplary illustration of theophanic vision. Before a gathering of people the apostle Peter refers to the scene of the Transfiguration that he had witnessed on Mount Tabor. And essentially all he can say is this: *Talem eum vidi qualem capere potui* ("I saw him in such a form as I was able to take in"). Now in this gathering there are several widows, afflicted at once with physical blindness and incredulity of heart. The apostle speaks to them in a tone of urgency: "Perceive in your mind that which ye see not with your eyes." The assemblage begins to pray, and thereupon the hall is filled with a resplendent light; it does not resemble the light of day, but is an ineffable, *invisible* light such as no man can describe. And this radiant "invisible light" shines into the eyes of these women, who alone are standing in the midst of the prostrate assemblage. Afterward, when they are asked what they have *seen*, some have seen an old man, others a youth, still others a little child who lightly touched their eyes and made them open. Each one has seen in a different form, appropriate to the capacity of her being; each one may say: *Talem eum vidi qualem capere potui.*[1]

The occurrence of perceptions possessing, like this one, a personal character is attested by a number of other passages in these "apocryphal" Acts. In the Acts of John, in the narrative of the calling of the Apostles, when John and his brother James return in their boat after a night spent on the

1 Cf. Acts of Peter XX–XXI; tr. M. R. James, *The Apocryphal New Testament* (Oxford, 1950), pp. 321–22.

sea, both of them behold on the shore a being who beckons to them. But their visions differ: one has seen a little child, the other a pleasant and comely man of noble bearing.[2]

Perhaps we shall find the key to these visions, the basis of their reality and their variations, in a few striking pages of these same Acts of John. On the evening of Good Friday the Angel Christos, while the multitude below, in Jerusalem, imagines that it is crucifying him, causes the apostle John to go up the Mount of Olives and into the grotto illumined by his presence; and there the angel reveals to John the mystery of the "Cross of Light." This cross is called sometimes Word, sometimes Mind, sometimes Jesus and sometimes Christ, sometimes Door, sometimes Way, sometimes Son, Father, Spirit, sometimes Life, and sometimes Truth. It separates the things on high that *are* from the things below that *become* (the things of birth and of death), and at the same time, being one, streams forth into all things. "This is not the cross of wood which thou wilt see when thou goest down hence: neither am I he that is on the cross, whom now thou seest not, but only hearest his voice. I was reckoned to be that which I am not, not being what I was unto many others. . . . Thou hearest that I suffered, yet I did not suffer; that I suffered not, yet did I suffer; . . . and in a word, what they say of me, that befell me not. But what they say not, that did I suffer." [3]

This brief quotation from the sublime discourse will suffice for our purposes. This mystery of the Cross of Light, which was one of the favorite themes of Manichaean piety, recurs explicitly in Shiite Ismailian Gnosis. The texts we have just cited from the so-called "apocryphal" Scriptures (like many others from the same source) give us the right tonality and may serve here as a prelude. If we reflect on the scene recorded in the Acts of Peter, we shall come to conclusions that will serve us as premises. We are dealing with visions, theophanic visions. There is actual perception of an object, of a concrete person: the figure and the features are sharply defined; this person presents all the "appearances" of a sensuous object, and yet it is not given to the perception of the sense organs. This perception is essentially an *event of the soul*, taking place *in* the soul and *for* the soul. As such its reality is essentially *individuated* for and with each soul; what the soul really sees, it is in each case alone in seeing. The field of its vision, its horizon, is in every case defined by the capacity, the dimension of its own being:

2 Cf. Acts of John 88–89; James, p. 251.
3 Acts of John 97–102; James, pp. 254–56.

Talem eum vidi qualem capere potui. The community of vision will be established not by reference to an external object, an evidence uniformly and fully given to all, but by reason of a dimension of being that is common to this or that group or family of souls. This adequation of vision to the dimension and capacity of the soul in which it takes place is the foundation of what we may call the *metamorphoses of theophanic visions.* We find a distinct formulation of these metamorphoses in Origen, where, speaking precisely of the Transfiguration, he declares that the Saviour existed not only in two forms—the one in which he was commonly seen, the other in which he was transfigured—but that in addition "he appeared to each one according as each man was worthy" (*sed etiam unicuique apparebat secundum quod fuerat dignus*).[4] This statement is in keeping with the conception of the metamorphoses of the Logos, no doubt derived from Philo and frequent in the works of Origen, according to which the Saviour appears to men as a man and to the angels as an angel.[5] It fits in with the vision of the steps of the Temple, in which the Saviour is, by reason of his humanity, the first and lowest step and, by reason of his angelic nature, the uppermost step dominating all the others, so that all the steps are the Saviour.[6] In Ismailian Gnosis we find a similar image: the Temple of Light of the Imām, who is constituted by all the degrees of the esoteric hierarchy, to each of which the divine Epiphany is manifested in the measure of its capacity.

We can dwell only on a few essential elements which have already been noted in the various schools of Gnosis and which reappear in this as yet little-known and scarcely studied form, Shiite Ismailian Gnosis. Among

4 "*. . . non solum duae formae in eo fuerunt* (*una quidem secundum quam omnes eum videbant, altera autem secundum quam transfiguratus est coram discipulis in monte . . .*) *sed etiam unicuique apparebat secundum quod fuerat dignus.*" In *Commentaria in Mattheum*, quoted with reference to parallel texts in Joseph Barbel, *Christos Angelos* (Theophaneia, 3; Bonn, 1941), p. 292, n. 459.

5 Cf. ibid., pp. 290–91 (on the creation of the *Gods*, Thrones, and Dominations, and on the theophanies as proofs of the Saviour's angelomorphosis): "*καὶ σαφῶς γέγονεν ἀνθρώποις ἄνθρωπος καὶ ἀγγέλοις ἄγγελος.*" *In Ioan.* I, 31. Compare the parallel texts of Melito of Sardis and Irenaeus (ibid., p. 294) as well as the verses of the poet Commodian, for whom there is only one sole God originated by himself, who is at the same time Father, Son, and Holy Spirit, God of the eternal light, who "*in primitiva sua qualis sit, a nullo videtur, Detransfiguratur, sicut vult ostendere sese, Praebet se visibilem angelis juxta formam eorum*" (ibid., n. 465); and lastly, the text of Philo commenting on Gen. 31 : 13: "I am the God who hath shown himself to thee *in the place of* (instead of) God"—Philo, *De somniis* I, 229–32 (ibid., p. 293); cf. our *Avicenna and the Visionary Recital* (New York and London, 1960), p. 153.

6 *Commentaria in Ioannem* XIX: 6, quoted in Barbel, p. 292, n. 457.

these the one element that determines all the rest is at once postulated and announced by the very nature of an event such as John's secret colloquy with *Christus impatibilis* on the Mount of Olives. In brief, it is the attitude that has been designated by the term Docetism, a conception which itself admits of numerous variants that are sources of no less numerous misunderstandings. What is of capital importance for our purposes is this: not only is the Christology professed by the Koran expressly Docetic (cf. 4: 156),[7] but moreover the doctrine of the Imām, the Imāmology peculiar to Shiite Gnosis is, in its broad outlines, conceived in Docetic terms. We know, moreover, that Mahāyāna Buddhism also conceived its Buddhology after a Docetic fashion.[8]

The conception with which Docetism contrasts is that of the hypostatic union, that is to say, the official dogma of the Incarnation as it was finally formulated by the Councils. In setting itself up against this dogma of the Incarnation, the Docetic conception consequently opposes the idea of a divine Incarnation occurring like a "material" fact which enters into the process of history and becomes its center and which may be invoked as an external and objective *datum*. We should probably gain a good deal by taking the term δόκησις not in its too current acceptation of "simulacrum" or "phantasm" but in its etymological sense of "apparitional" reality, that is to say, as an "appearance" or rather as a "real apparition" corresponding in every case to the faith, the mode of being, one might say the "a priori subjectivity" that is its foundation. Just this is the source of the metamorphoses of theophanic visions. It is implicit in the Docetic conception that the theophany is in every case proportionate to the theophanic dimension of the soul, that is, its aptitude for being shown a divine Figure (such is the meaning of the *qualem capere potui*). The dominant intuition is that the soul is not the witness of an external event but the medium *in which* the event takes place. In our days, too, phenomenology declares that knowledge does not bear upon Being, but it *is* Being, aware of itself. In this sense the Docetists may be regarded as the first phenomenologists.[9] But the term

7 Our Koran references are given according to the type of edition adopted in Iran; the numbering of the verses differs from the Cairo edition and accords with the Flügel edition. [The translator has quoted from and added references to *The Meaning of the Glorious Koran*, an explanatory translation by Marmaduke Pickthall (London, 1930)].

8 *ERE*, IV, 839ff.

9 Commenting on the passage from the Acts of John already quoted (n. 3 above), which states the mystery of the Cross of Light, C. G. Jung also observes that the teaching

is ambiguously broad: Docetism is not a set doctrine but a tendency.[10] Thus it can be reconciled with formulations which literally contradict one another: it can go hand in hand with a complete affirmation of human reality because what it perceives is at the same time not this reality; or it can—and prefers to—volatilize this reality (thus going from Nestorianism to extreme Monophysitism); or, lastly and better still, it can conceive of the reality of a body intermediate between the sensible and the intelligible.[11] Docetism can equally well accept or reject the virgin birth of the Saviour; it can also conceive of the Virgin Mother as having been an Angel, sent in advance of the Angel who was to "appear" to men as her son, their Saviour.[12]

of the Acts of John is far more subtle than the crude and current Docetic conception (or at least than the summary interpretation that is uniformly given of it), namely, that Christ possessed only the simulacrum of a body, which suffered only in appearance. Far from this, the Acts of John proceed in the manner of a critique of consciousness. "The historical facts are real enough, but they reveal no more than is intelligible to the senses of the ordinary man. Yet even for the knower of divine secrets the act of crucifixion is a mystery, a symbol that expresses a parallel psychic event in the beholder. In the language of Plato it is an event which occurs in a 'supracelestial place,' i.e., on a 'mountain' and in a 'cave' where a cross of light is set up, its many synonyms signifying that it has many aspects and many meanings. It expresses the unknowable nature of the 'Lord,' the supraordinate personality and τέλειος ἄνθρωπος, and since it is a quaternity, a whole divided into four parts, it is the classic symbol of the self. [Cf. the end of section 3 below, the Ismailian interpretation of the symbol of the Cross and of the *four* words of the Islamic profession of faith.] Understood in this sense, the Docetism of the Acts of John appears more as a completion of the historical event than a devaluation of it. It is not surprising that the common people should have failed to appreciate its subtlety, though it is plain enough from a psychological point of view."—"Transformation Symbolism in the Mass," in *Psychology and Religion: West and East* (CWJ, 11; 1958), p. 283.

10 *ERE*, IV, 832ff.

11 According to Apelles, the disciple of Marcion, Christ did not have the simulacrum of a body, but neither did he have the substance of a "real" body as the Gospel teaches. Rather, in his descent from the higher regions, he wove himself a body of sidereal and aerial nature (Adolf von Harnack, quoted in Barbel, p. 305, n. 502).

12 Cf. a fragment of the Gospel According to the Hebrews, quoted in James, p. 8; according to Pseudo-Cyril (of Jerusalem) an investigation revealed that a monk had in his possession a Gospel to the Hebrews, in which it was said that a heavenly Power, Michael, was sent from heaven to earth, where this Power was called Mary and bore Christ for seven months in her womb. After a solemn interrogation the poor monk's book was, of course, burned. On this same conception of Mary as a celestial Angel sent in feminine form to give birth to another Angel (Christ), cf. Hans Söderberg, *La Religion des Cathares* (Uppsala, 1949), pp. 183, 203; Henri-Charles Puech and André Vaillant, eds., *Le Traité contre les Bogomiles de Cosmas le prêtre* (Paris, 1945), pp. 207ff. (cf. below, the partial survival of this motif in the celestial origin of Fāṭima). Compare the Philomarianites, or Collyridians, a group of women who came to Arabia from Thrace and called themselves the priestesses of Mary as "goddess"—J. J. Herzog, *Realenzyklopädie für protestantische Theologie und Kirche* (3rd edn., 1896–1913), X, 649, and XII, 315.

These diverse tendencies can be distinguished in the Islamic forms of Gnosis.

What we perceive at once is that all Christology of this type moves against a background of angelology. This is the determining force in the "Angel Christology" or "Christo-angelology" (*Engelchristologie*), a thorough exposition of which by a historian of dogmas recently provoked some nervousness among certain theologians.[13] To tell the truth, such nervousness is quite comprehensible when we consider that the Christological dogma of the Church goes hand in hand with a certain anthropology that is shaken to its foundations by an "Angel Christology." Here we have an idea whose consequences are far graver even than Origen's "a man to men, an Angel to the Angels"—the idea, namely, that the divine anthropomorphosis as such, the theophany, occurs at the angelic level. On the one hand we have a simple "messenger" carrying divine orders: in his very person the Angel is "annunciation," that is to say, revelation of the divine mystery, since all theophany is in essence an angelophany.[14] Correlatively we have an exaltation of humanity in the sense that human nature ceases to be a "nature" as such and becomes a wholly transitory state: man is called, by right of his origin and if he consents, to an angelomorphosis (such is the doctrine also professed in the *Shepherd of Hermas*), his acceptance of which precisely regulates his aptitude for theophanic visions. All these features are sharpened and accentuated in Ismailian Gnosis. They presuppose the thesis that the human form perceptible to the senses cannot be the form of a divine Incarnation (*ḥulūl, tajassud*); at the very least it must undergo a transmutation by the internal organ of the soul in order to be perceived at the theophanic level, that is to say, as a *maẓhar*, an epiphanic Form (in the manner of a mirror in which the image is suspended). It goes without saying that this epiphanic relation,

13 We are thinking here of Martin Werner's important work, *Die Entstehung des christlichen Dogmas* (Bern and Leipzig, 1941), and the polemic raised by Werner Michaelis, *Zur Engelchristologie im Urchristentum* (Basel, 1942), which provoked "refutations" that were far from always being convincing. Cf. a first reply by Werner, "Christus Angelus" in *Schweizerische Theologische Umschau* (June, 1943), pp. 62ff. (containing, among other things, a comparison between Barbel's book cited above and that of Michaelis). Werner's work has just been republished (summer, 1954), too late for us to make use of it here; we expect, however, to return to it at a later date, for it is of the utmost significance for the relationships we are treating here.

14 Cf. in Dionysius and Proclus, the antithesis no longer of *σιγή–λόγος*, but of *σιγή–ἄγγελος*: the Angels as the interpreters of the divine "silence," announcing and revealing the Unity from which they issue. Cf. René Roques, *L'Univers dionysien* (Paris, 1954), p. 135.

like the metamorphoses which it makes possible and evokes, cannot be conceived or defined in terms of a hypostatic union.

If now we extend this law of essence which commands the succession of visions given to one and the same soul, just as it commands the variety of visions given simultaneously to several souls (as in the narrative of the Acts of Peter), if we extend it not in the dimension of our linear time but according to the curve of a cyclical time carrying back the past to its origin, we obtain the concept of a *cycle* of theophanies and their metamorphoses. If to this we add the notion of degrees of dignity or aptitude correlative to these metamorphoses which the law of an identical rhythm orders in *simultaneity* (to constitute a mystical Temple of Light) and in *succession* (to constitute a Cycle of Epiphanies), we possess the essential ideas by which to penetrate the heart of Shiite Gnosis and, most particularly, of Ismailian Gnosis.

Ismailian Gnosis—and this is one of its chief points of interest—presents both an actual extension (in history) and a virtual extension (for purposes of meditation or psychological analysis) of a Christianity that had long returned to the paradise of the archetypes. Not only Gnostic Christianity but eminently the Christianity that is designated as Judaeo-Christianity or Ebionism—a Christianity fundamentally hostile and alien to Paulinism, recognizing the primacy and presence not of Peter but of James, bishop of Jerusalem. We must not forget that Epiphanius, writing at the end of the fourth century (375), describes it as still existing at that time in southern Syria, only a little more than two centuries before the birth of Islam.[15] In general the historians and theologians who have dealt with the Christianity of the Ebionites have suggested and developed at greater or lesser length the idea that it was extended or amplified in Islam;[16] what they had in mind was essentially the conception of the prophetic mission, the Islamic prophetology as such. Here I cannot enter into details, but it is my belief that, if there are common traits, it is not so much in the general prophetology of Islam as in the doctrine of the Imām—the Imāmology peculiar to Islamic esoterism, to Shiism, and most particularly to Ismailian Shiism. Perhaps this thesis might be illustrated on the basis of the idea of the "True Prophet"

15 Cf. the remark of Wladimir Ivanow, *The Alleged Founder of Ismailism* (Bombay, 1946), p. 86.

16 See in particular Oscar Cullmann, *Le Problème littéraire et historique du roman pseudo-clémentin* (Paris, 1930), p. 260, and H. J. Schoeps, *Theologie und Geschichte des Judenchristentums* (Tübingen, 1949), pp. 337–42.

in Ebionism and of the Ebionite doctrine in regard to Adam, the essential features of which recur in the Ismailian Adamology. This Adamology is itself the consequence of an anthropology which goes hand in hand with a fundamental angelology; its keystone is an Imāmology which reveals an inherent "Angel Christology" and Docetism. We find, then, at the height of the Ismailian meditations the idea of a vision whose metamorphoses are correlative with the mode of "consociation" with the eternal Imām, consequently a perfect illustration of the formula *unicuique secundum quod dignus est.*[17]

Here we recall Harnack's proposed definition of Islam as "a transformation on Arab soil of a Jewish religion that had itself been transformed by Gnostic Judaeo-Christianity." [18] Like all such formulas, this one somewhat misses the mark and moreover has the drawback of embodying the type of causal reduction peculiar to historism (the concrete spiritual *fact* of "transformation" itself cannot be causally deduced). Nevertheless it has the merit of invoking not Ebionism pure and simple but Gnostic Ebionism, specifically the Elkesaism which has been called a pre-Manichaean Manichaeism.[19] And indeed we never cease to observe the importance of Manichaean ideas in the growth of Islamic Gnosis, for the Koranic revelation did not by itself institute a Gnostic religion but was, in fact, meditated and interpreted as the exoteric (*ẓāhir*) aspect of a Gnosis—of the Gnosis that concerns us here. The characteristic *theologoumenon* of Ebionite Christianity consists in the idea of the True Prophet and in a unique myth of Adam. For the Ebionites, the support of Revelation is the True Prophet (**προφήτης ἀληθής**) or the Prophet of Truth (**προφήτης τῆς ἀλήθειας**) and not a God incarnate, a God-man. "Running through the ages since the beginning of the world, he hastens toward the place of his repose" (*Nam et ipse Verus Propheta ab initio mundi per saeculum currens festinat ad requiem*).[20] Consequently the

17 Here we cannot even briefly describe the historical circumstances of the burgeoning of Shiism at the very beginnings of Islam, or the spiritual motivations that led to the formation of Septimanian or Ismailian Shiism and of the Duodeciman Shiism which for the last four and a half centuries has been the official religion of Iran; for Iranian Ismailism, cf. our *Étude préliminaire pour le "Livre réunissant les deux sagesses" de Nāṣir-e Khosraw* (BI, 3a; Teheran and Paris, 1953); see also W. Ivanow, "Ismāʿīlīya," *EI*, Supplement, and *Brief Survey of the Evolution of Ismailism* (Bombay and Leiden, 1952). Some of the problems treated in the present study are broached in our essay "Cyclical Time in Mazdaism and Ismailism," see above, pp. 1–58.

18 Adolf von Harnack, *Dogmengeschichte*, II⁴, p. 537 (quoted in Schoeps, *Theologie*, p. 334).

19 Cf. Schoeps, *Theologie*, p. 332.

20 *Recognitiones* 2, 9, 22; Schoeps, *Theologie*, pp. 98, 108–9.

question which the Jews asked the Ebionites was whether Jesus was the True Prophet foretold by Moses, he who is *Christus aeternus*.[21] This is all that separated the Jews from the Ebionites.

The True Prophet begins *ab initio creaturae* with the prophetic dignity conferred upon Adam. The first man was the first epiphanic Form of the True Prophet, that is to say, of *Christus aeternus*; he possessed *τὸ ἅγιον Χριστοῦ Πνεῦμα*, he was Adam-Christos.[22] This typology in itself puts us at the antipodes of the Pauline typology. This impression is intensified by a tenet that turns the Biblical narrative upside down, namely that of Adam's impeccability. For the True Prophet, having within him the breath of the divine nature (*πνέων θεότητος*) cannot sin: he is *ἀναμάρτητος*. To say that Adam sinned is to say that the divine Spirit sinned in him and by him.[23] Similarly the Ismailian theosophy will speak to us of a primordial, universal Adam (*Adam awwal kullī, πανάνθρωπος*) initially invested with the Imāmate and, as such, "immunized" (*ma'ṣūm*) against all impurity, all sin, as were all the Most Pure Imāms after him. And just as the Ebionites qualified Adam as *Anima generalis*, receptacle or treasure of souls, of all *his* souls, so the Ismailian Adam and after him all the Imāms sustain a Temple of Light built out of all the souls of their adepts.[24]

Now it is this Adam-Christos who is revealed through a succession of epiphanic forms, the "hebdomad of the mystery": Enoch, Noah, Abraham, Isaac, Jacob, Moses, Jesus. These are the Seven Pillars of the World, the Seven Columns of the House of Wisdom, the Seven Pastors, and (with Adam himself) the eight *Christs* among the men mentioned by the Prophet Micah, that is to say, the epiphanic forms of Adam-Christos for men.[25]

21 "*Si ipse* (*Jesus*) *erat propheta quem Moyses praedixit, qui est Christus aeternus*," *Recognitiones* I, 43 (quoted from Schoeps, *Theologie*, p. 87).

22 Schoeps, *Theologie*, pp. 100–101. In view of the perspective opened by this speculative Adamology, tending to express the rigorous unity of the prophetic Revelatory Principle in history, we may observe with Harnack that the dilemma of classical apologetics—"Is Christ God or man?"—gives way to an entirely different definition of his essence (*Christus praesens-vicarius Christi*, quoted in Schoeps, p. 108, n. 1).

23 Ibid., pp. 100, 102, 103.

24 Ibid., p. 99. *Anima generalis*, as the divine Treasure House of the souls, should be confused neither with the collectivity of the souls nor with the logical universal; cf. among the Catharists, the *Spiritus Adae* or *Anima* from which descend *omnes animae* (Söderberg, p. 157), the Angel Christ who is called *Anima* (pp.186ff.), the distinction between *Spiritus* or *Anima principalis* and the *Spiritus sancti* as tutelary spirits (p. 174).

25 Schoeps, *Theologie*, pp. 104–6 (Micah 5 : 4, *ἑπτὰ ποιμένες καὶ ὀκτὼ χριστοί—ὀκτὼ χριστοὺς ἀνθρώπων* = *Christos hominum* in St. Jerome).

Manichaeism professes a similar succession but includes figures from outside Semitic prophecy: Adam, Seth, Noah, Jesus, Buddha, Zoroaster, Mani. As for the Koran, it also has a succession of prophets, but the number of those it expressly names is very different from the number mentioned in the Traditions.[26] The idea of an exact periodicity is formulated only in Ismailian Gnosis with its Cycle of seven periods, the last Prophet of which will be the last Imām, the *Qā'im al-Qiyāmat* or Resurrector, corresponding to him in whom the True Prophet finds at last his "repose." And precisely this Figure enables us to point out the true nature of the correspondence. We know that Ebionism distinguished between the case of Moses and Abraham, to whom the True Prophet appeared, and that of Adam and Jesus, in whom the True Prophet was present and who in their person were the very foundation of the theophany.[27] The prophet Muḥammad may be likened to those to whom theophanic visions were given but whose person itself may not be called theophanic, whereas this epithet applies to the person of the Imām. That is why we have said that it is not Islamic prophetology in general but Shiite Imāmology in particular which prolongs and amplifies the Ebionite Christology as the summit of prophetology.

In this same connection, the idea of theophanic (*maẓhar*) persons and of their succession must be preserved in its original form. It would be quite incorrect to conceive of this succession as a series of reincarnations, as a metensomatosis. The *ἡγεμόνες τῆς προφητείας* are neither reincarnations of the True Prophet nor simple receptacles of the Spirit, to whom the True Prophet appeared.[28] The guiding idea is the idea of *ἀνακεφαλαίωσις*,[29] a recapitulation or, more exactly, an integration or reintegration into the whole. Just as all the Prophets since Adam are "recapitulated" in Christ, so all the Imāms, all the partial *Qā'im*, are recapitulated or integrated in the

26 Cf. ibid., p. 335. Here it may be well to recall certain aspects of Islamic prophetology: the distinction made between the *nabī* (the preacher with the divine mission) and the *mursal* (the Envoy who becomes the leader of a people). The *Biḥār al-Anwār* (Encyclopedia of Shiite Traditions) counts 124,000 *nabī* (including a great number of Biblical figures but many non-Biblical figures as well), among whom only 313 have the quality of Envoys; cf. our *Avicenna*, p. 312, n. 9.

27 Cf. Schoeps, *Theologie*, pp. 106–7, and *Aus frühchristlicher Zeit: Religionsgeschichtliche Untersuchungen* (Tübingen, 1950), p. 32.

28 Schoeps, *Theologie*, pp. 106–8.

29 Ibid., p. 104, n. 6, in which the author expresses the belief that Neander went too far in regarding this conception as a specifically Docetic Christology; one might well reconsider the question, taking into account what has been suggested above concerning the true meaning of Docetism (n. 9 above and related text).

last among them (whose *majma'* is the Temple of all their Temples of Light). It is then as a progressive integration that one must conceive the growth of an epiphanic Figure whose unity and totality imply a number of theophanies without confusion of persons. Further, if the last Imām, still to come, is called the Perfect Child (*al-walad al-tāmm*), he is so named in respect to the Angel of the pleroma, who is here the homologue of *Christus aeternus*. But "adoptionism" does not mean here that the Adopted One is exalted, or purely and simply metamorphosed, into the celestial person who adopted him; he is that person's ultimate, concluding Form. If he draws toward him in an ascending movement the entire pleroma of his souls, the adepts of the sodality down through the centuries, if he is enthroned as the substitute and successor of the Angel, it is because the Angel himself consequently rises into the celestial pleroma and from Cycle to Cycle continues to draw all those who follow him to ever higher abodes. Such are the consequences of a mighty dramaturgy to which we shall have occasion to return. Everything happens as though all the consequences of the rejection of the hypostatic union were preserved, down to the distinction of two persons: Christos Angelos *and* Jesus the prophet. And indeed Ismailism distinguishes a threefold notion of the Anthropos: there is the celestial, or spiritual, Adam (*Adam rūḥānī*), the Angel corresponding to Christos Angelos; there is the original, universal Adam (*Adam al-awwal al-kullī*) at the beginning of the Cycle of Cycles; and finally, there are the partial Adams (*Adam al-juz'ī*) at the beginning of each Cycle, our own for example: the Adam mentioned exoterically by the Bible and the Koran. Ultimately, then, the decisive interest is concentrated upon the person and the figure of Angelos Christos and his correspondences: in Ismailian Gnosis, the celestial Anthropos, the spiritual Adam; in Avicennism, the Tenth Angel, identified with the Holy Spirit and the Archangel Gabriel of the Koranic text.

The pattern of Ebionite Christology as contrasted with the official Christology of the Church is well known.[30] Adoptianist like that of the *Shepherd of Hermas*, this Christology considers Jesus as having first been a man among men. It looks on the scene of the Baptism as the Epiphany: a supernatural light descended from heaven, illumining and transfiguring the place (as in the narrative of the Acts of Peter), and the words of the Holy Spirit were heard: "Thou art my beloved son, *today* I have engendered thee" (words

30 Ibid., pp. 73–75, 78.

which are echoed by those of Jesus recorded in the Gospel According to the Hebrews: "*My mother the Holy Spirit* seized me by the hair and carried me up to Mount Tabor").[31] The consequences of this Christology are incommensurable: what interest now has the earthly genealogy of Jesus? Only Angelos Christos pre-exists, and all that need be meditated upon is his eternal birth in the pleroma. For beyond any doubt we find here a trace of the early hesitation to distinguish between Angelos Christos, the Son, and the Holy Spirit, the repercussions of which may be found in all Islamic theology (in the identification between the Holy Spirit and Gabriel the Archangel, who in Christian Gnosis was also Gabriel-Christos). But we know that this recognition of Christos as an Angel (who confers not his essence or his "person," but his name and his quality upon Jesus) was bound up, among the Ebionites, as may be seen in I Enoch,[32] with the idea of the Son of Man as originally a celestial Archangel and of Christos as one of the Archangels, at once prince of all the other Angels and celestial archetype of mankind.[33] And we also find Christos as an Archangel among the Seven, or identified with the Archangel Michael (as in Hermas or among the Catharists), and this identification becomes all the more comprehensible

31 Cf. James, pp. 2–5. (Here we have before us a third Judaeo-Christian gospel, the "Egyptian" Gospel according to the Hebrews. Cf. Schoeps, *Theologie*, p. 31.)

32 I Enoch 46: 1, and text of Tertullian quoted in Schoeps, *Theologie*, pp. 80–81: "*(Ebion) . . . non dei filium constituit Jesum . . . ut ita in illo angelum fuisse edicat, quemadmodum in Zacharia.*" Yet the difference is more profound than the author (alluding to the polemic mentioned above, n. 13) supposes, and the analysis should be carried further. It does not amount to the same thing whether an Angel acted in Jesus or whether Jesus was an Angel. Not Jesus is in question, but Christos Angelos and no one else. The union of the Angel Christos and of Jesus remains, then, to be considered; here the *unus ambo* is assuredly not equivalent to a hypostatic union; perhaps the old habits of thought that have decided otherwise do not at once provide us with the necessary categories in which to apprehend this mode of being in *duality*. It is fundamentally the problem of the mode of man's relation with his Angel, a problem which demands precisely to be reconsidered as soon as the pattern of an Angel Christology is put forward (that of Hermas, the Gnostics, Theodotus, etc.). It is also the problem raised in philosophical terms by Avicennism, where the figure of the active Intelligence as Gabriel-Holy Spirit dominates the theory of knowledge and of salvation by knowledge; it is under this aspect that we must analyze the reasons for the failure of Latin Avicennism, whose position in relation to orthodox Scholasticism was similar to that of Angel Christology in relation to the official Christology; see on this essential question (not hitherto considered) our *Avicenna* and the analysis outlined below of the notion of *maẓhar*, or "epiphanic form."

33 Cf. Schoeps, *Theologie*, p. 81 (quoted from Epiphanius: ὡς ἕνα τῶν ἀρχαγγέλων and *Homilies* 3, 20, *Recognitiones* 1, 45, in which God, deliberating with his Angels on his decision, institutes "princes" for all creatures—*Statuit angelis angelum principem . . . hominibus hominem, qui est Christus*).

in view of the contrast stated in one of the Clementine writings between the Demon as prince of the world and the Archangel Christ who will rule over the world to come.[34]

In all these variants, Angel Christology develops a soteriology that contrasts no less strongly with the orthodox soteriology. As the passage from the Acts of John regarding the mystery of the Cross of Light has solemnly told us, no soteriology attaches to the death of Jesus on the cross made of material wood. If he has been enthroned as a messianic Lord, it is not because his death effected a redemption; it is because the community was waiting for the Epiphany of the Son of Man, for Angelos Christos, the παρουσία τοῦ διδασκάλου, the return of him who dispenses the Knowledge that delivers and who will thereby establish a supraterrestrial kingdom, a kingdom of Angels.[35] It is not by shedding his blood that he saved the world (*Christus impatibilis* does not die); he is the Saviour because he has kindled for mankind the torch of perfect Knowledge.[36] The Clementine Homilies never speak of the Passion: redemption is effected by the Knowledge of the Truth. Jesus, the prophet of the Truth, is essentially an Illuminator, not a Redeemer in the Pauline sense. The traditional objection[37]—if Christ were an immortal Angel, he could not have become a true man and have suffered and died as a Saviour—always elicits the same reply: why should it have been necessary? And indeed this is a wholly Pauline objection. And although it is true that certain evangelical texts as well as the Apocrypha and certain Manichaean notions are known to Islamic theology and Ismailian Gnosis, there is no doubt that, like Mohammed himself, they know nothing of St. Paul.

34 Ibid.; on Christ as one of the Seven Archangels, cf. Barbel, pp. 192ff. Observe that the archangelical heptad so clearly represents an archetype that we encounter an extraordinary *revival* of the cult of the Seven Archangels, starting in Italy in the sixteenth century and spreading as far as Flanders and Russia; cf. Emile Mâle, *L'Art religieux après le Concile de Trente* (Paris, 1932), pp. 298ff.

35 Schoeps, *Theologie*, p. 76.

36 Cf. the quotation from Siouville in ibid., p. 111, n. 3.

37 This is one of the questions cited by Adolphine Bakker in an important article: "Christ an Angel? A Study of Early Christian Docetism," in *Zeitschrift für die neutestamentliche Wissenschaft* (Giessen), XXXII (1933), 255–65. The article's point of departure is an observation by Rendel Harris, the English theologian: from the Slavonic translation of Josephus it results not only that a collection of *Testimonia* quoted by Josephus forms the oldest document of known date that may be regarded as a source of Christology, but that in it Christ is constantly designated as an Angel; precisely the polemic in the Epistle to the Hebrews presupposes this Angel Christology, which it attacks and which is attested in the *Testimonia* (cf. also Werner, p. 66).

We have suggested above that an Angel Christology goes hand in hand with an angel anthropology;[38] the entire Adamology is affected, and the Ismailian vision concentrates on this theme. The dramaturgy embraces the events that befell the angelic, celestial Adam and the terrestrial Adam, or rather *Adams.* The traditional identification among the philosophers between Gabriel, the Holy Spirit, and the active Intelligence, which among the Ishrāqīyūn is the Angel of humanity and in Ismailism is *Adam rūḥānī*, or the Spiritual Adam, is only a commentary on the Koranic texts, where the identification Gabriel-Holy Spirit itself exemplifies a Gnostic Christology in which Angelos Christos assumes more particularly the features of Gabriel-Christos. Here I shall briefly set forth a few points: they will serve us as an introduction to the dramaturgy that has its source in this angel archetype of mankind—a dramaturgy in which our own history today is simply a phase, the crucible of the metamorphoses which must either lead humanity back to its celestial and angelical origin or consummate its demoniacal fall.

The identification of Christos with the Archangel Gabriel is the dominant trait of an entire Gnostic Christology.[39] If we consider at the same time the

38 Among other consequences, consider that mentioned in n. 22 above.

39 On Gabriel-Christos see Barbel, pp. 225–62. In the *Epistula Apostolorum* (p. 236) Christ tells how he took the form of the Archangel Gabriel in order to appear to the Virgin. Thence follows the idea that it is the Logos which "gives itself form in the Virgin" (p. 240), and we have a double equation—on the one hand between the Son and the Holy Spirit, on the other between the Son-Holy Spirit and the Angel Gabriel, as is suggested by this passage from the Pseudo-Ambrose: *Vides ergo Spiritum Sanctum, id est Filium Dei, venisse ad Virginem et inde Dei et hominis filium processisse* (p. 246, n. 282). It is texts of this kind (and particularly those concerning the Angels of the Holy Spirit) that should be systematically restudied if we are to interpret in depth the assimilation of the Angel Gabriel to the Holy Spirit in Islamic theology. The idea that the conception is accomplished by and with the annunciation of the Angel Gabriel brings up particulars that withdraw the Mystery from all physiological explanation: e.g., the idea that by the voice of the Archangel the ἰδιότης of the Logos penetrates the Virgin; or, rather, that the *voice* of the Archangel is itself a hypostasis of the Logos (p. 248); or that the conception did not last several months *sed ipsum per uterum ipsius instar aquae per canalem transiisse* (ibid.). Among the Gnostics (Book 8 of the Christian Sibylline Oracles), the Angel Gabriel acts "as God" (p. 254); the Angel Gabriel is the very form of Iao Sabaoth Adonai, the true Force that strikes down the demons, Christos (cf. section 5 below, Salmān the Pure, terrestrial typification of Gabriel, as well as the Veil, *ḥijāb*; the little known sect of the *Ahl-e Ḥaqq*, which still exists in Iran, possesses a book that is extremely rare though of recent composition, the *Shāh-Nāma-ye Ahl-e Ḥaqq*, or "Royal Book of the Gnostics," in the prologue of which the Angel Gabriel assumes the role of *protoktistos*). In the *Pistis Sophia*, Christ in the form of the Archangel descends with the twelve Saviours of the Treasures of Light, whom he projects into their mothers' wombs (p. 256), an image that we shall have occasion to remember in connection with the twelve Imāms in the Gnosis of Duodeciman Shiism.

primitive identification between the Holy Spirit and the Son of God (the "magnificent Angel" of the *Shepherd of Hermas*), we shall understand the contention that it is the Holy Spirit itself that is sent to Mary, that inspires her with its own breath and "takes body" in her with a reality which is not that of a material body but of a subtle celestial body. *Eo ipso*, this equation (Gabriel-Christos-Holy Spirit) that is discernible in Angel Christology, becomes an aspect of what has been called "Spirit Christology" (*Geisteschristologie*). The great majority of the *tafsīr* (Koran commentaries) are in agreement on this point (an entire book ought to be devoted to this pneumatology). The very details of the mental visions recur both in Christian Gnosis and in certain of our *tafsīr*,[40] for example the role attributed to the Archangel's *voice*, which is represented as being itself the hypostasis of the Logos. Hence the fine symbol of a virgin conception "by the ear," which means *by faith*, *ex auditu*, and suggests that the reference is to a theological dogma and not to a physiological problem. In other words, the miracle of the virginal conception is not the main point (as in the context of the dogma of the Incarnation); rather, it becomes a necessary correlate as soon as the vision is concentrated on the central problem, which is to elucidate the superior constitution of the celestial Aeon united with the man Jesus and the manner of their union. Correlatively certain *tafsīr*, amplifying the Koranic verses on the annunciation, disclose a relation between Gabriel and Jesus which would be expressed in Mazdean terms as a relation between

40 The equation, stemming from the Koran, between the Angel Gabriel and the Holy Spirit (*Rūḥ al-Quds*) and the correspondence (among the Avicennan philosophers) between Gabriel and the Angelos Christos of Angel Christology, is deserving of an entire study that would require a methodical analysis of the *tafsīrs*, or Koran commentaries. We hope to undertake such a study, for it would have the greatest consequences for an understanding of the differentials (and their sources) between a "philosophy of the Spirit," as conceived by a body of speculative thought developing in an Islamic world, and that "philosophy of the absolute Spirit," a secularization of several centuries of philosophical speculation, at which the Occident arrived in the nineteenth century. On Gabriel as Holy Spirit, cf. among others, Mullā Fatḥullāh Kāshānī, *Tafsīr* (Teheran, 1310 A.H.), I ad 2 : 81 and III ad 97 : 1–4; Muhsen Fayż, *al-Ṣāfī* (Teheran, 1282 A.H.), p. 253 (ad 16 : 104), pp. 264, 486; Maibodī, *Kashf al-asrār* (Tafsīr-e Khwāja Anṣārī) ed. Ḥekmat (Teheran, 1331 A.H.), I, pp. 258-63. Here again (cf. n. 39) Gabriel acts "like God" (Mullā Fatḥullāh, *Tafsīr* ad 4 : 169, mentions the exegesis that makes the *Rūḥ* cosubject of the verb *alqā-hā*: the Spirit, that is to say, Gabriel, who projected the Word, Jesus, into Maryam). Here we find the same conceptions as in Christian Gnosis: the voice of the Archangel as hypostasis, the time of conception in complete defiance of physiological laws (three hours!), the idea of the psychic, spiritual body, etc. (ibid., ad 2 : 254; 4 : 169; 5 : 109; 19 : 17–19, etc.). It goes without saying that to appreciate the Docetism of the *tafsīrs* one must bear in mind the remark made above (n. 9).

the Fravarti, the tutelary angel, the celestial archetype, and the terrestrial soul.[41]

Gabriel, the Angel of the Annunciation and the Revelations, is the Angel of the theophanies that were given to the prophet Mohammed. The Koran verses (53 : 3–4; 81 : 19–29) preserve the memory of the first grandiose visions when the Prophet, emerging from his tent, contemplated the majesty of the Angel whose outspread wings covered the whole horizon. In certain traditions invoked by the commentators these sumptuous angelophanies even recalled by contrast the memory of the refusal suffered by Moses on Mount Sinai when he asked to be favored with a direct vision and the Lord answered: "Thou shalt not see me" (*lan tarānī*). Mohammed also expresses the fervent desire to see the Angel in his real form. Although warned, he insists. The vision is not refused him, but he is thrown into a swoon by the beauty and majesty of the Angel in his superhuman form of Glory; henceforth a terrestrial human Form will be the epiphanic figure (*maẓhar*) of the Angel.[42] And marking the contrast with the dramatic episode experienced by Moses, a tradition establishes the angelic "numinosum" in a sense that is perhaps paradoxical if we compare it with the current acceptation of the term. Here it is far from being a *tremendum*, for it is in his form of Majesty, which nevertheless causes the Prophet to swoon, that the Angel reveals to him the imperatives and prohibitions of the Law.[43]

41 In agreement with the type of Gnostic who distinguishes between Jesus the man and the celestial Christ and who looks on the earthly phenomenon as a hidden image of the higher world but does not absolutely exclude all idea of a "corporeal" birth, cf. Barbel, p. 257, n. 316 (text of Carl Schmidt); cf. Maibodī, pp. 263–64. It is the Angel Gabriel who saves Jesus from death (Mullā Fatḥullāh ad 4 : 156, the Docetic verse par excellence of the Koran; the situation of the Angel corresponds here to the situation presupposed by the colloquy on the Mount of Olives in the Acts of John; and the application of this same verse came to be extended to all Imāmology, cf. section 4 below). Here we only arrive, by a different path, at the thesis of Rudolf Otto, *Reich Gottes und Menschensohn* (Munich, 1934), p. 146 (*The Kingdom of God and the Son of Man*, tr. F. V. Filson and Bertram Lee-Woolf [London, 1938], p. 182), showing the Mazdean idea of the Fravarti to be an exact prefiguration of the relations between Enoch and the celestial Man, between Jesus and the Anthropos. The present essay will show later on that the relation between the Imām-Anthropos and Salmān (the Gnostic True Believer) embodies a situation similar to that of Enoch when it was revealed to him: the Son of Man is *thyself*.

42 Cf. Muḥsen Fayż, pp. 432–33 (ad 53 : 3–5), p. 474 (ad 81 : 19ff.; on the two aspects, or "forms," of the Angel, cf. Mullā Fatḥullāh, ad 35 : 1; with this compare Abū'l-Futūḥ Rāzī, *Tafsīr* (the oldest Shiite *tafsīr* in Persian), ad loc., with certain variants of the narrative insisting on the Angel's feeling of compassion and tenderness.

43 Cf. Maibodī, pp. 301–2.

Mohammed, however, has only the vision of the Angel. Here, as we have pointed out, the distinction which the prophetology of the Ebionites makes between the cases of Adam and Jesus on the one hand and Moses and Abraham on the other will find a parallel in the transition from prophetology to Imāmology. A Koranic verse (33 : 33, *āyat al-taṭhīr*) rich in exegetic virtualities constitutes one of the Scriptural foundations of Shiism. I am referring to the scene in which the Prophet, having spread out his mantle over the members of his house (Fāṭima, his daughter; ʿAlī, his son-in-law; the two child Imāms Ḥasan and Ḥusayn), asks God to immunize them against all impurity (*taṭhīr*). These are the Five "Companions of the Mantle" (*Aṣḥāb al-Kisāʾ*), earthly epiphanies of the Five Pre-eternal Persons of the divine Mystery (*ashkhāṣ azalīyūn*), whose theophanies succeed one another on different planes of being and from period to period.[44] Thereupon the Angel Gabriel makes himself visible, proclaiming: "I am the sixth of you five" (*anā sādisukum*), which means the distinct personal unity that is also their totality; then he reveals the verse.[45] The vastness of theological meaning found in this scene by Shiite meditation may be measured by the fact that the *tafsīr* attributed to Imām Ḥasan ʿAskarī, the eleventh Imām of the Duodeciman Shiites, expressly establishes a typological relation between the Koranic verses evoking the Annunciation and the conjunction of the Holy Spirit with Jesus, and this scene in which Gabriel the Holy Spirit joins the five hypostases of the original Imāmate. It is precisely here that Shiism inaugurates the transition from Angel Christology to Imāmology.[46] Finally, the Angel Gabriel achieves his earthly typification, his theophanic person (*maẓhar*), in the person of Salmān the Persian, or Salmān the Pure, as the companion who initiates the Prophet into his vocation, and the figure of Salmān will indicate to us the ultimate and profound signification of personal experience that Imāmology can contain.[47]

44 On the metamorphoses of their theophanies (on the plane of the divine Throne, on the plane of the Five Archangels, on the plane of their earthly typifications), cf. particularly *Umm al-Kitāb* (proto-Ismailian treatise in Persian), ed. W. Ivanow, Questions 3 and 5.

45 Cf. Mullā Fatḥullāh, II ad 33 : 33; Muḥsen Fayż, p. 363; Muḥammad Bāqir-e Majlisī, *Biḥār al-Anwār* IX, pp. 39, 180–97.

46 Cf. *Tafsīr* attributed to the eleventh Imām (Ḥasan ʿAskarī) (lith., Teheran), pp. 150ff. and pp. 185ff. (for Gabriel and Salmān).

47 See particularly Louis Massignon, "La Mubāhala," in *Annuaire de l'École des Hautes-Études, Section des Sciences religieuses* (1944), pp. 19ff., in which it is the mission of Salmān as earthly homologue of Gabriel, Angel of the Annunciation, to make the

It is to this Angel of Revelation as Angel of Knowledge, of all knowledge, that the Avicennan philosophers "led back," by way of their own peculiar *ta'wīl*, the representation of the active Intelligence (*'Aql fa''āl*, Νοῦς ποιητικός) which they took from Aristotle and which Avicenna identifies with the tenth Cherub of the first celestial hierarchy. It is this active Intelligence that is worshiped as Madonna Intelligenza in the meditation of the *Fedeli d'amore*.[48] Among the Ishrāqīyūn it is the Angel of humanity, the celestial archetype of the human creature (*rabb al-naw'-e insānī*). All these variants merely define and amplify the original features of one and the same Figure: Angel, Holy Spirit, Gabriel, Christos, Sophia. In Ismailian Gnosis, to be sure, this Figure has its homologue in the tenth Angel of the pleroma, who is the celestial Adam, but here something more enters in: this tenth rank is not originally his. He must regain his original rank with the help of all mankind which issues from him, and he must draw all this mankind of his upward in his ascent. Here we have a dramaturgy of pre-cosmic origin, made explicit by the phases of Adamology. It is this Adamology that one must have in mind in order to conceive the Cycle of Divine Epiphanies, which is also the Cycle of the soul's metamorphoses.

2. *Ebionite and Ismailian Adamology*

It has been observed more than once that the Ebionite Adamology is characterized by a doctrine which is considered unique in Christian, Jewish, or Gnostic literature: the doctrine which absolves Adam of all sin and affirms

stupefied Christians recognize, in the theophany of the Five Mohammedans sitting haloed in Glory beneath the Mantle, a new manifestation of the Divine Spirit "which hath anointed the Messiah for the kingship," and pp. 25ff. (*nuṣayrī* liturgy) recounting the theophanic vision in which the Messiah (= Mohammed), his "Father" (= Salmān), and his Mother (Fāṭima = Maryam) are recognized beneath the Mantle. We might mention in passing that this would lead us to read the ideogram XΓM as Christos, Gabriel, Maryam, rather than Christos, Gabriel, Michael (according to the usually accepted hypothesis). On the "perpetual presence" of Salmān from Christ down to Mohammed, cf. our study "Le Livre du Glorieux de Jābir ibn Ḥayyān," *EJ*, XVIII (Jung Festschrift, 1950), 105; cf. section 5 below on Salmān as archetype of the perfect Gnostic, "Salmān of the microcosm."

48 Cf. our *Avicenna*, p. 267. To complete the mental image of Gabriel-Sophia-Holy Spirit, we may observe in passing that in Eastern Christian iconography, which traditionally represents the three persons of the Trinity by three Angels, the Angel seated on the right (i.e., to the left of the Central Angel) discloses more distinctly feminine features (e.g., in the famous icon of Andrei Rublev). [Cf. Rublev's "Old Testament Trinity" (c. 1410–20), in G. H. Hamilton, *The Art and Architecture of Russia* (Pelican History of Art, 1954), pl. 48 and p. 87f.—Ed.]

his impeccability.[49] Not only was Adam created in the image of God, but he was called Christos because God had anointed him with the Holy Spirit; the Spirit of the godhead dwelt in him and he possessed the Holy Spirit of prophecy, so that, if he had not dominated all the temptations of evil, the Holy Spirit would have had to sin within him. But in this case it becomes all the more urgent to ask: what, then, is the catastrophe that has *changed* man's original, celestial state and brought him sickness and old age, violence and death? The answer will be provided by a completely original exegesis of the famous motif known as the *descensus angelorum*, the fall of the angels, a dramatic episode conceived not as a second fall—as would appear from the letter of the Biblical narrative—but as a fall pure and simple of mankind. Down to the eighth generation (that is, according to the chronology of the Septuagint, down to the fortieth year of Jared, father of Enoch, or to the end of the first millennium) man had lived in Paradise. Then came the drama of the revolt and descent of the Angels upon Mount Hermon, the memory of which attaches chiefly to I Enoch 7.

But this drama itself may be interpreted in at least three different ways. One interpretation involves heavenly Angels who, led by two of their princes, descend from Heaven with the intention of uniting with the daughters of men. This interpretation suggests a certain malicious pleasure, a triumphant jealousy toward the Angel, who has at last fallen from his superiority to man. This Satanic depreciation is attenuated by another interpretation of the episode, that given in 2 Enoch, the Slavonic Enoch: the Angels descend to the earth, drawn not by human seductions but by indignation over the ingratitude of men, whom they plan to bring back to dignity and justice; but in their overgenerous boldness they merely succumb to the impossible task. Finally, there is a third form of interpretation, that of the Ebionites, which has no bearing on the heavenly Angels: the authors and actors of the drama are righteous men, the children of Seth as opposed to the posterity of Cain; up to that time the children of Seth had been leading the life of the Angels and for this reason are called the "sons of God."[50]

49 Cf. Schoeps, *Aus frühchristlicher Zeit*, pp. 7–10.

50 Ibid., pp. 10–13. The traces of this exegesis may be followed down to the traditions of Islamic Iran, where we find the children of Seth, a people of pious nostalgic foreigners, gathered together on Mount Hermon and identified with the Angels of Enoch, the Wakers, then with the antediluvian Chaldaean kings, and lastly with the first dynasty of Iranian mythohistory, founded by the Primordial Man, Gayōmart. Cf. the text of Jūzjānī's *Ṭabaqāt-i Nāṣirī* in Sven S. Hartman, *Gayōmart* (Uppsala, 1953), pp. 151–56.

It is this last interpretation that foreshadows the traits of the Ismailian Adamology, in which we encounter a conception of Adam's fault as radically different from the traditional exegesis of the Biblical narrative as is the Ebionite conception. In regard to the episode corresponding to the Mount Hermon episode, this conception results in an interpretation involving not heavenly but earthly Angels, that is to say, the "Angels *in potentia*" that are those human beings who correspond to the children of Seth. The drama itself will be seen to consist in the passage from a Cycle of Epiphany or Unveiling (*dawr al-kashf*) to a Cycle of Occultation (*dawr al-satr*). But this cyclical metamorphosis (corresponding to the Ebionite idea of the completion of the first millennium) does not imply the responsibility of Adam (that is, of the episodic Adam who is the only one known through the exoteric letter of the Bible and the Koran). It has far earlier causes.[51]

Far earlier, we have said. On the perspective opened up to us by the continuous presence of the True Prophet—Holy Spirit and ideal Anthropos—through the metamorphoses of his theophanies, Ismailism superimposes the perspective of a drama in heaven, the outcome of which is already decided but whose consequences will carry through the successive Cycles. The hero of this drama is not the "historic" Adam, he who is mentioned exoterically in the Bible and the Koran, but the Angel of the pleroma, the spiritual Adam or celestial Anthropos. In the hierarchy of the ten archangelical hypostases he originally occupied the third rank, that in which he was directly awakened into being by the original dyad of the First and Second Intelligences, Νοῦς and Ψυχή. What was his fault? In the Ismailian conception it was a retard in his own accomplishment of the Attestation or Unification of the Unity (*tawḥīd*), which constitutes the intimate being of the First Intelligence, the primordial Archangel who is the primordial Epiphany of the divine Mystery. Thus we can only gain an intimation of the meaning of this fault in the light of this initial *tawḥīd*, which orders the entire structure of the pleroma as a hierarchy of divine Epiphanies. We shall have more to say of it below.[52] But the decisive aspect of this dramaturgy is that its outcome is already decided, preoccurred. Shaking himself from his stupor, from the vertigo that had immobilized him and engendered this

51 On the beatific conditions prevailing in a Cycle of Epiphany and on the transition to a Cycle of Occultation, cf. our study "Rituel sabéen et exégèse ismaélienne du rituel," *EJ 1950*, pp. 201ff.

52 Cf. section 3 below, and for a more detailed analysis see our study "Cyclical Time," pp. 37–43 above, "The drama in heaven."

"retard over eternity," which is gradually absorbed by the cycle of the Times, the Angel tears out from himself his Iblīs, his "demon." All those of his pleroma who refused to follow him in his resurrection constitute throughout the Cycles the posterity of Iblīs. All those who have followed him carry on with his help the combat which finally, after innumerable Cycles, will destroy the progeny of Shadow and Negation. For far from being the evil archon of other Gnostic systems, the Angel whose "retard" sent him back from the third to the tenth rank of the pleroma becomes the creative demiurge of our world only out of compassion, only in order to help his followers in their combat. And thus, at the end of a very slow cosmic alchemy, a being of marvelous beauty and stature burst forth among beings who were still prehuman.

This being makes his appearance in a region of the Earth where the best climatic and astronomical conditions are fulfilled, namely on the island of Ceylon; here he appears simultaneously with twenty-seven other persons who resemble him—the total number of twenty-eight being related to the number of the lunar stations.[53] But this being is again not our "historical" Adam, who, like many of the Adams to initiate Cycles, was only a "partial" and episodic Adam. He is the original and universal Adam (*Adam al-awwal al-kullī*), a term recalling the *Anima generalis* and whose Greek equivalent would be *πανάνθρωπος*. For actually this original Adam, like the celestial Adam, Angel prince of a pleroma, is a receptacle of souls; and it is precisely as such that he became the "First Imām," that is to say, was invested with the primordial Imāmate. From the outset we have an essential reduplication, reflecting a form of consciousness that wishes to avoid any suggestion of an incarnation. The celestial Anthropos, the Angel, cannot be conceived as "incarnated" on earth: the initial Adam who represents him is his *maẓhar*, his epiphanic Form. Our texts tell us that he was his angel's first thought (*awwal fikrihi*), the end of his *knowledge* (*ākhir ʿilmihi*), the substance of his *action*: he was the project that concentrated (*maṭraḥ*) the radiation of his

53 Among these twenty-seven persons the primordial earthly Adam shines like the Sun amid the other heavenly bodies (the Brothers of Purity designate him as the Rising Sun, *shams ṭāliʿa*), like the red *yāqūt* amid the other precious stones. He was among them the *Sābiq* (the Precursor), just as the First Intelligence is the *Sābiq* of the spiritual world; he was the quintessence (*zubdat*) of all physical creation, the second *Nihāyat* (term, limit), just as the world of the *Ibdāʿ* is the first *Nihāyat*. First of the receptacles or repositories (*maqāmāt*) of the Imāmate, he was the Imām of the Imāms, their precursor in purity and innocence; cf. Idrīs ʿImādaddīn, *Zahr al-Maʿānī* (unpubl. MS), XII, pp. 72–75.

Lights; he is also his supreme *Veil* (*ḥijābuhu l-aʿẓam*), he through whom he shines (*tajallà bihi ʿinda ẓuhūrihi*). Each of these terms is carefully weighed: They show how with the primordial Adam, original repository of the Imāmate, Imāmology exemplifies an epiphanic relation, similar to that maintained in Angel Christology and precluding any idea of hypostatic union such as would be required by an Incarnation.

Here I can mention only very briefly the characterology of this primordial Adam whose figure appears at the dawn of mythohistory. Just as the Adam of the Ebionites is **ἀναμάρτητος**, so he too is immunized against all impurity, all sin (***maʿṣūm***, exact equivalent of the Greek term). And he will transmit this prerogative to all the Imāms from Cycle to Cycle. The first repository of the Imāmate, he institutes on earth the hierarchy of the esoteric sodality after the example of the celestial hierarchy. His Cycle was a cycle of Epiphany, of contemplative beatitude, of total spiritual freedom, in which man, even in his physical features, enjoyed a paradisiacal state. At the end of this cycle, set at fifty thousand years, he was "transferred" with all his followers who made up his Temple of Light, that is to say, he "emigrated" by means of a beatific death into the zone of the tenth Angel whose rank he took, while the tenth Angel rose one degree higher toward his original rank. Thus the primordial Adam, in inaugurating the Imāmate, is also the first Imām to accomplish the work which from then on will be the work of each final Imām in a Cycle, and particularly of the final *Qā'im* or Resurrector who, following his example, will lead all his adepts back to their Angel, so that the esoteric Church is drawn onward from Cycle to Cycle in a continuous ascending movement toward higher realms of the Pleroma.[54]

This cycle of Epiphany was followed by a cycle of Occultation, and so on; the alternation continues at a dizzy pace down to the Resurrection of Resurrections (*Qiyāmat al-Qiyāmāt*). Certain calculations of our Ismailian theosophers go so far as to evaluate the Grand Cycle (*kawr aʿẓam*) at three hundred sixty thousand times three hundred sixty thousand years.[55] Each

54 Cf. Idrīs. If the initial cycle inaugurating the mythohistory of our world was a cycle of Epiphany, it is because the drama in Heaven had ended in the victory of the Angel; thus this cycle was truly what the Brothers of Purity call, in their ritual, the Morning Sun, the festival of the springtime of the worlds.

55 The Persian book of *Taṣawwurāt*, attributed to Naṣīraddīn Ṭūsī, speaks in this sense of eighteen thousand worlds: it is impossible to say that there was "a time when the world did not exist," any more than that *our* Adam was the first man of the first

cycle of Epiphany marks a new triumph. But the passage from a cycle of Epiphany to a cycle of Occultation marks a fall which is the repercussion of a drama enacted in the Pleroma, and opens a new phase of the combat necessary to absorb its consequences. It goes without saying that the only case of which our theosophers can speak at length is the cycle of Unveiling, immediately preceding ours, including the vicissitudes which determined the transition to our actual cycle. It is in this sense that the Biblical narrative of the Creation is not the story of a beginning but actually deals with a state of affairs following terrible catastrophes. The cycle preceding them, during which mankind lived in a paradisiacal state, here corresponds to the millennium which among the Ebionites preceded the drama on Mount Hermon.

All our authors agree in their allusions to the catastrophes which afflicted the last three millennia of the cycle of Epiphany preceding ours. The high spiritual sciences were reduced to silence; abdicating their angelical condition, men turned away from that "religion of resurrection" (*dīn-e Qiyāmat*) which is the religion of the Holy Imāms. These last foresee the necessity of re-establishing the discipline of the arcanum; since mankind has become unworthy of the divulgation of the mysteries, a new religious Law (*sharī'at*) must be instituted, whose *ta'wīl* will liberate only those who pass through a new birth. This radical change is the fall that is designated as the "expulsion from Paradise."[56] Henceforth there will be only the "Paradise *in potentia*" constituted by the esoteric sodality, the Ismailian *da'wat*.

It is in this context that our Gnostics consider two episodes of pre-Adamic "history" recorded in the Koran. The first (2 : 28): "And when the

---

world, unless the meaning of the word "world" is restricted exclusively to the world of the present cycle, which is only a period in the ages of the world (*adwār-e 'ālam-hā*, an idea corresponding to that of the *Zeitalter* in Schelling); each change of period (*dawr*) signifies the coming of a world. Cf. *The "Rawdatu't-Taslim" commonly called Taṣawwurāt*, ed. and tr. W. Ivanow (The Ismaili Society Series, A 4, Bombay and Leiden, 1950), XVI, pp. 48–49 of the Persian text.

56 Our authors already analyze this "expulsion from Paradise" in phenomenological terms as a change of consciousness: in upsetting the angelical state in which they had been living, men radically pervert the perception and direct contemplation of the essences which gave them the pure knowledge of gnosis, transforming them into a knowledge of material things adjusted to material things and seeking to dominate them. This gave rise to the "practical" sciences (arithmetic, surveying, astrology, etc.). The Adversaries (the posterity of Iblīs), held prisoner in the world of the Mothers (the Elements) during the Cycle of Epiphany, are liberated: they multiply, corrupting beings and things. Thus the divine Epiphany (*ẓuhūr*) is weakened and effaced; Idrīs, pp. 78–79; cf. *Taṣawwurāt* XVI, pp. 48–49 of the Persian text.

Lord said unto the Angels: Now I am about to place a *khalīfa* (viceroy) on the earth, they said: Wilt thou place therein one who will do harm therein and shed blood?"[57] He who speaks in this verse is not, as the literalists suppose, the supreme God, the "All-Powerful." According to the Ismailian hermeneutics, it is the last Imām of the Cycle before our own who speaks to his "Angels," that is, to his dignitaries, to the purest members of his Temple of Light. He replies to them with grave melancholy, foreseeing the downfall to which humanity aspires: "Surely I know that which you know not." This Imām was named Hunayd; he was the father of the young Adam, our "historical" Adam, who was then enthroned on an Earth menaced by Darkness.

In the second episode (15:30–35),[58] known also to our Christian Apocrypha, the "Angels" are ordered to bow down to the youthful Imām, whose enthronement will transform him into the first Prophet (*Nāṭiq*) of our Cycle. But our Ismailian theologians are unanimous in repeating that the order was addressed to the "terrestrial Angels," that is, the members of the esoteric sodality, and definitely not to the celestial Angels of the pleroma. Thus Ebionism and Ismailism agree even in their profound intuition of Adamology and angelology; the Ismailian feeling for the hierarchy of the worlds would have been outraged by the degradation of the Angel involved in the literal interpretation of the book of Enoch. We gain an idea of the grave implications of such an interpretation if we consider the somewhat childlike satisfaction of certain Church Fathers who declared that by the Ascension of Christ mankind had been raised above the Angels, and this to punish them for having refused to worship Adam![59]

Moreover, only Iblīs and his followers refused. The malicious joy of the pious doctors would ultimately lead to a confusion between angelology and demonology, a confusion against which our Ismailians, it goes without saying, are "immunized." This Iblīs is actually the manifestation, at the beginning of our Cycle, of the spiritual Iblīs already conquered by the spiritual

57 Pickthall, p. 27 (Sūra 2 : 30).
58 Ibid., p. 263.
59 For the exegesis of these two episodes, cf. Idrīs, pp. 79ff.; *Taṣawwurāt* XVI, pp. 46–51 of the Persian text. The episode of prostration before Adam (if not the Ismailian detail, relating it only to the earthly Angels) occurs in our Apocrypha: cf. "Vita Adae et Evae," pars. xii ff., in R. H. Charles, *The Apocrypha and Pseudepigrapha of the Old Testament in English* (Oxford, 1913), II, p. 137, and the Gospel of Bartholomew IV: 52ff., in James, p. 178.

Adam, the Angel demiurge of our cosmos and our humanity. "At that time" he bore the name of Ḥārith ibn Murra; this is a dignitary belonging, like Adam himself, to the end of the previous Cycle of Unveiling. In his passionate refusal he is conscious of himself as a "terrestrial angel," initiated and initiating others into the gnosis of Resurrection; he knows that his nature is of *fire*, while the nature of Adam, appointed to teach men a religious Law whose truth is hidden beneath symbols, is of *clay*. By way of vengeance, he makes this suggestion to Adam: "Indeed, thou hast been given precedence over the Angels who have been commanded to bow down to thee and over whom thou hast been instituted as an initiator to initiate them into the names of all beings. Thou art still wanting only in the knowledge of one thing; if thou knewest it, thou wouldst be one of those higher Angels who have not been ordered to bow down, because they are beyond thine obedience." Then Adam cried out: "What then is this knowledge that *God* has hidden from me, although he knew that I need it and cannot do without it?" And the Adversary explained: "It is the knowledge of the Resurrection (*'ilm al-Qiyāmat*) and of the last things, and the knowledge of how the spiritual Forms, divested of their material envelopes, rise up free to the world of Eternity."[60]

Iblīs then attempted to stir Adam's compassion and generosity: why withhold from the mankind of his own Cycle what had constituted the glory and angelical condition of those of the preceding Cycle? And the young Adam yielded. He committed the error, the great error, of divulging the secret that should not have been revealed in his Cycle, so surrendering to the unworthy what must be reserved for "those who know." But our authors insist that his error was neither the fruit of obdurate pride nor a negation, nor a challenge to those whose superiority to himself he knew. Adam ceded rather to a nostalgia (*ishtiyāq*) for the Epiphany (*iẓhār*) of those higher celestial Powers, a nostalgia both for Resurrection and for the celestial Paradise,[61] as though all human beings shared in this nostalgia, whereas among most of them the mention of it provokes only demoniacal sarcasm. Here again the Ismailian intuition is close to that of the Ebionite Chris-

60 Idrīs, pp. 81–82; cf. *Taṣawwurāt* XVI, p. 50 of the Persian text.

61 Idrīs, p. 83. That is why, after Adam's fault, his wife Eve represents the hidden and salutary meaning of the positive religion (*Taṣawwurāt* XVI, p. 50) just as the nostalgia of the tenth Angel is his "eternal Eve," the "bride of the spiritual Adam returned to his paradise" (Idrīs, ch. X).

tians: Adam is not responsible for the fall, that is to say, for the "expulsion from the earthly Paradise." We have seen what far anterior causes necessitated this "expulsion." Adam's error was that by an excess of generosity he anticipated, we may even say usurped—he, a mere initial Prophet—the task reserved for the last Imām of his Cycle, the Resurrector (*Qā'im*). Up until then, up to the end of our Cycle, the knowledge of the Resurrection may be divulged only in symbols and always proportionally to the adept's degree of dignity and capacity. That is why Adam surpassed his "proper limit," his *ḥadd* (ὅρος).[62]

And here we encounter a term highly characteristic of the Ismailian lexicon (*ḥadd*, plural *ḥudūd*) and expressing a very complex notion. An analysis of this term will bring us close to the secret of Ismailian hierarchism, the principle which dominates the structure of the esoteric sodality, widening the field of theophanic vision as the adepts pass from degree to degree. Simultaneously, the same law of progression imposes the rhythm of the Cycles of Prophecy and, with each of these Cycles, the succession of Imāms which is its necessary complement, since the Imām is the repository of the esoteric meaning of the Revelation, that is to say, of saving Gnosis. Thus both the foundation and the meaning of Imāmology may be disclosed to us and disclose to us in turn a metamorphosis of "Angel Christology."

3. Hierarchies and Cycles: The Fundamental Angelology of Ismailism

In the principle by which the Ismailians deduced the degrees of Being and of revelation of Being in beings, we may apprehend a twofold axiom. On the one hand, he who knows himself (*nafs* = the soul, *anima*, and the self) knows his Lord (*man 'arafa nafsahu faqad 'arafa rabbahu*). *Who* is this Lord? Each of the degrees of the esoteric sodality, whose correspondence recurs in the different planes of being, in the angelic pleroma as well as in the astronomical cosmos, is designated as a *ḥadd*—in the literal sense a limit, a term, a definition. The word corresponds to the Greek ὅρος, or better still, one might render it literally by ὁρίζων, "that which limits or defines" the field of vision, hence the horizon Each of the archangelical degrees is a *ḥadd* (the lower *ḥudūd*, those of the terrestrial world, correspond to the upper *ḥudūd*, those of the celestial world). The word is often conveniently trans-

62 Idrīs, pp. 85–86.

lated as "dignitary," although this term in fact connotes an idea extrinsic to its etymology. The *ḥadd* defines for each degree the horizon of its consciousness, the mode of knowledge proportionate to the mode of being realized by the adept. The notion of *ḥadd*, or "limit," implies correlatively that of *maḥdūd*, or "limited." Each lower *ḥadd* is the *maḥdūd*, the "limited," of the *ḥadd* immediately above it, which is its "horizon." For every "limit," to know oneself is to know the *ḥadd*—the limit, the horizon—of which it is itself the "limited," the *maḥdūd*. The next higher *ḥadd* is, then, the Lord—that is to say, the *Self*—of its own *maḥdūd*, the Self of that which it limits, that whose horizon it is. But at the same time each higher *ḥadd* is the *maḥdūd*, the limited, of the *ḥadd* that is higher than itself. For each *maḥdūd*, to accede to the knowledge of the Self (i.e., of its *ḥadd*) is, then, simultaneously to rise toward the knowledge of the *ḥadd* which is the Lord both of *ḥadd* and *maḥdūd*.[63]

At each degree the mode of consciousness rises with the new mode of being. Each *ḥadd* is bound to its *maḥdūd* by a companionship of initiatory brotherhood; it must draw it along, lift it to its own rank, in order to raise itself to a higher *ḥadd*, or rank. The heavens of the esoteric Church are made in the image of the astronomical heavens, each encased in the next; here lies the secret of that perpetual ascending movement which draws the entire hierocosmos of the initiate from base to summit. Of course we are not speaking of empirical perception. At each degree the *horizon*, or limit, defines for the adept the measure of his being and of his perception; his knowledge of himself, like his knowledge of his Lord, rises from horizon to horizon, from Angel to Angel, that is to say, from metamorphosis to metamorphosis. It is the law of essence measuring its own field of theophanic vision, the same law expressed in the Acts of Peter by the attestation: *Talem eum vidi qualem capere potui.*

Up to what limit, it might be asked, will these ascensions and metamorphoses continue? Here we encounter a second axiom of Ismailian Gnosis: The supreme godhead is unknowable, inaccessible, ineffable, unpredicable—"that to which the boldest thought cannot attain."[64] The question is then transformed into this other question: at what *ḥadd*, or limit, at what horizon, does the godhead rise from its abyss of absolute incognoscibility? Or in other

63 Ibid., ch. XIX, p. 211.
64 Cf. Rudolf Strothmann, *Gnosis-Texte der Ismailiten* (Göttingen, 1943), p. 55 (*man lā tatajāsara naḥwahu 'l-khawāṭir*).

words, what is the limit at which it is personified, revealed as a person, eternally hypostatized, so that a definite personal relation of devotion and love toward it becomes possible? In Ismailian terms, this *ḥadd*, this absolutely original limit, is the primordial divine Epiphany, and as such the initial angelophany. Its mystery is that of an eternal liturgy, accomplishing in pre-eternity the Unification of the Unique (*tawḥīd*) that is reproduced in the Islamic profession of faith, the "*shahādat*": *Lā Ilāha illā'l-Lāh* (= *Non Deus nisi Deus*). It is to be feared that no translation into our languages can express the relation between two distinct phases disclosed by the Arabic sentence—these two phases to which Ismailian speculative meditation has applied the entire effort of its penetration, because in them it perceives the mystery which at once accomplishes the being of the First Archangel and is accomplished in his being as divine Ipseity.

First comes the absolute negation (*lā Ilāha*): the divine, unknowable abyss leaves no possibility of apprehending a divine person and of giving him predicates. This negative universal proposition is followed by a particular affirmative *exception* (marked by *illā* = *nisi*, except), or an absolute affirmation following from no logical premise. Between the two passes the fine line that the true Gnostic must follow without faltering: between the *ta'ṭīl*, or agnosticism which "evacuates" the godhead from the world, and the *tashbīh*, which "assimilates" it to an already given form. For him, the ideal realm whence burgeons eternally the dyad or syzygy of the First and Second Intelligences, Νοῦς and Ψυχή, overhangs this twofold abyss. The negative phase of the *tawḥīd* is that the godhead cannot take form (be theomorphosed) without limiting itself, that is, without an autonegation. The First Intelligence, as divine primordial Epiphany, constitutes the divine Ipseity itself,[65] *the* "theomorphosis"; but *eo ipse* it also limits it. It is the *ḥadd* or limit (the supreme *ḥadd*), because in it the godhead becomes its own *maḥdūd*, its own *limitatum*, and can know itself in this archangelic Ipseity only as a self-negation: *lā Ilāha* (= *non Deus*). And by this negation the Angel, worshiping his own Mystery, simultaneously refuses for himself that

65 On the idea that the divine Ipseity consists in the knowledge which the First Intelligence has of the Originator (*Mubdi'*) and that this knowledge, which is its Epiphany, is negativity (a negation excluding from the *Mubdi'* all ipseities and nonipseities), cf. also Abū Ya'qūb Sejestānī, *Kitāb al-Yanābī'*, *yanbū'* II (unpubl. MS): "On the pure Ipseity of the Originator" (*fī huwīyati' l-Mubdi'i' l-maḥḍa*). Hence there is no divine Ipseity (*al-Lāh*) to be sought beyond the *Sābiq*, who is the Archangel of the highest rank (*al-Malak al-muqarrab*).

divinity of which he is precisely the limit. But the negation is followed directly by the affirmation that absolves itself eternally from this negativity: *nisi Deus* (and yet . . . *this* God). Now this affirmation, which rises like a challenge, is the Calling-into-Being of the second Intelligence, the universal Soul; the being of this Soul concludes the liturgy of the primordial *tawḥīd*, attesting the divinity of the soul which precedes it (*Sābiq*), which is its limit, its horizon, *the* horizon to which the *personal* godhead raises itself. Thus the "origins" are seen in terms of phenomenology of the angelic consciousness; this phenomenology takes the form of a liturgy by which the divine Epiphany is eternally accomplished. The consequence is that all the affirmations concerning the personal divinity (*Al-Lāh* of the Koran) are taken in Ismailian Gnosis as referring to the Most Holy Archangel (*al-Malak al-muqaddas*) who *is* this divine Epiphany, that is to say, the *Deus determinatus*; it is to him alone that "divinity" (*ilāhīya*) can be imputed as a predicate.[66]

This dyadic relation constituted by the two first Intelligences and expressed in the two phases of the *shahādat* will be repeated from degree to degree of the esoteric hierarchy. Intelligence and Soul are called *Sābiq* and *Tālī* (Precedent and Successor); and each *ḥadd* will be the *Sābiq* of its *maḥdūd*, which is its *Tālī*. In the succession of these dyads is expressed a kind of kathenotheism whose "each instance" (καθ' ἕνα) is defined by each horizon, or *ḥadd* (here we have a kind of transcendental motivation of the *unicuique secundum quod dignus est*). The meaning and scope of the drama inaugurated in the Pleroma by the responsibility of the third Angel, the spiritual Adam (*Adam rūḥānī*), are then to be considered in the light of disintegration of the *tawḥīd*, brought on by his stupor, his retard in negativity on the level of his own being. Inversely our authors insist on the

66 Cf. Strothmann, IX, 1, p. 80 of the text (*lā yaqa'u'l-ilāhīyat illā 'alā'l Mubda'-i 'l-awwal*); cf. ibid. p. 80, lines 12–13, the strange etymology deriving the name of God (*Ilāh*) from the root *wlh*, conveying the idea of being stricken with stupor or sadness, with fearful sadness (like a traveler in the desert or a child separated from his mother). Doubtless there is here a pathetic presentiment proper to the divine Mystery, the idea precisely that the divine Ipseity is essentialized in negativity, in the stupor (or sadness) of the First Archangel, who recognizes his inability to attain the ipseity of the godhead which he becomes by refusing it for himself. Cf. the passage in which Ibn Ḥazm (*Fiṣal*, Cairo, I, p. 35), recording the doctrine of the Magi, speaks of the vertigo of sadness in the solitude (*istawḥasha*) that invades the godhead, Zervān or Ōhrmazd, or in Ismailian terms, the Third Angel who has become Tenth (cf. our "Cyclical Time," pp. 39–40), a sadness which "corporealizes" the corporeal world of non-light.

words attributed to the Prophet: "He who pronounces the *shahādat* in its purity and truth has entered into Paradise."[67]

In this sense Abū Ya'qūb Sejestānī, for example, calls the *shahādat* the *Key to Paradise.*[68] He believes that the four words that compose it typify the two principles, or Sources (*aṣl*), of the angelical *ḥudūd* of the upper world (designated as *Sābiq* and *Tālī*, Calamus and Tablet, Sun and Moon) and the two *ḥadd*, or "limits," which are the earthly correspondences of the principle of the *ḥudūd* of the hierocosmos—the Prophet and the Imām (*Nāṭiq* and *Asās*). The first Intelligence is the *key* to all spiritual and corporeal existence; the second Intelligence, or Soul, is the *key* to the composition and the "symphony" of beings. The Prophet (*Nāṭiq*, Enunciator) is the *key* to the utterances expressing the perfections of the Intelligence and the compositions of the Soul. His *Waṣī*, or spiritual heir, foundation of the *ta'wīl* (etymologically the *exegesis* which "causes to return" to the origin), is the key to "that to which return" (*mā āla ilayhi*) the meanings of these Utterances and the existents that have emanated from the Intelligence. And furthermore, an ecumenical feeling that seems quite appropriate in an esoteric leads him to proclaim that the four branches of the Christian Cross have the same meaning and the same symbolical significance as the four terms composing the *shahādat.*[69]

On the other hand, all those who cling to exoteric and literal understanding—that is to say, all those who reject Ismailian Gnosis and its Imāmology—remain in the negative phase of the *tawḥīd.*[70]

Through fear or ignorance of angelology the simple monotheism which affirms the predicates of the *Deus determinatus*, professing them to be valid as attributes of the supreme godhead, is indeed, whether consciously or not, a disguised theism. All these divine Names[71] refer not to the "originating"

67 Idrīs, ch. XIV, p. 109.

68 For all these considerations on the *shahādat* and the analysis reproduced here, cf. particularly Abū Ya'qūb Sejestānī, *Kitāb al-Yanābī'* (The Book of the Living Sources), *yanbū'* 30–32; see also the fine chapter 54 of Nāṣir-e Khusraw in *Khwān al-Ikhwān* (The Table of the Brothers), ed. Y. al-Khashshāb (Cairo, 1940), pp. 137–39, on the cosmic liturgy of the First Archangel.

69 Sejestānī, the whole of *yanbū'* 32: *fī ittifāq al-ṣalīb wa'l-shahādat* (On the Concordance [of the symbol] of the Cross and of the *shahādat*).

70 Idrīs, p. 109.

71 Ibid. The Prophets of our Cycle preceding the period of Mohammed gave God divine Names which veiled him successively beneath their Veils. God, to be sure, is existent where his Names exist: in so far as there is Wisdom, he is the Wise; in so far as there is Power, he is the Powerful. However, the divine Names refer not to the Prin-

Principle (*mubdi'*), which is unknowable, but to the *ḥudūd*—that is to say, the "horizons" to which the theophanies rise. The First of all (*Sābiq*) is both the supreme Veil and the supreme Name of the godhead, and this name is none other than *lā Ilāha illā'l-Lāh* (this is why, symbolically, in the *Mi'rāj Nāmah* commented on by Avicenna, the Prophet sees the words *lā Ilāha illā'l-Lāh* in letters of flame on the forehead of the Archangel, on the diadem of light enclosing his hair).[72] It is, then, through knowledge of the spiritual *ḥudūd*—that is, of the Archangelical hypostases which are theophanies—that the worship of the unique Worshiped One (*ma'būd*) is accomplished; it is by knowledge of their correspondences, the terrestrial *ḥudūd*, that knowledge is gained of these spiritual *ḥudūd*. Hence the importance of the fundamental angelology that determines the succession and correspondence of these hierarchies, which find their closest Christian analogy in the work of Dionysius the Areopagite, though Dionysius cannot be said to have carried the parallelism between celestial and earthly hierarchies as far as, for example, Ḥamīdaddīn Kermānī (eleventh century).[73]

As in Avicennism, there are, in all, ten higher *ḥudūd*, that is to say, archangelical Intelligences; their existence flows from the first among them, each being the immediate cause of the one next following (as a torch kindles another torch).[74] This decad is divided into two distinct groups, the Three and the Seven, a *triad* and a *heptad*. The primordial dyad gives rise to the third Intelligence, the spiritual Angel Adam, protagonist of the drama in Heaven. Whereas the vertigo of his stupor immobilizes the accomplishment of his *tawḥīd*, seven Cherubim designated as the Seven Divine Words,

ciple, to the Originator, but to the Archangelical hypostases which are the "horizons" of the Pleroma—the *ḥudūd*, or degrees, to which the theophanies rise (cf. the procession of divine Names as hypostases in *3 Enoch, or The Hebrew Book of Enoch*, ed. and tr. Hugo Odeberg (Cambridge, 1928), Part II, pp. 123ff., 160ff.

72 See our *Avicenna*, p. 172.

73 Each Intelligence comprises a multitude of celestial Angels composing its own pleroma; the structure accords with the hierarchy of the Ten Cherubic Intelligences that dominate the system of Avicenna (cf. his *Risālat al-Malā'ika* (Epistle on the Angels) ibid., p. 62). In studying the parallel, one should consequently remember that the entire Avicennan pleroma has been made to correspond with the Dionysian hierarchies (ibid., pp. 112–13). However, the characteristic feature of the Ismailian angelology remains the parallelism between celestial and terrestrial hierarchies, verified point for point; these correspondences both ground and express what we might, as a parallel to *Engelchristologie*, call an *Engelanthropologie*, so close is the connection (here as in Christology) between one's idea of the Angel and one's idea of man.

74 Cf. Idrīs, XIX, pp. 211ff., which quotes at length the *Kitāb Rāḥat al-'Aql* of Ḥamīdaddīn Kermānī (passage corresponding to pp. 134ff. in the edition of K. Ḥusayn).

come into being.[75] These seven Cherubim mark the ideal distance which the Angel, the celestial Anthropos, who by his "retarded eternity" has become the tenth in the Pleroma, must reconquer for his followers and with their help—that is to say, with the help of the angel-souls, today those among humankind who follow him in his glorious conversion against Iblīs. But they mark also the degrees of the higher aid (*ta'yīd*) which helps him to attain this victory. Just as the spiritual Adam, the Angel of our mankind, received aid and compassion from their heptad, so this heptad will command the rhythm of the cycles of Prophecy and Imāmology. The same rhythm of three and seven determines "vertically" the structure of the esoteric sodality—that is, the organization of the degrees into which the companions in one and the same combat, the members of one and the same spiritual chivalry (*javānmardī*), are drawn up—and also determines in time the order of succession of the cycles of Salvation.

Ḥamīdaddīn Kermānī schematizes as follows the correspondences determined by the repetition of the same rhythmic law:[76]

1. The first of the three higher degrees involves the prophetic mission (*risālat*). The Envoy (*rasūl*) inaugurates a new religious period; he is the Enunciator (*Nāṭiq*) of a new Law (*sharī'at*) which he receives from a celestial Angel as *tanzīl*, "revelation," dictated from a revealed text; he enunciates the letter of this text in exoteric (*ẓāhir*) form as positive religion. It is his mission to establish the rules of the practical, active cult—we should say the "religion of works" (*'ibādat 'amalīya*)—thanks to which the souls open up to their *first birth* as souls and receive their *perfectio prima*. Just as the First Intelligence governs the uppermost Heaven (*falak al-aflāk*) which his thought originates, so the *Nāṭiq* presides over the uppermost Heaven which embraces all the other Heavens or "horizons" (*ḥudūd*) of the esoteric religious cosmos (hierocosmos, *'ālam al-Dīn*).

2. The spiritual successor of the Prophet, the *Waṣī* or "diadochos" (διαδόχος), is also designated as *Asās*, "foundation," that is to say, foundation of the Imāmate. His proper function as repository of the spiritual secret of the positive religion is the *ta'wīl*, the esoteric exegesis which "carries back" the exoteric (*ẓāhir*) to its hidden interior (*bāṭin*) meaning. It is his mission to establish the esoteric spiritual cult (*'ibādat bāṭinat 'ilmīya*) whereby the souls are molded in the image of the eternal Forms; for the adepts

75 Strothmann, XIII, 1.

76 Cf. Idrīs, pp. 211ff., and Kermānī, pp. 134ff.; cf. the recapitulatory table below.

this is the ***second***, or spiritual, ***birth***. His rank corresponds to that of the second Intelligence, who governs the Heaven of the Fixed Stars.

3. Next comes the Imām (the *Asās* is actually the first Imām, but as "foundation" he remains distinct from the series).[77] He assumes authority over the community, essentially in the esoteric and spiritual sense—and actually, in exceptional cases, in the exoteric and temporal sense. In the course of the Cycle he must perpetuate the balance and indispensable connection between *ẓāhir* and *bāṭin*, the necessary transmutation of literal facts into symbols, which conditions the spiritual birth of the adepts. His rank is similar to that of the Third Intelligence, and here lies the secret of Imāmology: the Imām is the Perfect Man, the epiphanic (*maẓhar*) Form of the celestial Angel Anthropos. Just as the third Angel, having become Tenth by his "retard," must as Saved Saviour lead his own pleroma back to its original rank, so the last Imām, the Resurrector (*Qā'im*) in whom is recapitulated the entire line of the Imāms, leads their Temple of Light back to the realm of the Angel, of which he is the diadochos.

The three figures of this triad—sometimes placed in correspondence with the theophanic designations of Seraphiel, Michael, and Gabriel,[78] which

77 This contrasts with Duodeciman Shiism where 'Alī ibn Abī-Ṭālib, foundation of the Imāmate, is designated as the first Imām and causes a discrepancy throughout the series (for example, the sixth Imām, Ja'far Ṣādiq, so important for Duodeciman Shiism, will appear here as the fifth Imām; cf. also n. 85 below). Thus to consider the "foundation" of the series as a unit distinct from the whole and added to its component parts typifies a method of calculation that is specifically Iranian but well known elsewhere (cf. the six Amahraspands *of which* Ōhrmazd is the seventh! By analogy, as we have seen above, the Angel Gabriel says to the Personages of the Mantle: I am the sixth of you five).

78 The homology between the celestial functions of the three first Intelligences and the sacral functions of the three highest degrees of the religious cosmos resides in the fact that in both cases the first function produces the original archetypal Forms, the second creates the concrete Forms, and the third composes them and orders them; each gives rise to the Heaven that it governs, Heaven of the physical cosmos or "Heaven" of the initiatory religious cosmos. "He is the Creator, the Shaper out of naught, the Fashioner. His are the most beautiful Names" (59 : 24; Pickthall, p. 577). While literalist exegesis naïvely relates this Koran verse to the supreme God (thus committing the error of *tashbīh*), our theosophers meditate on it as enunciating the functions and prerogatives of the supreme archangelical Triad, the "most beautiful Names" referring to these Intelligences (cf. Kermānī, p. 136). To them correspond on earth the three supreme *ḥadd*; now in the order of priority between them there will be variants which abstruse discussions represent symbolically by the letters 'AIN, SĪN, MĪM (on which the entire concept and destiny of the Imāmate depend. Cf. section 5 below). It is this same triad which in Nāṣir-e Khusraw (but within a pentadic and not decadic scheme) corresponds to the theophanic designations of Seraphiel, Michael, Gabriel; cf. our ***Étude préliminaire***, pp. 91ff.

further emphasizes the parallel between the Imām and Gabriel-Christos-Holy Spirit—are followed by the heptad of degrees considered as a homology to the Seven Cherubim intermediate between the third and tenth rank of the Angel, just as the terrestrial *ḥudūd* are intermediate between the Imām from whom emanates their spiritual quality and the Resurrector for whose assumption they prepare the way.

4. The *Bāb* or "Threshold" of the Imām. The capital importance of his role follows from the features in which Imāmology reveals its affinity with Angel Christology, principally in the late Ismailism that has become once more a personal religion of mystical salvation; here, assimilated to the following degree, that of the *Ḥujjat* or "Proof," it becomes the epiphanic Form of the Imām, the sign of his Invisibility. This eminent rank of mediator, on which rests the articulation of the visible with the invisible, is expressed in his function as *faṣl-al-khiṭāb*, a technical term which in Arabic grammar designates the moment of the "entrance into matter," articulated according to the exordium.

5. The *Ḥujjat* or "Proof" of the Imām, whose responsibility is great. We know the principle of Balance (*mīzān*), particularly essential in the alchemy of Jābir ibn Ḥayyān, in so far as it permits the universal application of the law of correspondences.[79] It is incumbent on the *Ḥujjat* to see that proper use is made of it, that is, to see that the operations of the *ta'wīl* ("to reveal the occult, to occultate the apparent") conform to the equilibrium, the correspondence of beings (*muwāzanat al-khalq*); in this sense he must decide (*ḥukm*) between the authentic (*ḥaqq*) and the inauthentic (*bāṭil*).

6. The two preceding degrees (4 and 5) form a transition or mediation between the upper triad (1–3) and the group of the last five ranks (6–10) headed by the *Dā'ī al-Balāgh* (*dā'ī*: literally, "he who calls, invites"; *da'wat*, the term designating the Ismailian sodality, signifies literally "call, vocation"). To the *Dā'ī al-Balāgh* falls essentially the task of preaching (we shall see below in section 6 that this does not consist of sermons in public places); the great Nāṣir-e Khusraw was invested with this function for Khurāsān. He must provide the adept who has been admitted to initiation and has received the teaching of the first *ḥudūd* with all the proofs and arguments regarding the higher *ḥudūd* (that is to say, the secrets of angelology) and *ma'ād*, individual eschatology, the posthumous development of the human being.

79 Cf. our study on "Le Livre du Glorieux," pp. 75ff.

7. Below him come two "dignitaries" who have the same title but modified by an adjective. First, the *Dā'ī muṭlaq*, who has full, "unrestricted" authorization. The level of initiatory knowledge corresponding to this degree is expressed in his task: to *initiate* into the higher *ḥudūd*, that is to say, into angelology; to initiate in the *ta'wīl*, that is to say, in esoteric exegesis; to initiate in the spiritual cult (*'ibādat 'ilmīya*).

8. Below him is the *Dā'ī maḥṣūr*, or *Dā'ī* with limited, "restricted" authority. He must initiate the adept into the lower *ḥudūd*, that is, into the secrets of the hierarchy of the sect.

9. The *Ma'dhūn akbar*, literally, the "higher master"; it is he who receives the neophyte's oath and concludes the pact of initiation with him.

10. Lastly, the *Ma'dhūn maḥṣūr*, literally, the "limited master" with "restricted" authorization. His function is to attract the souls capable of "responding to the Appeal" (*mustajīb*) of the esoteric Church. Though restricted, his function is extremely delicate; it consists in provoking a break[80] with social and religious conformism, in asking disturbing questions, in observing their effect on the individual selected, etc.[81]

The correspondences between the terrestrial and celestial hierarchies are summed up in the following table:[82]

80 Cf. Strothmann, p. 57 of the Arabic text, in which the word *mukāsarat* is associated with *al-Iksīr* (the elixir).

81 Just as the Tenth Intelligence marks the lower limit of the archangelical pleroma, below which begins the world of *physis* and change, and just as no other Intelligence emanates from it as there does from those above it in the hierarchy, its function being to send out into the cosmos the Energies from which result the corporeal births, so similarly from the last degree of the esoteric hierarchy there emanates no lower degree; below it there is only the profane world consisting of the ignorant and of literalist believers. Like the Tenth Angel, the Tenth *ḥadd* must cultivate the spiritual births that may blossom in this world (those who respond to the Appeal, *mustajīb*) by drawing souls to the Temple of the Spiritual Cult (*Bayt al-'Ibādat*) (cf. Idrīs, p. 216, and Kermānī, pp. 137–39). The Tenth Angel corresponds to the active intelligence of Avicennism, identified, as we have said, with the Archangel Gabriel as Holy Spirit. It is here the celestial Anthropos, the spiritual Adam (for the *Ishrāqīyūn*, the Angel of mankind), and assumes the role of Saved-Saviour, homologous to Gabriel-Christos. This homology does not appear as such in the vertical structure of the hierarchies. One must bear in mind that the Tenth Angel originated in the third rank and must regain this rank. This is precisely what creates the homology between him and the Imām; the drama enacted in Heaven between the third and the tenth rank (descent and reascent) becomes visible by homology in the relation between the Imām and the *Qā'im*, that is to say, in the cyclical schema of a period of prophecy; cf. the schema below.

82 Cf. Idrīs, ch. XIX, p. 215, and Kermānī, p. 138.

Ḥudūd or degrees of the angelical world	Their function	*Ḥudūd* or degrees of the terrestrial world	Their function
1. First Intelligence	Uppermost Heaven (*falak al-aflāk*)	1. Nāṭiq	*Tanzīl*. Literal or exoteric (*ẓāhir*) statement of positive religion (*sharī'at*).
2. Second Intelligence	Heaven of the Fixed Stars	2. Asās	*Ta'wīl*. Exegesis of the esoteric (*bāṭin*) meaning. The spiritual cult.
3. Third Intelligence	Heaven of Saturn	3. Imām	Personal mastery over the community: *ẓāhir-bāṭin*.
4. Fourth Intelligence	Heaven of Jupiter	4. Bāb	Faṣl al-Khiṭāb.
5. Fifth Intelligence	Heaven of Mars	5. Ḥujjat	*Ḥukm* (authority of decision; cf. *Mīzān*, principle of Balance in *ta'wīl*).
6. Sixth Intelligence	Heaven of the Sun	6. Dā'ī al-Balāgh	Preaching. Initiation into the *Ma'ād*.
7. Seventh Intelligence	Heaven of Venus	7. Dā'ī al-Muṭlaq	Initiation into the celestial *ḥudūd* and the esoteric cult.
8. Eighth Intelligence	Heaven of Mercury	8. Dā'ī maḥṣūr	Initiation into the earthly *ḥudūd* and the exoteric cult.
9. Ninth Intelligence	Heaven of the Moon	9. Ma'dhūn muṭlaq	To receive the undertaking of the new adept (*'ahd wa mīthāq*).
10. Tenth Intelligence	Sublunar World	10. Ma'dhūn maḥṣūr	To attract neophytes.

Particular attention must be paid to the homologous relations that recur at every degree of this vertical structure. As we have already indicated, every dyad or pair of degrees within the hierarchy exemplifies a relation analogous to that between the first and second Intelligences forming the original dyad. Every "precedent" (*sābiq*) stands to his "successor" (*tālī*) in the same relation as the Νοῦς, or Intelligence, to the Soul; each is the *Sābiq* of his *Tālī*. It follows that each "preceding" (*sābiq*) *ḥadd* is the ***Imām*** for him who follows; in other words, it is the horizon of his "theophanic vision," progressively proportional to the metamorphosis of his being and to the new mode of knowledge attained in each instance; each horizon realizes the *individuation* of the relation with the godhead, which is the function of angelology and which, as we shall see, is experienced as the relation of a "one to a one" (*wāḥid li-wāḥid*) (cf. section 6 below). Already we gain an intimation of how, at all the stages of the theophanies, the concept of the Imām can be analyzed as a symbol of the Self in so far as each of these degrees defines the relation that was expressed in the *qualem capere potui* of the Acts of Peter. This *qualem* is amplified from individuation to individuation with the ascent of degrees that mark the spiritual career of the adept, the Cycle of his Resurrections: the attainment of each higher degree, or "horizon," is indeed called a *qiyāmat*, a "resurrection." This is the esoteric meaning meditated upon in the saying attributed to the Prophet: "He who dies, his resurrection is already risen."[83]

Now if we consider this same rhythmic law no longer in the vertical structure of the esoteric hierarchy but as it operates in the unfolding of time, we shall see a periodization which knows none of the difficulties with which historians struggle in their attempts to establish the chronology of the Holy Imāms. But here precisely we are dealing neither with positive history nor with a chronology of material facts; here we can have only the temporalization of time, which is itself a hierophany, because it is the order of succession in which the sacral persons appear to the visions of the soul. Each cycle of Prophecy will be in its turn inaugurated by three Figures homologous to the three first archangelical Intelligences of the pleroma; they are followed throughout the Cycle by a heptad of Imāms, or several heptads of Imāms (homologous to the Seven Cherubim), who find their completion—their "recapitulation"—in an eighth, who is Tenth among the Figures taken as a whole, namely the *Qā'im*, or Resurrector.[84] The esoteric representation of the cycle of the Islamic religion established by the Prophet Muḥammad will yield the schema shown on page 96.

This schema makes quite clear the homology noted above according to which the Imām is *maẓhar*, the "epiphanic person" of the third Angel. Just as there are the Seven Cherubim between the third rank to which the spiritual

83 Cf. the idea of these "resurrectional" metamorphoses as set forth by Naṣīraddīn Ṭūsī in our "Cyclical Time," pp. 53–55. In Idrīs, p. 222, we also find a schema of twelve degrees resulting from the addition at the bottom of the ladder of the *mū'min bāligh* (the major believer) and of the *mustajīb* (the neophyte, he "who responds to the Appeal"). Both represent the world of "spiritual births"; the schema of correspondences indicated above is not affected by this modification.

84 Cf. Idrīs, p. 216, and Kermānī, p. 137.

1st Intelligence	2nd Intelligence	3rd Intelligence	4th Intelligence	5th Intelligence	6th Intelligence	7th Intelligence	8th Intelligence	9th Intelligence	10th Intelligence
Nāṭiq	Waṣī (Asās)	1st Imām (= 2nd)	2nd Imām (= 3rd)	3rd Imām (= 4th)	4th Imām (= 5th)	5th Imām (= 6th)	6th Imām (= 7th)	7th Imām (= 8th)	Qā'im
Muḥammad	'Alī ibn Abī-Ṭālib	Ḥasan	Ḥusayn	'Alī Zayn ul-'Ābidīn	Muḥammad Bāqir	Ja'far Ṣādiq	Ismā'īl	Muḥāmmad ibn Ismā'īl ↓ ...	— ... ↓

Angel Adam must remount and the tenth rank to which he has descended, so similarly a heptad of Imāms measures the unfolding of the Cycle from the third rank, which is that of the first Imām, to the tenth, which is that of the Qā'im, the Imām Resurrector who closes the Cycle. From one term to another, without confusion of persons, extends the unity of an Epiphany whose completion will be the full divulgation of the *ta'wīl*, that is, the resurrection of the souls whom the last Imām will lead triumphantly to the pleroma of the Angel, whose diadochos or *khalīfa* he in turn will become in order that the Angel may raise himself one more degree toward his original rank. It is in this anticipation that the visions of Imāmology culminate.[85]

Such is the schema of one of the cycles of Prophecy. The sum of the cycles composing our present cycle of Occultation (*dawr al-satr*) has again a sevenfold rhythm. There are seven successive cycles, each inaugurated by a Prophet: Adam (the "partial Adam"), whose *Waṣī-Imām* was Seth; Noah, whose Imām was Shem; Abraham, whose Imām was Ishmael; Moses, whose Imām was Aaron; Jesus, whose Imām was "Sham'ūn al-Ṣafā," under which name we read "Simon bar Kepha," but under which our Ismailians, guided

85 According to the computation of the Duodeciman Shiites, the Imām Ḥasan ibn 'Alī is actually the second Imām; on the discrepancy that runs through the heptad (or ogdoad) when the first Imām as Foundation (*Asās*) is counted separately, cf. n. 77 above.

by the Gnostic traditions that had come down to them, also read other names, among which we may note particularly Mary of Magdala.[86] Lastly, Muḥammad, whose *Waṣī-Imām* was 'Alī ibn Abī-Ṭālib. Under each one of these cycles our authors' ecumenism leads them to comprise allusively one of the great religious groups of mankind (respectively, Sabaeans, Brahmans, Zoroastrians, Jews, Christians, Musulmans). These six periods represent the hexaemeron, the six days of the creation of the religious cosmos or hierocosmos.[87] As for the seventh day, it will be precisely the day of the *Qā'im*, the final Imām (who occupies tenth position in the cycle outlined above). Just as each of the partial cycles, when a religion has exhausted its spiritual potentialities, is closed by a *qiyāmat*, a resurrection that marks the passage from one Revelation to another, so the totality of the Cycles will be closed by the Grand Resurrection (*Qiyāmat al-Qiyāmāt*): this will be the completion of a world, the dawn of a cycle of Epiphany (*dawr al-Kashf*) which will succeed ours.[88]

Here two observations come to mind: this advent of the *Qā'im*, the Imām who will even have the power to abrogate the *sharī'at*, is a belief common to all the Shiites (Duodeciman and Ismailian). To Sunnite orthodox Islam

86 "*Sham'ūn al-Ṣafā al-mu'arrab 'anhu bi-Maryam al-Majdalānīya*," Idrīs, p. 100. This transference becomes understandable if we consider the prominent role played by Mary Magdalen in certain earlier Gnostic texts, such as the *Pistis Sophia*. Cf. certain variants (*Kalāmi Pīr*, p. 67 of the text): the Imām of the period of Adam is also called Malik Shūlīm, i.e., Seth; that of Noah is called Malik Yazdaq; that of Abraham Malik al-Salām (another name for Ishmael; ibid., p. 49), etc. Each Nāṭiq has as his "awakener" (*muqīm*) the last Imām of the period of Epiphany which closes the religious cycle preceding his own. Our Adam, as we have seen, was "awakened" and enthroned by his own father, the Imām Hunayd, last Imām of the cycle of Epiphany which preceded our present cycle of Occultation. Noah had as his *muqīm* Lamech, grandson of Idrīs or Enoch, whom our authors identify traditionally with Hermes; Ṣāliḥ was Abraham's *muqīm*; 'Adnān was that of Moses; Khuzayma that of Jesus. Here we find the key to an esoteric exegesis of the Annunciation: Maryam, as *Ḥujjat*, receives the *Rūḥ* (Spirit) from Khuzayma (Strothmann, XII, 12, p. 117 of the text). A special study ought to be devoted to this conception which invests *feminine* figures with the eminent dignity of the *Ḥujjat* who "initiates" the future Prophet: Maryam for Jesus, Khadīja for Muḥammad, Fāṭima for 'Alī (cf. below, n. 115ff.). Finally, Abū Ṭālib, 'Alī's father, was Muḥammad's *muqīm* (Idrīs, p. 216). Here again we have an eloquent indication of the priority of the Imāmate over prophecy (*nubuwwat*); it is the father of the *Waṣī*, foundation (*Asās*) of the Imāmate and repository of the esoteric *ta'wīl*, who enthrones the Prophet Enunciator of the exoteric Law (*sharī'at*).

87 Cf. *Kalāmi Pīr*, pp. 64–65 of the text. Compare the fine chapter devoted to this hexaemeron by Nāṣir-e Khusraw, *Jāmi' al-Ḥikmatain*, ed. H. Corbin and M. Mo'īn (BI 3a; Teheran and Paris, 1953), sections 164ff., and our *Étude préliminaire* to this book of the "two wisdoms," pp. 81ff.

88 Idrīs, ch. XX, p. 230.

it represents an outrage, for in one way or another it offends against the dogma according to which Muḥammad is the "seal of the Prophets." And a good many philosophers and mystics have been included in this reprobation.[89] Our second remark concerns the whole of the triple schema that we have considered. The systematization and rhythm are so strict that Ismailian meditation might provide a system of co-ordinates, on the one hand, for the Ebionite Epiphanies of the True Prophet "running through the centuries" to his place of rest and, on the other hand, for the ladder of spiritual metamorphoses by which each initiate's capacity for theophanic vision is enhanced—up to the summit which is the Imām of his time. Only here the True Prophet has not yet attained his place of rest, as he had in the person of Jesus for Ebionite Christianity and of Mohammed for Islamic prophetology. And this difference, this opening of the schema toward the future, is precisely Imāmology. Here the Seven Imāms, or the heptads of Imāms, are the Seven Pillars of the House of Wisdom. For the final "repose" will be more than a Prophet *Nāṭiq*; it will be an Imām, and the Imām is a *Ṣāmit*, a Silent One: he does not proclaim a new Law; rather he liberates by disclosing the symbols.[90] But the Imām as *maẓhar*, that is to say, as epiphanic Figure, exemplifies a mode of presence analogous to that of the Angelos Christos in Jesus. And it is precisely this that led us to say that the fulfillment of Ebionite prophetology is to be sought not in orthodox Islamic prophetology but in Shiite Imāmology.

It is indeed in the person of the last Imām that the idea of the ἀνακεφαλαίωσις, the "recapitulation," the "reunion into a whole," is realized. This is expressed in numerous symbols. It is said, for example, that the *Qā'im*, the aim and goal of all the *ḥudūd*, the degrees or "horizons," is the Grand Cycle (*al-kawr al-aʿẓam*) of which the Imāms are the periods or partial

89 Such was the case of Suhrawardī, the master of "eastern philosophy" (*Ishrāq*), to judge by his trial in Aleppo, in which he was condemned to death at the age of 38 (1191) on the strength of the concept of the Imām set forth in the prologue of his basic work *Ḥikmat al-Ishrāq*.

90 On the "absolute Silent One" (*Khāmūsh-e muṭlaq*) who is at the same time the "absolute Speaker" (*Gūyā-ye muṭlaq*), cf. *Taṣawwurāt* XXV, p. 100 of the text (Persian *Khāmush* = Arabic *Ṣāmit*). Cf. our study "Le Livre du Glorieux": whereas the official doctrine of the Fāṭimids upholds the priority of the *Nāṭiq* over the *Ṣāmit*, Jābir ibn Ḥayyān, in agreement with the underlying tendency of Ismailism (which achieves its full flowering in the Iranian Ismailism of Alamūt), professes the priority of the *Ṣāmit* over the *Nāṭiq* (pp. 57ff.); and this contrast supports our thesis that, from the spiritual point of view, the political and official triumph of the Fāṭimids can only be regarded as a regression. On the *symbol* that is both word and silence, cf. ibid., pp. 69ff.

cycles, just as each Imām is himself a cycle in relation to his *ḥudūd*: each *ḥadd*, each "companion" or member of the initiatory sodality, is himself a "period" of the Imāmate; in other words, he himself *is his own* time, posited and defined by the elevation of his horizon.[91] It is also said that the *Qā'im* is the "coalescence" (*majma'*), the *corpus mysticum* of all the *ḥudūd*; each of the Imāms has his own *corpus mysticum*, his Temple of Light, and all are gathered together and integrated in the Sublime Temple of the Resurrector.[92] In this sense, as seal of the Imāmate, the *Qā'im* is termed "the second breath of the Trumpet of Resurrection," the first breath having been emitted by the first Imām, foundation and origin of the Imāmate.[93] This first breath was the blowing of the Spirit (*Rūḥ*) into the letter of the positive legalist religion (*sharī'at*), the Calling (*da'wat*) of the souls to Religion in spirit and truth, made possible by the *ta'wīl*, the esoteric exegesis of the Spirit to which the Imām is the Key. The last Imām announces the consummation of the positive religions: he is the full Epiphany of what had been alluded to in the letter of the Revelations uttered by the prophets, namely, a "return" to the pure spiritual sense. He is the "Perfect Child" (*al-walad al-tāmm*), who was the initial project of the celestial Adam, Angel of our mankind, just as he will be the final fulfillment of his demiurges.[94]

91 Cf. Idrīs, ch. XIX, p. 223, and XX, p. 226: at every epoch there is a unique individual (*fard wāḥid*) to whom falls the humanity, the reality of the Anthropos in the absolute sense (*al-insānīyat 'alā'l-muṭlaq*). The Imāms of the posterity of the *Waṣī* are, each in his turn, the absolute Anthropos (*al-Insān al-muṭlaq*), the Adamic in the true sense (*al-Adamī al-muḥaqqaq*). The closer an adept is to the Imām—this is not a material proximity (*qurbat al-jism*) but a proximity of faith and gnosis (*qurbat dīnihi wa 'ilmihi*)—the closer he is to the full reality of the Anthropos; cf. section 4 below, on the Imāmate as *lāhūt*, divinity of the Imām, and compare among the Brothers of Purity the notion which crowns the anthropology that we are here setting forth, namely, the *insān malakī* (*homo angelicus*), in *Rasā'il* (Cairo, 1928), IV, p. 280.

92 Idrīs, p. 226.

93 Regarding the two breaths of the Trumpet of Resurrection, cf. the *shaykhī* (Gnostic school of Duodeciman Shiism) exegesis in our "Terre céleste et corps de résurrection d'après quelques traditions iraniennes," *EJ 1953*, pp. 181ff.

94 Idrīs, p. 230; in a way, the designation *al-walad al-tāmm* (Strothmann, p. 154, lines 14ff. and p. 176, lines 5ff.) recalls the "youth" Enoch-Metatron (in *3 Enoch*). Here, as last of the demiurges (*ākhir al-ṣanā'i'*), this figure points to the relation conceived by Ismailism between the celestial Angel Anthropos and the terrestrial Anthropos who finds his completion in the Perfect Child, or *Qā'im*. There is neither confusion nor identification, but rejunction: at the advent of the Perfect Child, the Angel, *Adam rūḥānī*, who in the Pleroma was himself the *Qā'im in potentia* in relation to the higher degrees, becomes *Qā'im in actu*; through this "angelomorphosis" the Perfect Child, the *Qā'im al-Qiyāmat*, once transferred to the Pleroma with the entire *corpus mysticum* of his *ḥudūd*, succeeds him in his regency over the sublunar world, while the Angel, celestial

This fulfillment marks what Ḥamīdaddīn Kermānī also calls the "rejunction" or "conjunction of the two extremes," namely, of the original archangelical dyad and of that Perfect Child for whose advent the seven Cycles —thanks to the efforts of the spiritual Angel Adam—are a preparation. Thus the total Cycle closes: the celestial Angel Adam—back to whom the final Imām, his "Perfect Child," his terrestrial Epiphany, leads his followers —rises one step closer to his initial rank and to the archangelical dyad in which he originated. As a Yemenite *dāʿī* remarks, the entire edifice of Ismailian Gnosis rests on the idea of this rejunction.[95]

It is reflected in the most sumptuous symbolic descriptions of Paradise, with its Seven Gates, its castles of light, its innumerable lofty halls, each containing twelve assemblies, its gardens and its streams of running water, its Angels and its houris. The *ta'wīl* takes all these symbols in a threefold sense: eschatologically they refer to the coalescence of all the souls of light that have realized their "second perfection," that is, their Angelic state.[96] The Sublime Temple is the celestial City the Most Pure Imāms are said to

---

Archetype of mankind, rises from his tenth to the next higher rank (the ninth, eighth, etc.), drawing along the entire Pleroma in his ascending movement and also summoning all the "Angels" of future mankind to this ascent toward the "lotus of the limit" (cf. ibid., pp. 26 and 113).

95 The "second blast of the trumpet," the final triumph of Gnosis revealed *in actu*, the appearance of the souls emerging liberated from the fetters of initiatory pedagogy— this is the conjunction (*ittiṣāl*) of the Energies of the First Limit (*al-nihāyat al-'ūlā*), which is the dyad of the First and Second Intelligence (cf. above, Seraphiel and Michael), with the Second Limit, which is the completion of the Anthropos (the *Qā'im*, the Perfect Child), and this last depending on the completion of the seven Cycles as the work of those who were commissioned and assisted (*mu'ayyadūn*) by the Third (> Tenth) Intelligence (Gabriel, Adam Rūḥānī). This conjunction is the new and final Creation, which contains and gathers together all the souls that have been called into being from the beginning to the end of the Aeon (*dahr*), those who, having achieved Gnosis, are able, by separating themselves from their mortal envelope, to resuscitate in the *corpus mysticum* of the eternal Imām; cf. Idrīs, p. 230, and Kermānī, p. 367. Sayyid-nā Ḥātim b. Ibrāhīm b. Ḥusayn was right in saying that Kermānī's whole book, from beginning to end, rests on this chapter!

96 The descriptions of Paradise agree (1) that all the Angels *in actu* are gathered in the Temple of Light of the Soul of all the worlds, which is the Second Intelligence; this is the Paradise *in actu*, the Paradise of the Haven "by the lotus of the utmost boundary, nigh unto which is the Garden of Abode" (53 : 14–15; Pickthall, p. 548); (2) that all the souls which have achieved their second perfection, i.e., the Angelic state, coalesce to form the Temple of Light of the *Qā'im*, the Resurrector; (3) that the "Paradise *in potentia*" (*jannat fi'l-quwwat*) is formed by the *da'wat*, the Ismailian sodality, in which each adept achieves through the *ta'wīl* his spiritual birth, the fulfillment of his "angelicity *in potentia*." Cf. Idrīs, ch. XX, pp. 234–36 (citing at length the Yemenite *dāʿī* Ibrāhīm b. Ḥusayn al-Ḥamīdī, d. 537/1162). Here it is impossible for us to discuss at length the *ta'wīl* that determines this topology of Paradise.

have built from time immemorial "out of their souls by their souls," the celestial City whose *visio smaragdina* will rise at the end of the mysterious Night, the Night of Destiny (*laylat al-Qadr*) celebrated in three Koran verses (97 : 3–5) for which the Ismailian Gnostics have a special predilection—a Night which "is better than a thousand months," a Night in which "the Angels and the Spirit descend. . . . That night is a peace which endures until the rising of the dawn." This Night is said to be the typification of "our sovereign Fāṭima" (*mawlātunā Fāṭima*), daughter of the Prophet, mother of the line of Holy Imāms, who, endowed with attributes similar to those of the Virgin Mother, gave birth to the succession of Epiphanies of celestial beings "until the rising of the dawn," that is to say, until the advent of the Perfect Child who will lead mankind back to its celestial archetype.[97]

The person of Fāṭima is indeed the basis of a whole Shiite sophiology. But here the motif takes on an unsuspected scope. It is not without surprise and emotion that we discover how Ismailian meditation on the Night of Destiny explicitly utilizes an essential motif of pre-Islamic Gnosis, namely the mystery of the Cross of Light set forth in the above-cited passage from the Acts of John. We have already heard one of our Ismailian theosophists, Abū Ya'qūb Sejestānī, declare that the four branches of the Christian Cross have the same symbolic content as the four words composing the Islamic *shahādat*. This same writer, meditating on these same symbols, mentions a sacred tradition concerning the Night of Destiny.[98] "In this Night," says the tradition, "the Light pours forth and spreads over Earth. Before this Light the stone walls, trees, all material things bow down and pray. Jesus announced to his people that the Resurrector would have the power to bring

97 Cf. Idrīs, ch. XVI, p. 127, and ch. XX, p. 227; Strothmann, XII, 7, p. 114. The "descent of the Angels" in this Night which *is* Fāṭima is the Epiphany of the Imāms to whose line she gives birth, of those Imāms upon whom it is incumbent to safeguard the pure spiritual meanings, to activate the symbols which inspire life to the positive religion (*sharī'at*). The "Spirit" is the inspiration and the celestial assistance which descend from each and all the Sublime Archangelical Intelligences to join them to the Most Pure Imāms "until the coming of the dawn," i.e., the parousia of the Resurrector. Thus the Night of Destiny, at the end of which mankind finds its redemption and apotheosis, is not simply one of the last nights in the month of Ramażān; it is the whole of our present Cycle of Occultation. And the Niche of Lights (*Mishkāt al-Anwār = Lampas luminum*) that illumines this Night is Fāṭima, the Virgin-Mother (*Fāṭima Batūl*) of the Holy Imāms; cf. our "Rituel Sabéen," pp. 236ff.

98 *Kitāb al-Yanābī', yanbū'* 31: *fī ma'na'l-ṣalīb li-millat 'Isā* (On the Meaning of the Cross for the Religion of Jesus).

out the spiritual meaning of all things,[99] even of a religion in which there had been no idea of this exegesis of the Spirit; similarly, it is possible to say that all the *ḥudūd* are gathered together in the inert wood of the Cross. Yes, in this Night of Destiny, whose mystical *Light* has power to transfigure all things, it is given to the *Qā'im*, the Resurrector, to metamorphose this inert wood, to transfigure the apparent, exoteric evidence of the crucifixion. Then it becomes a prodigious Sign for the totality of the *ḥudūd*, the companions of the esoteric sodality from Cycle to Cycle down to the consummation of our Aeon."[100]

These lines disclose a perfectly conscious Gnostic assertion, which bears witness to the extraordinary continuity of Gnosis. The gathering of all the *ḥudūd*, discernible in the transfiguring light, is a vision similar to that of the Acts of John. We are entitled to say that the symbol of the Cross, as understood by our Ismailian, *is* and can only be the mystery of the Cross of Light of Gnostic Christianity, the Christianity which the Angel Christos revealed to John in the secret colloquy on the Mount of Olives. And if we were to speak here of a "speculative Good Friday," it would be in a sense totally alien to our theological and philosophical habits, those habits which are still at work in the thinking of Hegel.

This is an aspect of Ismailian Gnosis that has gone entirely unnoticed up to now and concerning which there is assuredly a good deal to be learned. We shall again encounter this mystery of the Cross of Light in the very heart of Imāmology, precisely at the point where the union of the divine and the human in the Imām will, in its own special way, explicate the true meaning of Docetic Christology. Here precisely is the source of the feeling of the Imām's priority over the Prophet, a priority generally accepted in Duodeciman Shiism and accentuated in the reformed Ismailism of Alamūt. We can already measure its importance by the correspondence between the pairs *Nāṭiq*-Imām and First Intelligence-Soul, symbolically designated also as Sun and Moon; thus the Imām corresponds to the feminine principle; and he is also called the "spiritual mother" of the adept.[101] Thus the affirma-

99 Here, no doubt, we have an echo of the Gospel of St. John (14 : 26): "The Comforter, which is the Holy Ghost . . . shall teach you all things."

100 For, as an anonymous glossator adds in the margin of the manuscript, it is the *ḥudūd* which the *ta'wīl* discovers and identifies in these trees and stone walls that begin to pray in this Night; all are gathered together and transfigured in the Cross of Light. Cf. n. 123 below.

101 Cf. Nāṣir-e Khusraw, *Jāmi' al-Ḥikmatain*, section 341, pp. 298–99.

tion of his priority reflects a slow transformation of consciousness which is at the heart of the adept's spiritual birth and of the cycle of his soul's metamorphoses.

4. *Imāmology and Docetism*

Any study of the different forms taken by Christology presupposes, as we have said, an inquiry into the anthropology that goes hand in hand with it. Any attempt to discover how Shiite Imāmology in general, and Ismailian Imāmology in particular, reproduces certain traits of Angel Christology must begin with an inquiry into the relations between anthropology and angelology. And the very nature of the question leads us to accord to angelology, not the minor significance attributed to it by a schema of the world in which the Angel is all in all only a kind of metaphysical luxury, but the primary significance ascribed to it in a world where it assumes a twofold—theophanic and soteriological—function. The Ismailian indications are precise; they carry us back to certain traits common to all varieties of Gnosis, traits which put us in the presence of an anthropo-angelology, that is to say, an anthropology which is itself only a phase of angelology. In other words, there are no Angels separate both from Matter and from the Souls destined by nature to animate a material organic body. Both are *substantiae separatae*: there are Angels who have remained in the pleroma, and there are Angels who have fallen to the earth, Angels *in actu*, and Angels *in potentia*. Or this cleavage may refer to a single being, an *unus ambo*: the πνεῦμα, the Spirit or Angelos (Spiritus Sanctus or Paracletus in the Manichaean sense),[102] is the person or Angel who has remained in Heaven, the "celestial twin," while the soul is his companion who has fallen to the Earth, to whose help he comes and with whom he will be reunited if he issues victorious from the contest. But for a Gnostic the idea, conforming to Aristotelian anthropology, of a soul made by nature to animate a material body can only constitute an offense against the Creation of Light. Correlatively, the soul is not the unconfigurable entity generally assumed by a philosophical dualism for which the incorporeal is reduced to an abstraction or concept. If etymologically the soul (*anima*) has as its function to *animate*, if it is a complete substance independent of the organic material body which temporarily holds it, it is because this soul has left in the world of Light its

102 Cf. H. Söderberg, *La Religion des Cathares* (Uppsala, 1949), pp. 132, 174, 208ff.

"real body," the celestial body of a pure, still "immaterial" matter, or the "garment of light" which it must don once again.[103] In short our authors, Nāṣir-e Khusraw for example, conceive the human lot—the "horizon" that we call by this name—as a transitory status. What we call "man" is only a Not-yet: *either* an Angel *or* a demon *in potentia.*[104]

Now—and here again we shall encounter the premises opposed to the idea of an Incarnation realizing a hypostatic union—how is this potential angelicity of the human being fulfilled? The intermediary can only be an angel or else a being or beings in whom angelicity *in actu* is in one way or another already present. And these beings are the Most Pure Imāms.

Two Koran verses that have been meditated conjointly show one of the bases from which Imāmology arose. Here we shall follow Idrīs 'Imādaddīn (a Yemenite *dā'ī* of the fifteenth century), who in turn refers to Ja'far al-Manṣūr (*dā'ī* for Yemen in the middle of the tenth century of our era).[105] The Ismailian exegesis of these verses already discloses the priority of the Imām. The basic idea is this:[106] the Prophet as Envoy is entrusted with the mission of proclaiming the exoteric aspect of the Revelation; like those believing souls to which he addresses himself, he shares in the condition of an angelicity *in potentia.* But this potentiality can flower only through the revelation of the esoteric sense; this revelation is the condition of the second

103 Cf. Söderberg, pp. 135ff., *Anima* as *corpus spirituale*, pp. 243ff., 261; Acts of Thomas (motif of the "robe") in James, pp. 411–15, and Hans Leisegang, *La Gnose*, French tr. J. Gouillard (Paris, 1951), pp. 249ff.; cf. our *Avicenna*, pp. 157ff., and "Terre céleste," pp. 176ff.

104 Cf. notably Nāṣir-e Khusraw, ch. XI, and our *Étude préliminaire*, pp. 120–22.

105 Cf. Idrīs, ch. XIII, p. 84, citing a long passage from the *Ta'wīl al-Zakāt* of Ja'far ibn Manṣūr.

106 Just as the heavenly bodies are the visible aspects intermediate between the invisible Angels and humans (Nāṣir-e Khusraw, *loc. cit.*), so the Prophets and Imāms are intermediaries between the Angels *in actu* of the Pleroma and the earthly Angels, or Angels *in potentia*, who, captive in material bodies, can receive knowledge of the angelical world (*malakūt*) only through an intermediary and gradually (Idrīs, p. 83). But between the Prophets and the divine Mystery, the *ḥudūd*, or spiritual Angels, stand as intermediaries. Hence the name of "Messenger" (*rasūl*), which may fall to both ("Allāh chooseth from the angels messengers, and [also] from mankind" [27 : 74]; Gabriel is the *Rasūl Karīm*, the Noble Messenger). Similarly in Manichaeism, Mani is designated as *fereshtag rōshn*, messenger of light, and this epithet is current both among the Khorramdīnān and the Ahl-e Ḥaqq. This does not mean, however, that the Pehlevi term *fereshtag* has two different meanings, or that it designates a function rather than a nature. Actually the Persian *fereshtag* is equivalent to *Izad* (Avestan *Yazata*, "adorable," just as *Angelus* is equivalent to *Spiritus*, spiritual being). And the quality of *nuntius*, messenger, presupposes precisely the *nature* of the (celestial or terrestrial) Angel as fulfilling, par excellence, the theophanic function; cf. n. 14 above.

birth and the work proper to the Imām, master of the *ta'wīl*. The Prophet's impeccability is not total; even immunized against "sin," he can commit an error. This was the case with Adam, as we have seen (not the Adam-original Imām, but the "partial" Adam of our Cycle); it was the case with Moses and even Muḥammad.[107] The idea of the "impeccable" (*ἀναμάρτητος* = *ma'ṣūm*) is applied in the full and proper sense to the Imāms, who are the earthly typifications, the epiphanic Figures of the Angels of the highest degree, those who are called the "bearers of the Throne." From a Koran verse (6 : 9) which taken literally would signify only a hypothesis, our exegetes have constituted a fact, giving it the following sense: if ever God sent an Angel as messenger, he assuredly assumed earthly, human form; hence only this disguise was visible to the eyes of men, who hastened to say: he is only a man like ourselves.[108] Such precisely was the case of the Holy Imāms.

But this is not all. In the same context our authors refer to the verse (4 : 156) which explicitly states the Docetic Christology of the Koran. Since this verse is immediately transposed to the case of the Holy Imāms, we have here an explicit grounding of Imāmology in Docetic Christology. The verse in question is the vibrant reply to the contention that Christ was really crucified: "They slew him not nor crucified, but it appeared so unto them, and lo! those who disagree concerning it are in doubt thereof; they have no knowledge thereof save pursuit of a conjecture. They slew him not for certain."[109] The association of the two verses is immensely significant. On the one hand the disguise, the *dissimulation* (*talbīs*) which *dissimulates* the

107 Muḥammad's fault (Idrīs, ch. XIV) was to have laid claim to the Imāmate, to have believed himself *mustaqarr* (titular Imām), whereas he was only *mustawda'* (depository; on this distinction, cf. *Taṣawwurāt*, introduction by W. Ivanow, p. lvii). He understood only later that he had thus laid claim to a spiritual power that belongs to the *Qā'im*, the Resurrector, whose precursor was the Imām 'Alī. However, like that of Adam, his fault was not a deliberate "sin" nor a revolt. He repented, and commanded his *ḥudūd*, to reveal, each in its place, the high position of the *Qā'im*, the "seventh *Nāṭiq*." Here we have a specifically Shiite locus which would call for thorough study; we shall see its crucial importance.

108 The exegesis of the verse, without contradicting the general idea, modifies the current interpretation and translation which, in view of the immediate context, take it as an unrealized hypothesis; cf. *Taṣawwurāt* XV, p. 44 of the text.

109 Idrīs, p. 84; this is a key verse for our discussion. An extensive comparison of its *tafsīr* would be in order (cf., among others, Mullā Fatḥullāh, *Tafsīr* ad 3 : 48 and 4 : 156; Muḥsen Fayż, *Ṣāfī*, pp. 82 and 119). On their indications (attesting the contribution of highly varied pre-Islamic sources) depends the nuance given to the passive locution (*shubbiha lahum*).

spiritual Angels who came down to Earth for the salvation of men; on the other hand the *tashbīh*, the mental act which for our theosophers is the great sin of the literalist theologians, the *assimilation* of this *dissimulation* to what it dissimulates (corresponding to the assimilation of the attributes to the divine essence, which is a deviation from the line that passes between *tashbīh* and *ta'ṭīl*). But the *talbīs*, the dissimulation, is a trap only for those who commit the *tashbīh*, the assimilation.[110] Here the conditions of the *phenomenon* are lucidly set forth, and that is why we said a few pages back that our Docetists deserve to be regarded as the first phenomenologists. To anyone who might argue: "Are we not then dealing with appearances?" they have the ready answer: this *appearance* must become *apparition*; and this it will never do if precisely we assimilate it to the reality it veils, if we do not make it *transparent*—in short, if instead of thinking in terms of "*zuhūr*," or *epiphany*, we think in terms of "*ḥulūl*," or *incarnation*.

Here we may set forth the contrast in a very few words: on the one hand Angel Christology, which coincides with Imāmology; on the other hand the ideal of Incarnation, invoking a Christology of hypostatic union. Indeed, the differential is constant. What we have agreed to call "Docetism" constitutes a mode of perception, a fundamental intuition, which for oriental spirituality in general has the value of a "category" (its recurrences may be ascertained in Christianity as well as Islam or Buddhism). It corresponds to a mode of being so fundamental that we find its whole "style" in the Iranian Sufis, those *Fedeli d'amore*. The Beauty that is the object of their adoration is not exterior to the human Form in which it is epiphanized (since it is here that it shows itself), and yet it is extrinsic to it, for it is other than this Figure which can show it only in veiling it, just as the First Archangel is at the same time the supreme Name and the supreme Veil—just as the mirror is the "place" where the Image shows itself but is not its substrate. Rūzbehān Baqlī, the great twelfth-century mystic of Shīrāz, developed the psychological analysis of this epiphanic sense of love in great detail and with infinite delicacy.[111] It is disclosed in the attitudes common to the Shiite devotion to the Holy Imāms and to the adoration of Beauty among the *Fedeli d'amore*: in every case those whose devotion takes a person as its object and support are conscious of addressing themselves to a person

110 Idrīs, p. 83: *Fa'l-talbīs huwa'l-tashbīh lahum.*
111 In his Persian book *'Abhar al-'Āshiqīn* (The Jasmin of the Faithful of Love; BI 8, Teheran, 1958).

who transcends the empirical individuality that is subject to empirical conditions; what they perceive in this person is rather an eternal individuality. This presupposes the conviction (allowing of variable degrees of consciousness) that what constitutes the *maẓhar*, the epiphanic Form as such, is an event that takes place in the soul, which is its scene and organ, and whose mode of perception is entirely different from that of sensible or logical evidences that may be apprehended by everyone indifferently; otherwise, its perception would belong to every man alike.

And precisely because the soul is the "place" of metamorphoses, the plurality of Epiphanies by no means involves the idea of "reincarnations" (*tanāsukh*, expressly rejected by our Ismailian thinkers); on the other hand, statements which an "incarnationist" would regard as contradictory can coexist. The Koran verse relative to the person of the Prophet is extended to all the Imāms: "Thou seest them looking toward thee, but they see thee not" (7 : 197).[112] All regard the same being, but do not see the same being. It is not even necessary to deny the reality of the carnal body in order to affirm that the perception of this being is in every case *qualem capere potui*.[113] And this is not all. We have indicated above that the person of Fāṭima is the source of an entire Shiite sophiology. As an object of common perception she was the spouse of the first Imām, 'Alī ibn Abī-Ṭālib, and the mother of the two young Imāms Ḥasan and Ḥusayn. This representation does not infringe on the "natural laws." But simultaneously epiphanic faith endows her person with prerogatives equivalent to an Immaculate Conception, or to the Gnostic intuition of the Angel sent to Earth ahead of Christ to be the Virgin Mother.[114] Fāṭima was indeed born from

112 Cf. Idrīs, ch. XVI, p. 131.

113 For what changes and varies is the appearance, the *phainomenon*, of this body as object of the vision which shows it to itself. This accounts for the coexistence among the Duodeciman Shiites of what has been called their "dolorism"—their extraordinary cult of the Passion of the martyrs of Kerbalā—with the clearest Docetic statements. In one of the books devoted to the martyrdom of the Imām Ḥusayn, for example, we find the following literal quotation from the Koran: "No, they did not kill you; a *semblance* of your body was made for them, O son of the heroic knight" (quoted in Strothmann, p. 121). The material body is restored (or raised) to the level of a likeness or image of the Temple of Light. Accordingly, the Imām Muḥammad Bāqir (Idrīs, p. 131) declares that the sufferings, trials, and misfortunes of the Holy Imāms were apparent, *'alā'l-khayāl*, which is the literal equivalent of δόκησις (as of the corresponding term *putative*, which occurs among the Cathari; cf. Söderberg, p. 204); cf. also Massignon, p. 21, where, in the Nuṣayri poems of Khaṣībī, the Imām Ḥusayn is presented as a reapparition of *Jesus impatibilis*.

114 Cf. n. 12 above.

a fruit of Paradise, which the Angel gave the Prophet to taste in the course of his celestial ascension.[115] She is called *Fāṭima-Batūl*, that is to say, the Virgin Fāṭima; on the plane of theophanic vision, she is really the mother of the divinity (*lāhūt*) of the two young Imāms; she has the power to bear them to the Imāmate.[116] These traits that I briefly outline suffice, no doubt, to show us how in Imāmology thought operated very differently from the Christian speculation which was to culminate in the Christological formulas of the Councils.

Our authors, we may say, bear witness to the simultaneity of a twofold plane of vision corresponding to a twofold plane of happening: the whole question changes the moment one passes from one plane to another. And that is why, when it comes to understanding the humanity (*nāsūt*) of the Imām, that is, to translating Imāmology into anthropological terms as an event lived by the soul, the data of the problem will not partake of the physiology that imposes itself on sense perception and ordinary consciousness. It is an archetypal Image which will function as an organ of perception, replacing the faculties of sense perception and making perceptible an object that might correspond to the "body of transformation" in Mahāyāna Buddhism—and yet the humanity of the Imām is not reduced to what our "realist" exigencies would qualify as a "hallucination" and does not fit in with the idea of a hypostatic union. The problem is, then: how can a humanity that is the *maẓhar* of the godhead be constituted, to what order of

115 Idrīs, ch. XVI, p. 128: "Let him who wishes to breathe Paradise in the manner of Muḥammad breathing his daughter's perfume turn his mind upon her and upon what she reveals of the Secret hidden in her person; for she is the *Ḥujjat* of 'Alī, she establishes the esoteric sense of his Knowledge and guides those who attain to it. Through her, then, Paradise is breathed, as the essential sense (*ḥaqīqat*) of the *da'wat*."

116 Because the fruit of Paradise from which Fāṭima was born signifies the reunion of the two functions of the Imāmate (*istiqrār* and *istīdā'*). In the person of Fāṭima the two functions of the Imāmate are combined, but they separate once more in her sons, Ḥasan and Ḥusayn (Idrīs, p. 130). The two little Imāms were not born of her as other children of men are born, or rather they were the children of Fāṭima in the physical sense *and* in the most concrete spiritual sense (*fī'l-jismānīya wa'l-rūḥānīya*). Ḥasan issued from her *left side* because he *is* the *istīdā'* and also the exoteric law to which the *ta'wīl* must apply. Ḥusayn issued from her *right side* because he is the *istiqrār* and the esoteric *ta'wīl*, the essential sense (*ḥaqīqat*). In this sense (and not by virtue of a physiological process), Fāṭima is the *mother of the divinity* of the Imāms (their *lāhūt*, cf. below) for she herself possesses a Temple of Light, she is a repository of *lāhūt* (cf. Idrīs, pp. 127–32). These are brief indications suggesting the research that remains to be done; the image of Fāṭima, Virgin-Mother and mother of the divinity of the Imāms, shows that a parallel study of Imāmology and Angel Christology should have as its prelude an analysis of this aspect which corresponds in Shiism to a Mariology and Sophiology.

reality must it belong, that is to say, what *trans*figuration of it is presupposed in order that the epiphany (*ẓuhūr*, *iẓhār*) of this epiphanic Figure (*maẓhar*) may be produced not to the eyes of the body but to the soul's "eyes of light"?[117] Clearly we are dealing with something very different from an attempt to define some sort of somatic reality. Here the active Imagination is at work, producing the "body of metamorphosis" that is the support of its theophanic vision.

Now the active Imagination is the organ par excellence of the alchemical operation.[118] This is no incidental remark, for the meditations that our authors elaborate with a view to composing a mental representation of the humanity of the Holy Imāms will develop a vast operation of cosmic alchemy, which, moreover, offers the extreme interest of being only a variant of Manichaean conceptions.

We know that according to the Manichaean conception of man's posthumous development, the purified souls, having become once more pure lights, rise toward the Column of Glory that is the Perfect Man, then toward the Heaven of the Moon that is the Vessel of the Night, inhabited by the Primordial Man, then toward the Vessel of Living Fire, the Sun, which is the vessel of the Day and the abode of the Third Messenger.[119] The entire scheme of this process recurs in the Ismailian representations, with this particularity, that there is a duplication. Manichaeism had no need to worry about the ulterior destiny of the body of flesh, which was produced by demons; similarly for Ismailism, since the angel-souls are complete substances in themselves, the vicissitudes of the mortal remnants are without importance for the triumphant return of the souls of light to the angelic pleroma. Here cosmic alchemy responds to another preoccupation; to it we owe the notion of the subtle body, the delicate, pure, already angelic humanity, which is the only "true appearance" that the "apparition" of the Most Pure Imāms can assume. This alchemy must sublimate the mortal remains of the adepts, the true Gnostics. Its initial phases are a repetition

117 This is also the problem eminently represented for Shiite Gnosis by the scene of the Mantle: this Mantle that is a veil before the Knowledge that sees the "Five Persons," because they themselves are the Veils closest to God; common mortals regard only the Veils; what is at once veiled and manifested by the veils remains hidden to them (under the Mantle that is the *Sharī'at*, positive religion); Idrīs, p. 129 (for Koran 33 : 33); cf. also Louis Massignon, pp. 24ff.

118 Cf. C. G. Jung, *Psychology and Alchemy* (CWJ, 12; 1953), pp. 243ff.

119 Cf. *Manichäische Handschriften* . . . Vol. 1, *Kephalaia* (Stuttgart, 1940), p. 20.

of those which punctuate the Return of the souls in Manichaean soteriology. The subtle aerial and igneous elements of the adept's body, the vital spirits, sources of vital heat, rise like a diaphanous vapor drawn by the Moon's force of attraction; refined and sublimated, they are transmitted to the Sun, and after rising from Heaven to Heaven, they fall back to earth like a celestial dew that settles on certain of the most exquisite fruits or on the surface of an absolutely pure body of water. Through the providence of the Angel demiurge, the Imām and his consort will taste of these fruits and drink of this water; thus the humanity (*nāsūt*) of the future Imām, the subtle envelope of his Temple of Light, will be made of this subtle substance elaborated in the secret heights of the Heavens.[120] Our theosophers admit that the child will then be born like all other children of men; however they have opened a field of vision that enables the True Believer to perceive this humanity as not homoousian, or identifiable with common humanity; and yet the eyes of the flesh discern only this latter humanity, "even though a flash of light may shine through, a beauty and a purity defying all description."[121]

The humanity (*nāsūt*) of the Imām is thus conceived as the result of a cosmic process exemplifying an archetypal Manichaean representation. And it is in accordance with another Manichaean archetype that Ismailian Gnosis conceives the divinity (*lāhūt*) of the Imām. The conjunction of these Manichaean motifs in the heart of Imāmology is truly striking if we consider how little we still know about the sources of Ismailism. We have noted in Abū Ya'qūb Sejestānī a distinct allusion to the mystery of the Cross of Light proclaimed in the Acts of John. In Manichaeism this conception goes hand in hand with that of the Pillar of Light or Pillar of Glory; the two motifs typify the two phases, the *descensus* and *ascensus*, of the souls of Light. And here this Pillar of Light is presented as the mystery of the Imāmate.

For the Manichaeans the Cross of Light is the mystery of the descent of the souls of Light, of the energies and particles of Light held captive in the prison of Darkness, in the Gehenna of material bodies.[122] Twice a day, this

120 For a description of the process, cf. Idrīs, ch. XVIII, pp. 207–8, and Strothmann, I, 2, pp. 6–7 of the Arabic text.

121 Humanity so pure and subtle that, when the Imāms die, the body evaporates like *jism kāfūrī* (a body having the whiteness of camphor), so subtle that the celestial alchemy renders it fit to be united with the souls of the Bāb, the Ḥujjat, and the Dā'ī; cf. ibid., I, 1.

122 Cf. *Kephalaia*, p. 177; cf. also ch. LXXXV, pp. 208ff.

mystery is announced: at dawn and at dusk.[123] The ascent of the Pillar of Light, leaving the darkness to itself, is the triumphant response to the descent of the Cross of Light: it is the ascending procession of the elements of Light, of the angel-souls saved from their captivity, returning to their original world. Let us examine the details of this conception, for we shall meet with them again in Imāmology.

This Pillar of Light that is formed of all the souls of Light returning triumphantly from affliction to their original world is called the *Pillar of Glory*, or more precisely, the *Pillar of Glories*; the plural stresses the multiplicity of the individual souls that compose it, while the souls themselves are designated by a term that carries us back to the old Iranian notion of *Xvarnah*, "Light-Glory."[124] However, the representation of this Pillar of Glory does not coincide purely and simply with that of the *collectivity* of souls that composes it. Thanks to a specifically Iranian mode of thought, it is *also* a Person, a personal unity distinct from the totality whose parts are thus considered as the Person's members. This Person is the great Νοῦς of Light, he whom the Iranian texts call the Great Vahman (name of the first archangel after Ōhrmazd in the Zoroastrian heptad), or Manvahmed.[125] This Person is also designated as the Perfect Man[126] who transfers the elements of light from the earthly Church to the celestial pleroma. This action in itself individualizes the Person and distinguishes him from his own souls which he saves; and moreover, the Person is invoked in a hymn which

123 When the sun rises at dawn and the creatures begin to move on earth to break the Cross of Light that stands there in silence, the same thing happens as happened to the primordial Man; when from the heights of Light he rose up against the sons of Darkness, the sons of Darkness mounted from the depths and strove to corrupt the body of his sons in which his body was clothed (his "armor"). And at dusk, when men return to their abodes, it is the mystery of the end. All the purified light rises once more in a last *column* toward the Aeon of Light; never again will the word Light be uttered over those who have so hated it and so much loved the Darkness (*Kephalaia*, pp. 164–65). This *Pillar of Light*, the mystery of which is the triumphal answer to that of the Cross of Light, is therefore the ascending procession of the elements of light, the angel-souls delivered from their captivity. And Abū Ya'qūb Sejestānī had an intimation of precisely this (above, section 3, end) when, in the symbol of the Cross transfigured at the end of the Night of Destiny, he discerned the multitude of the *hudūd* of the Esoteric Church.

124 Cf. E. Waldschmidt and W. Lentz, *Manichäische Dogmatik* (Berlin, 1933), pp. 27–28 (the hymn, and commentary p. 123); *Die Stellung Jesu im Manichäismus* (1926), p. 57; on the Xvarnah as *Imago Gloriae*, see our "Terre Céleste," pp. 121–35.

125 Cf. George Widengren, *The Great Vohu Manah and the Apostle of God* (Uppsala, 1945), pp. 12–34.

126 See texts cited in ibid., p. 14.

addresses him as Srōsh (the Zoroastrian Angel Sraosha), who is the homologue of Gabriel just as the *Νοῦς* of Light is identified with Christ. This central figure of Gabriel-Christos brings us back once more to Angel Christology. And indeed this *Νοῦς* of Light, the Great Manvahmed, a total Person, yet distinct from the totality of its souls, is designated as Angelos Christos, or as Sophia, the personal Angel of Mānī, who conferred his prophetic mission upon him at the age of twenty-four[127] and remained his eternal companion even after death.

Thus we may first of all note that the Pillar of Light has a twofold aspect; it is the collectivity of the souls of Light, *and* it is also a Person distinct from this Totality. Thus distinct, it appears to Mānī as an individual person in a strictly individuated relation, that is, as a personal Angel, Manvahmed, appearing to *his* terrestrial soul. And this relation is reiterated for every soul. It is grounded in the very relation which posits the great *Νοῦς* (Srōsh, the Perfect Man) *and* the Column of Light as two distinct terms: here is born the idea of "geminity," the idea that every earthly soul has a celestial "twin."[128] We have, then, an analogy of relations presupposing four terms: the great *Νοῦς* of Light is to the totality (the Pillar) of the souls of Light as every *Νοῦς* or Angel is toward its Soul. And it would not be sufficient to say that the souls of Light are each one of them a part of the Great *Νοῦς* of Light. We may speak neither of fragmentation nor of incarnation, but only of an individuation, an individuation of relations: a perfect homology of structure between the *each* and the *All*, so that the *All* is present in the *each*.

All these features recur in Ismailian Imāmology. Idrīs 'Imādaddīn[129] repeats that the Imāmate is the coalescence (*majma'*) of all the souls of Light, who have been dyed with the precious spiritual Dye, substantialized by the teachings of Gnosis, and carried to the degree of subtlety of the spiritual world, and who have migrated from the material body and been drawn to join the Pillar of Light (*'amūd al-Nūr, al-'amūd al-nūrānī*), the summit of which reaches into the pleroma of the Archangels.[130] With a

127 Cf. Widengren, pp. 26 and 27n.
128 Sharing the name of "Angel" by reason of their common origin (cf. Söderberg, p. 129, n. 1).
129 Idrīs, ch. XVIII, pp. 206–7, and ch. XX, pp. 240–42.
130 Cf. also Strothmann, p. 53 of the Arabic text; the same representation occurs in the "oriental theosophy" of Suhrawardī; cf. our edition of *Ḥikmat al-Ishrāq*, p. 233, and our *Prolégomènes* in French, p. 52.

lyricism equal to that of the Manichaeans, our texts describe the power of this Pillar of Light, whose prodigious magnetism reaches down to the last ranks of the initiatory sodality to raise them upward from degree to degree, reaches down even to the neophytes (*mustajīb*, the "hearers" of the Manichaean hierarchy) and gathers them together in the Bāb, the "Threshold" of the Imām.

Such is the Imāmate, the Pillar of Light that constitutes the divinity (*lāhūt*) of the Imām. This highly complex conception is elucidated by its homology to Manichaeism. To understand the relation of the Imām with his divinity, that is, with the Pillar of Light constituting his Imāmate—a relation that is very different from an incarnation—let us turn to the Ismailian conception that is the homologue of the Perfect Man: the conception of man in the true sense (*insān ḥaqīqī*) and in the absolute sense (*'alā'l-iṭlāq*). We are told, for example, that the archangelical Forms of the celestial pleroma (*dār al-ibdā'*) have human form, "for it is the most beautiful of forms"; but it is made clear that this refers to Man in the true and absolute sense, that is to the Imāms, and most particularly to him who completes their line, the "Perfect Child," the Resurrector (*Qā'im*).[131] Here it is implied that the celestial pleroma is not limited to ten archangelical Figures; each Archangel is an aeon, and his person stands in the same relation to the Angels of his own pleroma as the Perfect Man, that is the Imām, to the souls of light constituting his Imāmate. Perfect, divine humanity, that of the Imām, corresponds to the archangelical archetype in the sense that it is the earthly support, the receptacle of a coalescence of souls of light, which is his *lāhūt*, his divinity, his Temple of Light (*haykal nūrānī*). Thus the conjunction of the divine and the human in the person of the Imām follows the example of the pleromatic relation between the Angel of humanity and the race of celestial humanity issued from him, because the Imām is precisely this Angel's terrestrial support. And that is why, in his individual person—that is to say, in that subtle superhumanity which alchemy, as we have seen, meditated upon and elaborated—the Imām is the *maẓhar*, the epiphanic Form (not the Incarnation) of the celestial Angel Adam.

In this exemplification we also find the process of individuation repeated in multiple geminations analogous to those which joined Mani and the

131 Cf. Strothmann, I, 1, p. 6; also Kermānī, p. 145 (the second term of the creation, the perfect human being, resembles the first, the Angel of the pleroma, as a child resembles his parents).

Angel Christos, each soul with its Angel or "Holy Spirit." The Sublime Temple of Light (*haykal nūrānī sharīf*) of the last Imām gathers together, integrates, all the Prophets, *Waṣī*, Imāms, all the *ḥudūd* and true Gnostics who have preceded him in the course of the Cycles. He contains each of the Temples of Light of each Imām (*haykal imāmī sharīf*), progressively erected by the Angel demiurge to constitute the resurrective Form (*ṣūrat qā'ima*), the Temple of the Resurrector (*haykal al-Qā'im*).[132] Without fusion or confusion of persons, in the image of the Heavens encased one in the other, *each* Form subsists as a member in the *Whole*, just as each *ḥadd* subsists in the Temple of Light of its Imām, and each Form is preserved in its perfect living individuality that is all life, all power, all knowledge. What the Temple of each Imām is to the Sublime Temple of the *Imām Qā'im*, each *ḥadd* is to the Temple of his Imām; what this Imām is for the *ḥadd*, the *ḥadd* himself is for his own *maḥdūd*, the "companion" who follows him. In these individuations and their law of homology, the presence of the *All* in the *each*, we once again encounter the principle that we found at the source of the maxim: he who knows himself knows his Lord. This verification of homologies, defining the dyadic height of each soul in the *Corpus mysticum* and hence, with the horizon of its being and its knowledge, the rhythm of its metamorphoses, is carried so far that we should have difficulty in finding a parallel except perhaps in Swedenborg, where, for example, he says: "Each soul is the whole Church; to each angelical consociation the Lord appears as an Angel corresponding to the very form of this consociation."[133] And such words are perhaps the most satisfying commentary on the sentence "Whoever knows himself (= knows his soul), knows his God."

In this very brief sketch we have indicated the structure of the Pillar of Light that constitutes the Imāmate, the *lāhūt* or divinity of the Imām. Now, we may ask, what is the event that brings about the conjunction of the

132 See n. 129 above.

133 Swedenborg, *Heaven and Hell*, 52 and 72. The Swedenborgian idea that every heaven or company of Angels has the form of a human being (*homo maximus* = *insān muṭlaq*) may be compared to the Ismailian parallel between the progress of the soul rising from degree to degree of the hierarchy and the phases of embryology (Idrīs, ch. XVIII, p. 207), or better still the idea that in the Temple of Light that is the *lāhūt* or divinity of the Imām the souls are disposed in a certain order, in function of their rank, their knowledge, their activity: some are in the heart, others in the brain, others in the limbs, etc., according to their degree of maturity and elevation. All together form the sublime and luminous Imāmic Temple, each one rejoicing in his fellows (ibid., p. 209).

Imāmate with the Imām, of the *lāhūt* with the *nāsūt*, of the divine with the human? When the young Imām attains a certain age,[134] the Imām his father confers on him the investiture (*naṣṣ*), a solemn act that does not make him an Imām—this he already is potentially by virtue of his birth—but enables the adepts to recognize in him the mystical presence of the Imāmate. The mystery is accomplished: the Temple of Light assembled in the Bāb, the "Threshold" of the previous Imām, is transferred invisibly to the young Imām in the manner of the Angel Christos descending upon Jesus on the *dies natalis* of his baptism. The young Imām is henceforth the epiphanic Form, the *maẓhar* of the celestial Angel Adam, because he is the terrestrial support of the Pillar of Light whose summit rests on this Angel's Heaven.[135]

When the Imām departs from this world,[136] he draws with him this entire Pillar of Light. All together its component souls dwell in the realm of the Tenth Angel, the celestial spiritual Adam, the Angel Gabriel-Holy Spirit of the philosophers. Here, according to our theosophers, they live in an expectation of still new spiritual upsurges, new burgeonings of light and perfection—until the total Cycle is consummated, that is, until Man in the true sense, the last Imām of the Cycle, the *Qā'im* or Resurrector, having completed the work of the Seventh Day and erected the Throne that he himself is "in person," also rises to that realm in which all the Temples of Light of the Imāms who have preceded him are awaiting his apotheosis. Then there occurs in Heaven an Event as inscrutable to our imaginations as the prologue of the drama, the stupor that "retarded" the Angel of our humanity. And yet this Event is the response to that other Event, its denouement. The Resurrector, support of the Sublime Temple of Light, the Perfect Man after the example of the archangelical Forms of the Pleroma, so totally exemplifies the Image of the Angel that he is worthy to succeed him. He is enthroned as his *khalīfa*, his successor, while the tenth Angel rises to the next higher degree (the ninth, eighth, etc.), thus reconquering the "retarded eternity," the rank lost in pre-eternity—not as though reconquering it over the other Archangels of the Pleroma but raising them too in this vertiginous ascent which draws the entire universe of being

134 There are variants: when the child has attained the age of education (*tarbiyat*), that is, the age of four (Idrīs, p. 208), or when the Angel demiurge recalls the Bāb to him (Strothmann, p. 8).

135 Idrīs, ch. XVIII, p. 208.

136 For this whole paragraph, cf. ibid., ch. XII, pp. 75–7, and ch. XVIII, pp. 209–10; cf. n. 94 above.

toward the "lotus of the limit," that is, to the threshold of the primordial Archangel whose Form of Light emerges eternally from the inscrutable night of the deity, in the sublime self-abnegation of the "No God outside of Him," that abnegation which makes *Him*, precisely, the one and primordial theophany.

I hope that this brief sketch of a very complex doctrine will suffice to suggest how Imāmology both extends and modifies an Angel Christology. We have pointed out that the Docetism of our theosophers was situated in the context of an affirmation of the Imām as an Angel *in actu, dissimulated* beneath the garment of a body. We have just examined the relation between the *nāsūt* and the *lāhūt*, in other words, the "how" of the angelicity that has the power to unfold the angelicity of those souls whose Saviour (through the Imām) is the Angel, because their own nature is originally and eschatologically also that of the Angel. The Saviour need not assume an alien *nature* inferior to his own; on the contrary, he saves his followers by awakening them to their primitive nature that is also his. In this sense we may say that the divine Epiphany as anthropomorphosis is accomplished on the level of the Angel (the Archangels of the pleroma have the perfect human Form). And if it is on the level of the Angel that the divine becomes *man* and that the divine and the human meet, it is precisely because the human being by his origin is an Angel *in potentia* and because such a theophany presupposes the "opening" of this very dimension in the soul, the realization of its angelical potency, which is the measure of its *qualem capere potui*. Here the *descent* of the divinity is conceivable only through a simultaneous *assumption* of man, a bursting of the human condition that passes as "natural." Anthropomorphosis and *theōsis* (our authors say "angelomorphosis," in Persian *be-fereshtagī rasīdan*), are here correlative terms. *Eo ipso* such an Angel Christology, either in itself or in the Imāmology that is its extension, marks the sharpest contrast with the Christological dogma of the Councils: the godhead incarnated in man, assuming all the miseries of the human lot in order to save mankind, inspiring a cult of human suffering, the contemplation of the "outraged Christ." The contrast throws a blinding light on what was—and perhaps remains—a crossroads in the destiny of each man, in the destiny of humanity, in the destiny that mankind has prepared for itself according to the manner in which it has understood itself.

It is perhaps at this point that Imāmology discloses the degree and form of spiritual energy which dominates it and shows how it absorbed and surpassed simple prophetology. It has already gone beyond Ebionite prophetology; we no longer have merely the one True Prophet "running through the centuries" and through his metamorphoses to his repose which is already at hand. Rather we must note the *plurality* of the persons of the Imāms and the *unity* of Imāmic epiphany or existence (*wujūd* as *ẓuhūr* and *ishrāq*). This unity is the Sublime Temple of Light of the Imāmate, with which these Persons are integrated each in his turn while still preserving their individuality. But the dome of the Temple will rise only in the dawning light of the Seventh Day! The predominance of Imāmology, of the figure of the Imām over that of the Prophet, did not result from phases comparable to the exhausting controversies which led in Christianity to the formulation of the Christological dogma. Since the idea of an eternal Imām imposes itself upon the horizon of the soul, it is in its own secrecy that the soul verifies his theophanies. The process rather resembles the transfer of interest in Mahāyāna Buddhism from lived religion, from the "historical" Buddha perceived in his "body of transformation," to the Buddha meditated upon in his "body of the law" (Dharmakāya).

5. *The Eternal Imām*

It would even be difficult to consider this idea of the priority of the Imām as the result of a historical process. The idea is discernible at the very beginning of Shiite Gnosis and is no doubt the most compelling force in its development. On August 8, 1164, the Great Resurrection was proclaimed at Alamūt (the Ismailian "commandery" erected in Iran, in the chain of mountains southwest of the Caspian Sea). In settling the statute of the Law (*ḥukm-e sharī'at*) against the statute of Resurrection (*ḥukm-e qiyāmat*[137]) and in proclaiming itself a religion of Resurrection (*dīn-e qiyāmat*), Ismailism merely returned to its origins after the closing of the Fāṭimid episode, the political success of which was a paradox doomed to failure on the spiritual plane, since it presupposed the accomplishment of an eschatology. Reformed Ismailism established once and for all the priority of the Imām and the Imāmate, since the Resurrection is the application of the *ta'wīl*, the spiritual exegesis that carries every exoteric figure back to its tran-

137 Cf. *Taṣawwurāt* XXIV, pp. 79–80 of the Persian text.

scendent origin,[138] and since the Imām is the key to Resurrection. Here precisely is the paradox, the permanent challenge of this Shiite Gnosis: to experience the religion of Resurrection, the religion of the Imām, is to penetrate the hidden sense of the positive religion and at the same time to surpass it. And yet the positive religion must be retained, precisely in order to constrain men to exceed it, to call forth the resurrection of the adepts.

Such is the meaning of the six periods of the exoteric revelation of the Prophets, which one of the rare Persian texts in the Alamūt tradition to have survived the Mongol tempests describes as the "Night of the True Religion" (*shab-e Dīn*[139]), a Night that is the veiling (*ḥijāb*) of the Imām just as in the physical world the night is the hiding of the Sun—and we already know that it is the "Night of Destiny." Is then a Moon not necessary to illumine this night with the True Faith? In response to this question, a distinction is made between two Epiphanies of the Imām: one Epiphany that we may designate as corporeal and plastic (*ẓuhūr-e shaklī*) and which has always been exceptional in our Cycle, and another spiritual or mental Epiphany (*ẓuhūr-e ma'nawī*), that of his true hidden (*bāṭin*) meaning, visible only to the soul of the initiate, forever invisible to the profane, even when the corporeal Manifestation is present to his eyes. And an Ismailian poet, Gharīzī, asks: "If the spiritual Epiphany today is without profit, what will the corporeal Epiphany avail tomorrow?"[140] In the foreground of this spiritual Epiphany the figure of the *Ḥujjat*, the "Proof," the "Witness" of the Imām, will stand out, assuming the role that previously fell to the Bāb, the "Threshold." This promotion is of inestimable importance for the re-junction of Ismailism and the mystical religion.

To understand its repercussions in the individual being of each adept, let us consider the ontological aspect in which the concept of the Imām is now perceived. With great psychological subtlety a treatise attributed to Naṣīraddīn Ṭūsī observes that the measure of a True Believer, what he is in his innermost being, can never be understood by others. And he goes on to infer: "How then will it be with him in whom the True Believer puts his

138 Definition of the *ta'wīl*: (Arabic) "*raddu shay'in ilā awwalihi*" (*Yanābī'* 30–31) = (Persian) "*chīzī be-aṣl-e khwōd rasānīdan*" (*Kalāmi Pīr*, 57).

139 Cf. the little treatise on Imāmology published in Persian by W. Ivanow under the title *Faṣl dar bayān-e shanākht-e Imām* (Leiden, 1949); *On the Recognition of the Imām* (Bombay, 1947), pp. 1^b–2 of the text (abbrev. here = *Shanākht*).

140 Ibid., p. 2^b.

faith?"[141] Concerning the object of this faith, the Imām, we are told that knowledge must avoid both his *tashbīh* and his *ta'ṭīl*; one can neither affirm nor deny the resemblance of the Imām to creatures.[142] The Imām as Imām is unknowable for men; he is knowable only in his being that is relative to the creatures, to each according to his rank in being (*unicuique secundum quod dignus est*, to cite Origen's formula). But have we not here the entire problem concerning knowledge of the godhead? Assuredly; and the thesis is precisely that knowledge of the Imām is knowledge of God.[143] Thus a decisive change has been made in the system of correspondences that we have found established among the thinkers of the Fāṭimid tradition, such as Ḥamīdaddīn Kermānī. The Imām is no longer the epiphanic Figure (*maẓhar*) of the second Intelligence or universal soul, but, extending over the entire hierarchy of the pleroma, it is the Epiphany of the existentiating Word (*Kalimat*), the creative Fiat (KN)[144] of eternal existentiation (*ibdā'*), the being in the imperative and the imperative of being that vibrates in every being. In his essence he is essentially this Epiphany, that is, the possibility of giving attributes to the godhead; concretely, he is the godhead itself clothed in these attributes,[145] that is to say, not Epiphany of the divine Essence but Epiphany of those attributes that are entirely relative to men. There is a saying in which Imāmology coincides literally with Christology: "He who knows me knows God";[146] here it is not this or that Imām who speaks in his own name, but an eternal Imām. And as primordial Epiphany it is, in proto-Ismailism, the Five Pre-eternal Persons (*ashkhāṣ azalīyūn*), who are epiphanized in the successive stages of the cosmology (the Five Archangels, the Five "Persons of the Mantle")[147] as Manifestations of the godhead (*ṣūrat-e ẓāhir-e Khodā*), as his Attributes, his eternal theophanies. "We are the beautiful Names of God and his supreme attributes, that is to say, the supreme Name and the concretized and hypostatized Attributes."[148]

141 Cf. *Taṣawwurāt*, p. 87.

142 Ibid.; cf. Shihābaddīn Shāh Ḥusaynī, *The True Meaning of Religion or Risāla dar Ḥaqīqat-e Dīn*, tr. W. Ivanow (2nd edn., Bombay, 1947), pp. 20–21 (hereinafter abbreviated as *True Meaning*).

143 Ibid., p. 20.

144 [The consonants of the Arabic word *kun*, "Let there be," from *kāna*, "to be."—Tr.]

145 *Taṣawwurāt*, p. 88: "His word, his action, his knowledge, his face can be called the word, action, knowledge and face of God."

146 *True Meaning*, p. 20: *Har kas mārā shanākht, Khodā shanākhtah*. Cf. Gospel of St. John 14 : 7 and 9: "He that hath seen me hath seen the Father."

147 Cf. nn. 44, 47, 117 above and the end of section 6 below.

148 *Taṣawwurāt* XXIV, pp. 88ff.: "I knew God before the Heavens and the Earth were

The Prophets pass away and change, while "We are an eternal people" (*naḥnū anās ṣamadīyūn*).[149]

We must take note of this *plural.* It marks the plurality which from the outset attaches essentially to the very notion of a theophany. Yet we must take care not to interpret it as indicating quantitative fragmentation, as though each Imām were a fragmentary Imām. Here we see at work the notion of individuation, having as its corollary the homology between the *each* and the *All* that we stressed above. Each Imām is the Epiphany of a degree, a mystery, a beneficence,[150] a gradation relative to him to whom he "shows himself," but each one homologically contains the totality. To make it clear that he is not speaking of the fragmentation of a species into individuals differing numerically (and only numerically) among themselves, Naṣīr, drawing on the lexicon of Avicennan angelology, points out that the individual person of the Imām is itself his entire *species*, that his *species* is his *person.*[151] The plural refers to what we have called above the "metamorphoses of theophanic visions"; it is the basis of the distinction that we have just remarked between plastic or corporeal Epiphany and spiritual or mental Epiphany.

Now this fundamental distinction encompasses another: the modes of manifestation (or theophanic visions) vary according to the modes of knowledge, which vary according to the mode of consociation (*payvastagī*) with the Imām. This consociation itself presents a threefold variety, determining a threefold mode of being which differentiates human beings and to which corresponds a threefold mode of perception or knowledge of the Imām.

There can be a purely physical bond with the Imām (as in the case of those of his lineage who have not been invested with the Imāmate); there can be a purely spiritual bond (this will eminently be the case of Salmān the Pure); and lastly, there can be a consociation realized at once on the physical and spiritual plane and on the plane of Essence (this in general is

---

created. . . . We stand in such a relation to God that being with Him, we are He. I am he who raises the Heavens and he who lays out the Earth. I am the First and the Last, the Manifest and the Hidden. I am cognizant of all things." In such texts we gain an intimation of the figure of eternal Sophia through the eternal Imām.

149 *Taṣawwurāt,* p. 90.

150 Ibid., p. 94. Through the unity of the *οὐσία* (*ḥaqīqat*) of the Eternal Imām, the persons (*shakhṣ*) of the Imāms are conceptually and ontologically (*dar ma'nawīyat wa ḥaqīqat*) both distinct; it is in this sense that one may speak of the "return" (*raj'at*) of the Imām.

151 Ibid., p. 89.

the case with the twelve Imāms of Duodeciman Shiism, who comprise the first heptad of Imāms recognized by Ismailism).[152] To the threefold mode of consociation corresponds a threefold division of human beings: there are the Exoterists (*ahl-e ẓāhir*) who require a material presence and attach themselves to the genealogy of the Imām, to his carnal lineage. There are the Esoterics (*ahl-e bāṭin*), who discern and examine hidden meanings and forms; they are open to the mental Epiphany, and what they perceive in the genealogy of the Imāms is a spiritual perpetuation. Finally, there are the Gnostics of the Essence (*ḥaqīqat*), the esoterics of esoterics, for whom the Imām is *himself* this Essence, the eternal Imām. To the three modes of being correspond, then, three modes of knowledge: there is a perception of the Imām in his physical person (but of this animals are also capable), or in his common name, his carnal genealogy (but of this his enemies and negators are also capable); there is the knowledge of his Imāmate, corresponding to the Self (*dhāt*) of the Imām, or rather of the Self that is the Imām, of the Essence which creates the truth of his attributes (*ḥaqīqat-e ṣifāt-e ū*), that is to say, which is the foundation of his very being as primordial Epiphany, *Deus determinatus*. Only the *Ḥujjat* possesses this knowledge.[153]

All these functional relations between modes of consociation with the Imām and modes of being and knowing, combine to determine the very concept of Epiphany, to define what may be meant when it is said that an "Imām has come to this world." Of course, this coming cannot (any more than in the case of Angelos Christos) be an incarnation into this world nor an entrance into becoming. This "coming to the world" is essentially an Epiphany, a Manifestation, which is equally present in the three worlds (the physical world, the psychospiritual world of the *da'wat*, the spiritual world of the heavenly Angel), a Manifestation that is the cause of their being, of their revelation to being.[154] This means that his coming consists in his making himself visible in the Form in which he is contemplated and that the eternal Imām epiphanizes himself *to* this world without coming *into*

152 Here, of course, we leave out of account the divergence concerning the person of the Seventh Imām (the successor of the Imām Ja'far Ṣādiq).

153 *Taṣawwurāt*, pp. 89–90, 93; *Shanākht*, p. 22. This law of essence that defines the relation between the subject's mode of being and his mode of perception of the Imām may be compared with the discussions on the Light of Tabor among the Byzantine Hesychasts: an animal, an unbeliever, would not have perceived this light.

154 *Taṣawwurāt*, pp. 90–92, 95; *Shanākht*, pp. 28 (= 6 of the text), 29; compare the admirable phenomenology in Naṣīraddīn Ṭūsī (ibid.) of "coming into this world" and "departing from this world"—"Cyclical Time," pp. 57–58.

this world; his epiphany does not reveal his essence—it is always "relative to" (that is to say, relative to the capacity for vision of) him who contemplates it.[155] Thus, so far as the eternal Essence (*ḥaqīqat al-ḥaqā'iq*) is concerned, the Imām has never come and never does come *into* this world; but in regard to the relation of which we have been speaking, he has had and will have, down through the ages, his Epiphanies *to* this world. Thus he is at once father and son, sometimes a youth, sometimes an old man. Trait for trait, we recognize the theophanic visions of the Acts of Peter and the doctrine they imply: *qualem capere potui*. Such and such a vision is the relation *in actu* with such and such a divine attribute "in person"; the Imāms are the Manifestation, the hypostasis of these attributes ("We are the beautiful Names of God and his attributes"). In short, each being to whom he epiphanizes himself *is* the coming of the Imām into this world. Of course our familiar consciousness of the "real" will mobilize our anti-Docetic instinct to utter the objection: but what guarantees the *truth* of this vision *relative* to myself? Our Gnostics foresaw this objection and answered it: it is the truth of the Imām that makes the vision true and not, inversely, some external criterion that makes the vision of the Imām true. The setting up of a relation between the two terms, the contemplator (or, him who contemplates) and the contemplated, results from an individuation, the truth of which does not arise from the contemplant alone but also from the Figure individually contemplated. The only criterion, the Imām, formulates this by declaring: "He who recognized me in pre-eternity will recognize me."[156]

Once we have taken together these considerations regarding the plurality of theophanies as individuations of the eternal Imām, the functional relations that condition them, their nature as spiritual events—not as visions of

155 *Shanākht*, p. 26.

156 *Taṣawwurāt*, p. 96, going as far as the paradox "Without him, the truth itself is impious error (*kufr*); with him even pluralism (*shirk*) is Truth and True Faith." With this idea of pre-eternal recognition we may connect the motif of an Epiphany of the Imām which is consonant with the Christology of Origen (Christ an Angel for the Angels, a man for men): "Thou appearest a man among men, an Angel among Angels" (*Shanākht*, p. 26 = 5[b] of the text, dealing with the distinction between the world of the *khalq* and the world of the *Amr*). Cf. the names of the Five Persons written in letters of light on the Throne (Idrīs, ch. XIII) and the Angels contemplating 'Alī (which is only the kyriological name of the eternal Imām, *Excelsus*) in the form of an Angel (*Kalāmi Pīr*, p. 88, and *Ta'wīl al-āyat* of Sharafaddīn 'Alī Astarābādī, *in fine*); compare also the idea of the *personal* form of every Epiphany (Paradise is a person, Prayer is a person, etc.) and the idea of *maẓar* among the *Fedeli d'amore* (*Rūzbehān*).

the Imām in his epiphanic *essence* (which would be to penetrate the mystery of the creative Fiat) but as epiphanic *relations* constituting, as such, the only coming of the Imām into this world—it becomes possible for us to gain an intimation of the meaning of the *Ḥujjat*, the Witness, the Proof of the Imām, and the reasons which impose this Figure on Imāmology carried to this speculative height.

Two characteristics define the *Ḥujjat*. This Moon, we are told, "illumines the Night of Faith"[157] just as the Moon illumines the world in the measure in which it receives from the Sun a light proportional to its capacity: in itself it is nothing and has nothing, but the radiant brightness of the Imām makes it incandescent, and it is his substitute (*khalīfa*, diadochos) during his "occultation." The *Ḥujjat* is described to us as the person who from pre-eternity is the perfect homologue of the Imām; their concepts are one.[158] It is the true kyriological name (*ism ḥaqīqī*) of the Imām; it is the "Door of Compassion" (*dar-e Raḥmat*), the "Threshold of Knowledge" (*Bāb-e ma'rifat*) of the Imām. By virtue of the identity of their concept (*ma'nā*), the *Ḥujjat* is the mental or spiritual Epiphany (*ẓuhūr-e ma'nawī*) of the Imām; in other terms, his person is not an Incarnation of the Imām but is the form of his "coming *to* this world." That is to say, that since the Imām, as epiphany of the divine attributes, is knowable only *relatively to* human creatures, the *Ḥujjat*, the "Threshold of Consciousness," is precisely this *relation*.[159]

The second trait that completes the characterization of his person brings us to the striking convergence of Imāmology and Angel Christology. The mode of "consociation" which places the person of the *Ḥujjat* in respect to the Imām is by no means the mode of carnal descent, of genealogical legitimacy. He is the Spiritual Child (*farzand-e ma'nawī*), the Adopted Child of the Imām.[160] It is no accident that this term should remind us of the adoptianism of the Christology of the Ebionites and of the *Shepherd of Hermas*; indeed, the convergence of which we have just spoken becomes clear as soon as we give the *Ḥujjat* his archetypal proper name, the name of

157 *Taṣawwurāt*, p. 97.

158 *Shanākht*, p. 28.

159 Ibid., pp. 36–37 (=10–10b of the text). To enter by the Threshold is to enter the house, but it is by the Threshold that one must enter. God cannot be known by the creature, and the knowledge of the Imām cannot be realized in this Night of the Faith without the *Ḥujjat*, who is the spiritual or mental Epiphany (*ẓuhūr-e ma'nawī*) of the Imām (ibid.).

160 Ibid., p. 23 (=4 of the text).

Salmān the Persian or Salmān the Pure (Salmān Fārsī, Salmān Pāk). The Imām may be said to stand in the same relation to Salmān, his Adopted Child, his Spiritual Child, as the Angel Christos to Jesus. If we recall the equivalence between Gabriel and Christos professed by an entire Angel Christology, we shall not be far from the secret of the enigmatic figure of Salmān, in whom our texts show us the earthly typification of the Angel of Revelation, and as such the Angel of initiation. The intervention of Salmān inaugurates a process that will make esoteric Imāmology a paradox in Islām, for Salmān will outrank the Prophet himself, and this priority will derive from his quality as *Ḥujjat*, as Witness and Spiritual Child of the Imām. Since in this capacity he will be presented as the archetype of the Gnostic, of the True Believer, he may be said to mark the most personal spiritual experience to which Ismailian Imāmology can lead.

Who is Salmān? A dominant figure of this Islamic esotericism: the Expatriate, the Exile, he who comes from a distant horizon: he is the Orphan (*yatīm*) and also the Adopted One, the Spiritual Child of the Imām.[161] Historically an Iranian, son of a Mazdean knight of Fārs; after attending a liturgy he became a Christian and set out on a pilgrimage in quest of the True Prophet, in the course of which he came into contact with Mohammed. Magnified to the gnostic dimensions of the Ismailian consciousness, his Person rose to an extraordinary rank. Salmān is he who initiated the Prophet, who helped him to gain awareness of the scriptural antecedents of his Revelation. He is the "epiphanic form" of the Angel Gabriel, his human, earthly form, since the Prophet could not sustain the brilliance of the Angel's original form.[162] Thus he was the Prophet's companion of initiation, the *ḥadd*, whose *maḥdūd* is the Prophet, the exegete of the esoteric meaning of the words "dictated" by the Angel—in other words, he to whom it is given to demonstrate the recurrences and correspondences in the Revelations communicated by the Angel. Accordingly he alternates with the Angel Gabriel as "sixth" by the side of the Five Persons of the Mantle.[163]

161 Cf. Louis Massignon, *Salmān Pāk* (Paris-Tours, 1934); our study on "Le Livre du Glorieux," pp. 60ff.; on the motif of the Expatriate, cf. also our *Prolégomènes II* to the Works of Suhrawardī, pp. 87ff., 97ff.

162 Cf. n. 42 above (the two forms of the Angel): Thus the story that Mohammed received the initiation (*ta'līm*) from Gabriel, the Angel in human form, is to be referred to the *Ḥujjat* of the Imām; cf. also n. 86 above: Maryam, as *Ḥujjat* of Jesus, receiving the *Rūḥ* from the Imām, or from the *Ḥujjat* of the Imām of the preceding period.

163 Cf. nn. 43–47 above; Massignon, *Salmān Pāk*, pp. 16ff.; our "Le Livre du Glorieux," pp. 64ff.

All these indices of superior rank are alluded to in enigmatic *ḥadīth*,[164] but above all they are motivated by the solemn attestations of Salmān's adoption, given by the Prophet and, with still more weight, by the first Imām. Such attestations are known in many variants, pointing to different sets of circumstances. This variant, for example, emanates from the Imām: "Salmān is one of us, the members of the House (*Salmān minnā, Ahl al-Bayt*), a Sun of the divine Light, an integral part of ourselves. The heart of the True Believer is the Light of God; no one measures his measure, for the True Believer is forever living in the two universes."[165] Or yet again: "Salmān is part of myself, and I myself am part of Salmān."[166]

In primitive Shiism, or more precisely in proto-Ismailism, this assumption of Salmān is reflected in the speculations developed around the three symbolic letters 'AYN, SĪN, MĪM, typifying respectively the Imām, Salmān the Adopted One (his Spiritual Child), and the Prophet. The "Book of the Glorious One" of Jābir ibn Ḥayyān starts from these highly abstruse speculations.[167] The order in which the three symbolic letters have just been enumerated corresponds to the order of rank adopted by the reformed Ismailism of Alamūt, which thus returned to its primitive inspiration. Considered on the plane of hierarchical archetypes, according to the law of homology that we have discerned in the basic angelology, this order of rank introduces a radical and highly meaningful change into the schema of correspondences established by the thinkers of the Fāṭimid tradition.[168] And indeed this modification is the direct consequence of the promotion of the Imām, who is now meditated upon as a typification not of the second

164 "If Abū Dharr knew what there is in the heart of Salmān, he would hurl the anathema against him" or even (in an alternative reading) "would wish to kill him." The Imām explains: "If Salmān declared to Abū Dharr that his own rank is superior to that of the Prophet (priority of the *Sīn* over the *Mīm*, n. 78 above and n. 167 below) and that the Imām is the Creator and Former of the World, Abū Dharr would regard him as an infidel and would wish to kill him" (*Shanākht*, p. 7^{a-b}). Thus the Ismailian exegesis of this *ḥadīth* makes it a witness attesting the superiority of the *'Ayn* and the *Sīn* over the *Mīm* (see references in preceding note). I shall also mention the exegesis given me recently by an Iranian friend (a Duodeciman Shiite): the secret of Salmān is the secret of *each* believer: each believer has secretly *his* own Imām; perhaps if he divulged his secret, he would pass as an infidel! This exegesis strikes me as characteristic of Iranian individualism; it amply justifies the idea of Salmān as archetype of the True Believer (cf. also n. 176 below).

165 *Shanākht*, p. 7^{b}.

166 Ibid., p. 9^{b}.

167 Cf. the references given in nn. 163 and 164 above and n. 169 below.

168 See section 3 above, the table of hierarchies.

Intelligence but of the creative Logos which dominates the entire hierarchy of the Emanations to which it gives rise. The entire doctrine of epiphanic Forms (*maẓhar*) is thus reformed from the top down: the Imām is the *maẓhar* or epiphany of the creative Logos; the *Ḥujjat* (or Salmān as human correspondence of Gabriel) that of the first Archangel; the Prophet (who is initiated by Gabriel-Salmān) that of the second Intelligence, the universal Soul. Thus the *Ḥujjat* stands in the same relation to the Imām as the first Archangel to the creative Logos: he is the *Factum* (*mubda'*) of this *Fiat* (*ibdā'*). As for the Prophet (*Nāṭiq*, Enunciator), he now takes his rank simply among the *Dā'ī*, the Preachers: "Each time that the *Dā'ī* ('he who calls') is mentioned, we are told, it is an allusion to the Prophet, as for example in this Koran verse: And as a *Summoner* unto Allah, by his permission, and as a lamp that giveth light" (33:45).[169]

We need hardly point out that we are far from Islamic orthodoxy. To follow the road opened up by Ismailian Gnosis to its end, we must now compare the texts celebrating the apotheosis of Salmān with those which show him as archetype of the True Believer, as the Adopted One, the Spiritual Child, exemplifying the bond between the True Believer and the Imām. The "Glorious One," the hero of the alchemist Jābir ibn Ḥayyān, already gives an intimation of this Glory: he is the Expatriate, come from afar, who required no master nor any long initiation and familiarity with the Imām, as did the Prophet, but who learned everything from the presentiment of his Quest, from the direct magnetism of the Imām upon his person.[170] But let us now consider the significance of declarations such as this: "Salmān is the Threshold of Paradise. . . . Since the Threshold of Paradise is a human being, the place of Paradise must also be a human being." And elsewhere: "I am with my friends wherever they seek me, sometimes on the mountain, sometimes on the plain, sometimes in the desert. He to whom I have revealed my Person, that is, the knowledge of myself, has no need of proximity in

169 *Shanākht*, pp. 1^{a} and 8^{b}. This little treatise on Imāmology begins with a theory of the "epiphanic Forms" (*maẓhar*) in accord with that put forward by *Taṣawwurāt* XXIV, p. 82; the Imām is eternally the Throne, and the "pillars of this throne" are the *Ḥujjat*; the Angel-princes (Gabriel and Michael, Seraphiel and Azrael) named in the positive religion have their earthly typification in these figures (*Shanākht*, p. 7^{a}). The four other ranks (*Dā'ī*, to which rank is assimilated that of the Prophet, the two "licentiates," the Auditor) are the epiphanies of the universal Soul and stand in the same relation to the *Ḥujjat* as the Second Intelligence to the First (ibid., p. 1^{a}).

170 Cf. our "Le Livre du Glorieux," pp. 66–67, 74, 103ff.

space; this is the Great Resurrection." And lastly, this sentence in which Imāmology offers the decisive fulfillment: "Consecrate to me thy devotion and thy knowledge,[171] and thou wilt become, *as Salmān, like unto me*."

"To become as Salmān" is to become oneself a *Ḥujjat*, the Imām's Proof and Adopted One, and thereby to become "like unto the Imām"; such is the ultimate metamorphosis to which the initiate will aspire. Now we may understand the resonance of these verses by Ra'īs Ḥasan, an Ismailian poet:

> Thou art He whose *Ḥujjat* is the Threshold in this world;
> In a symphony of a hundred thousand voices,
> Wisdom proclaims in the Kenoma and the Pleroma,[172]
> His rank is symbolized by the distance of the "two arrows' flights."[173]

Thus Salmān the Mazdean, then the Christian, the Exile in "Quest" of the True Prophet, then the Spiritual Child of the Imām who solemnly attests his "adoption," has become the "Threshold"; so will it be with all the "Salmāns," with every soul that exemplifies his case; each one, as a very ancient text declares, becomes the "Salmān of the microcosmos."[174] We have already pointed to the homology of this adoptianist relation: the Angel Christos is to Jesus as the Imām is to his *Ḥujjat*. To "become like unto the Imām" corresponds here to an *Imitatio Christi*, no longer in the context of an incarnation Christology, but in the only sense that this "imitation" implies for a Gnostic: as exemplifying a similar relation with Angelos Christos, which Theodotus's Gnostics also expressed as a conjunction of the soul with its Angel.[175] And this essentially is the conception and vision of the Imām attained by Shiism at the limit of its spiritual maturity. Mullā Ṣadrā of Shīrāz, one of the greatest philosophers of seventeenth-century Duodeciman Shiism, gives us this edifying definition: "There is in the human being a reality of the angelic world, a divine thing, which comes to it from God and is absolutely proper to it; this thing that is absolutely proper

171 *Farmān-e man bar*, obedience which is at once *'ibādat* and *ma'rifat* (ibid., p. 9ᵃ).

172 *Shanākht*, p. 9ᵇ.

173 Allusion to Koran 53 : 9: the distance from Muḥammad at which the Angel descending from heaven stands at the time of the first revelation, and the distance from the divine mystery to which the Prophet (and in imitation of him the mystic, here the *Ḥujjat*) approaches. This verse represented a particular challenge to the sagacity of the *tafsīr*.

174 *Salmān-e 'ālam-e saghīr*: technical term in *Umm al-Kitāb*, question 34.

175 Cf. *Extraits de Théodote*, ed. F. Sagnard, pp. 137–39, 187; Söderberg, p. 249.

to the human being *is the Imāmate*."[176] In meditating this message we shall discover the ripened fruit of that other maxim that has guided us from the start: "He who knows himself (*nafs*, his *Anima*) knows his Lord."[177]

Illustrations might be drawn from all the surviving Ismailian literature and from Shiite literature in general. In these illustrations the same constants are confirmed: nostalgia for the vision refused and at the same time granted by the epiphanic meaning of the symbols, the nostalgia whose premises and fulfillments we have attempted to analyze here; and dominating the whole, the sense of the incommunicable, of the intransmissible personal secret. We still find it in a little book composed at the end of the last century, by a man whose premature death was an inestimable loss for the Ismailian community: Shihābaddīn Shāh Ḥusaynī.[178] Certain traditional sayings, or logia, which our author recalls and enchases in his own text, propagate the same flame of intrepid devotion. This one, for example, attributed to the first Imām: "I would never worship a God whom I did not see." And this other, which comes as an answer to the challenge of the impossible vision: "He who does not know *his* Imām does not know God."[179]

But we must take care: this vision is given not to the eyesight (it does not even reside in the material "data" of the past) but to the vision of the heart: what the heart sees is pure Light;[180] it is not an object that one can point to with the finger, that one can find, identify, impose on others, not even by invoking the materiality of what we call a "historical fact." To attain to this vision which others do not see, to this audition that others do not hear, a long, very long struggle is needed. "How might one say these

176 Quoted in Shaykh Āgā Bozorg, *Zarī'a* (Shiite Bibliography) II, 1325. In the course of our conversation about Abū Dharr's *ḥadīth*, the same Iranian friend to whom I have referred above (n. 164) also said to me apropos of this definition of Mullā Ṣadrā: "So you see, each one of us has indeed *his* Imām. Basically the Imām is for us what the Fravarti was to the ancient Iranians." Any commentary would weaken this testimony to a lived religion, which in its conciseness expresses what is perhaps the most original spiritual message that Iran has ever given to mankind.

177 *Kalāmi Pīr* (p. 73 of the text), citing this verse of Nāṣir-e Khusraw (*Dīwān*, Teheran edition, p. 528, line 7): "Become conscious of thine own being and then hold thy head high among the multitude (or else: take the head of the multitude)," adds: "The knowledge of the Imām is then achieved."

178 Died in 1885 at the age of 40. He left a short treatise which he had composed not for the higher initiates but for the Ismailian community in general. Its Persian text along with an English translation was published by W. Ivanow, *True Meaning* (Bombay, 1933; 2nd edn., 1947) (cf. n. 142 above).

179 *True Meaning* (2nd edn.), p. 21.

180 Ibid., p. 48.

things to the firstcomer, and how might the firstcomer see them, hear them, and understand them? No, only those who see with the eye that sees the truth can do so."[181] And so the enigmatic allusions are illumined for us too in the transparency of a wholly interior light; such allusions, for example, as those referring to Adam's Paradise, Noah's Ark, Abraham's vision, the Mount Sinai of Moses, Maryam mother of Jesus, Gabriel Angel of the Prophet, as so many forms of the *Ḥujjat*.[182] For in the context of the Ismailian spirituality that repudiates all purely abstract or anecdotic significance, these are all metamorphoses of theophanic visions, always perceived as personal presences (Paradise is a person, Hell is a person, Prayer is a person, etc.).[183] And it is precisely as such that they can neither be communicated nor made comprehensible to the firstcomer, any more than they can be rationally demonstrated or dogmatically imposed. The discovery of the *Ḥujjat*, or epiphany of the eternal Imām, remains the most intimate of secrets in the depths of the heart, the secret which the True Believer discloses to no one; here the "Docetic" consciousness attains its profound truth through the sentiment of its essential individuation. Witness also this tale upon which our author invites us to meditate:

> The Imām Ja'far Ṣādiq replied one day to a man who asked him whether it was true that on the day of the Resurrection God would be visible to all: "Yes," said the Imām. "He is visible even before that day; he has been visible since the day when he asked, 'Am I not your Lord?'[184] The True Believers have seen him even in this world. Dost thou not see him?" And the man replied: "O my Lord, I see *thee*. Permit that by thy authority I go and announce it to the others." But the Imām said: "No, say nothing to anyone, for the people are stupid and ignorant, they will not understand; they will disavow you and hurl the anathema at you."

And our author comments:

> Know, O my brother, that this subject was always kept hidden from the unworthy and the incompetent; it has been confided only to a small number. If one of the True Gnostics (*Ahl-e ḥaqīqat*)

181 Ibid., p. 22.
182 *Shanākht*, p. 8ᵃ (translation, p. 31).
183 Ibid., translation, p. 47; cf. our "Rituel Sabéen," pp. 232ff., 239ff.
184 Allusion to the pact concluded in pre-eternity, in the Night of the Covenant, when God asked future humanity, present in its archetypes: "Am I not your Lord?" (Koran 7 : 171).

> is somewhere, the people slander him and mock him. . . . Each thing, whether it be exoteric or esoteric, can be for you yourself a form of worship (*'ibādat*). Worship, assuredly, is identical with Knowledge (*ma'rifat*), but worship in every case forms a thing in itself, different from every other thing. Knowledge by the organ of your eyes means that you know this human Form that guides you, which is proper to the person who bears outwardly all the features of simple human reality (*insānīyat*). But it is not with the eyes that you can obtain a representation of the heart. The Knowledge of the heart is different from that of sight: it is pure luminescence, shining for itself. And neither have I the power to tell you more nor you the capacity to hear more.[185]

Theophanic vision is experienced by each man alone; it is revelation and pure luminescence of the "Alone for the Alone," a full spiritual event the evidence of which is incommensurable with the norms governing common evidence, that which imposes itself on the senses and on common reason, or that which is recorded in history and profane chronology. The only transitive action that is conceivable and effective is that of helping each man to encounter *his* Imām, and this is eminently the role of Salmān the Pure, the "companion of initiation," who in his dealings with the Prophet typifies the ministration of the invisible Angel. "No more than this?" it may be asked. But "this" alone is perhaps the total encounter to which every soul aspires.

6. *The "Quest of the Imām"*

We may thematize the search for this encounter as the "Quest of the Imām." Since the reasons and the vicissitudes of this Quest are the same as those which motivate and guide all the doctrinal expositions of Ismailism, the aspects we have so far considered will suffice to provide the foundation of an inquiry into it. At this point a brief recapitulation may suggest the main lines of such an inquiry. One of the questions raised by an initiatory sect such as Ismailism is this: Is there any trace of an experimental spiritual pedagogy, of a "psychagogy," that is specifically Ismailian, leading the soul to "birth," to metamorphosis, making it apt for theophanic visions, as the widows in the Acts of Peter are made accessible to the story of the Transfiguration? Unfortunately, few documents relating to such a pedagogy, and

185 *True Meaning*, pp. 23–24, 48 (Persian text, pp. 38–40, 73–74).

particularly to the reformed Iranian Ismailism that most interests us here, have come down to us.

We do, however, have a little romance of initiation, dating from a remote period, preceding the Fāṭimid era. It retraces the phases which put the neophyte upon the "way of the Quest" and lead him to final membership in the esoteric sodality. Its possible author is Manṣūr al-Yaman, the first Ismailian *Dā'ī* sent (in 266/879) to southern Arabia, where his mission was to be crowned with great success. Its title is simply *The Master and the Disciple* (*Risālat al-'ālim wa'l-ghulām*).[186] Here I cannot undertake to summarize it, but shall merely point out certain of its characteristics. The essential is that it is not an anecdotic history but an archetypal narrative.[187]

In the Iranian province of Fars (Persis), amid general ignorance, there lived a man who attained True Knowledge (that is to say, an Ismailian). Endowed with a sensitive heart, a penetrating intelligence, and a lofty moral sense, he understood the illusion and the emptiness of the mirage of life. He abandons his home and his people, becomes a pilgrim wandering through the world, among the Persian populations and the Arab tribes. Directly our protagonist, Abū Malik, becomes the type of the spiritual Exile, the Expatriate after the manner of Salmān the Persian or Jābir's "Glorious One," or the hero of Suhrawardī's *Recital of the Western Exile*; he is the Stranger, the *Allogenos* of the Sethian Gnostics (the children of Seth). He enters a town unnoticed or unrecognized; this incognito is an essential condition of his *mission*—a mission totally different from what the history of the Christian Churches has accustomed us to understand under this word, implying a different aim and different triumphs. His mission is neither to speak in the public square nor to convert the crowds. Abū Malik mingles with a group of pious Moslems who are conversing; of course he does not say who or what he is; he presents himself as a pious foreigner on a journey and contents himself with seizing the opportunity, between sentences, to inject discreetly a question, edifying perhaps, assuredly disturbing, if only his interlocutor were capable of grasping it. But soon, called back to their affairs, all arise and disperse except for a single one, a youth who, like

186 W. Ivanow has given a summary of this little spiritual romance in his *Studies in Early Persian Ismailism* (Bombay and Leiden, 1948).

187 The names of the two principal heroes are also those of archetypal characters: the master is called Abū Malik (*Pater regis*) and the disciple Ṣāliḥ (*Idoneus*).

Parsifal, asks in his turn the question which none of the others has even thought, or will ever think, of asking. This is the "disciple," the second protagonist of the romance.

Then there opens a series of dialogues which progressively awaken the young man's curiosity, arousing a desire to know ever more, to enter upon the path of the "Quest." These dialogues reveal the entire Ismailian art of pedagogy, or let us rather say "psychagogy," which awakens the meaning of symbols, the desire for a spiritual *exegesis* (*ta'wīl*) as the necessary *exodus* from the letter. But the first decisive step is taken only after a conversation full of pathos, in the course of which the *Dā'ī* receives from his disciple the first solemn promise not to reveal to anyone what he will learn in the course of their ensuing conversations. And these conversations initiate him gradually into the fundamental questions, some of which we have discussed here. They dazzle the youth; from now on he is dominated by the attraction of an unsuspected dimension that opens up access to spiritual liberation. It is not only the opposition between the exoteric and the esoteric (*ẓāhir* and *bāṭin*) that is revealed to him; this is known also to the Sufis. For there is more, namely, the esoteric of the esoteric (*bāṭin al-bāṭin*), that is to say, that which underlies the organic connection between *ẓāhir* and *bāṭin*, that which, in Ismailian terms, is its key—to wit, the third world, the cosmos of the esoteric Church, the hierocosmos, a world intermediate between the physical and the spiritual cosmos: this is the "Paradise *in potentia*," "the potential angelical world," structured in imitation of the celestial hierarchies. Then the metamorphosis of the disciple is announced; this potentiality is awakened in him too; he asks to see and to know more concerning the "person" who symbolically holds in his hands the keys of Paradise, i.e., the Imām.[188]

188 The knowledge of the exoteric, our author points out, corresponds to the degree of the animal; that of the esoteric, to the degree of human beings: to possess it is to be a True Believer, that is to say, a man in the true sense. Lastly, that of the esoteric of the esoteric is an attribute of the Angels. To acquire it is to become a spiritual being in respect to knowledge, while remaining a human being in respect to physical appearance. It is thus that the Envoy of God is called the Veil which dissimulates the Angels (*ḥijāb al-Malā'ika*, ibid., p. 96). The angelomorphosis toward which initiation starts the young adept presupposes an anthropology whose conclusions are perfectly clear. In this world there are only two types of men in the real and true sense: (1) *'ālim rabbānī* (corresponding to the *ḥakīm muta'allih* of the Ishrāqīyūn, the "theosophianic Sage"), who has attained the summit of religious knowledge and whose spirit has experimentally realized the Spirit of certainty, and (2) the *muta'allim*, the disciple who seeks the Way and progresses, an angel *in potentia*. All the rest are human only in a purely metaphoric sense (ibid., p. 97).

At this moment the master vanishes. He has gone to consult the youth's "senior parent" (*wāliduhu'l-akbar*),[189] that is to say, the *Dā'ī* of the next higher degree. Soon he returns in haste to inform his disciple that the "gates of Compassion are wide open to him." The two depart together, like Gurnemanz and Parsifal, toward the "Threshold of Compassion," taking good care to tell the youth's blood father nothing about the journey.

Here begins the scene of the "Transformation," the ritual of the initiation proper. Admitted one evening to the presence of the Shaykh, the senior *Dā' ī*, and of his assembly, the two pilgrims soon withdraw; they pass the night with their companions in friendly and edifying discussions; at dawn they return to the house of the Shaykh. The assembly takes place and after a solemn sermon by the Shaykh, there opens a dialogue that lays the groundwork for the liturgy of initiation. In the course of it the neophyte learns that the name which he bears by virtue of his earthly genealogy is not his real name, that for the moment he has no name—a situation corresponding to his status as a spiritual "newborn babe." It is the Shaykh who must give him his *real* name, his initiatory Name, the Name which will be his God and which he will serve.[190] This investiture in his real Name, marking his *dies*

189 Cf. in Suhrawardī's *Récit de l'Exil occidental*. In revealing to his adept the existence of the Angels or Intelligences preceding him, the Angel Gabriel-Active Intelligence speaks, despite their eternal youth, of their *parentes seniores* (*jadd, ajdād*). In addition, we have here the homology between Heaven and Earth required by the parallelism between the Ismailian hierarchies.

190 Fragment of the dialogue (Sh = the Shaykh, D = the disciple): "Sh: O young man, thou hast been favored by a friend come to thee as an Envoy, beloved of a Messenger come to visit thee. What is thy name? — D: 'Ubaydallah ibn 'Abdallah (little serf of God, son of the serf of God). — Sh: This name describes thy qualities and we have already heard tell of them (here an unspoken question is implied). — D: I am a *free* man, son of the *serf* of God. — Sh: Who, then, has freed thee from thy servile state, that thou hast become a free man? — D: (pointing his finger at him who initiated him) This Sage. — Sh: But dost thou not see that he is himself a serf, not the owner? How can he have freed thee? — D: No, indeed, he cannot have done so. — Sh: Then what is thy true name? — D: (vainly seeks the answer.) — Sh: O young man, how shall a thing, any more than a newborn babe, be known if it has no name? — D: It is to thee that I have been born. It is then incumbent on thee to give me a name. — Sh: I will do so when seven days have passed. — D: Why delay? — Sh: For the profit of the newborn babe. — D: And if the newborn babe should die before the seven days have passed? — Sh: Nothing will befall; he will receive his name once the time has gone by. — D: But will this name that thou art preparing to give me remain mine? — Sh: As long as it is thy God. — D: How can one speak thus? — Sh: Thy Name is thy Lord and thou art its serf. Do not engage in discussions out of turn. Go now, until the appointed day." (Ibid., pp. 101, 102.) The closing words of the dialogue, which seem strange at first (D is surprised at them), become clear if we compare them with the teaching of Qusṭā ben Lūqā cited below (in response to the question "Who is my

natalis, will take place seven days later. The ceremony does indeed take place at the end of the week: in the midst of the Assembly the Shaykh and the new adept stride solemnly toward one another. Then, says our text, "the Shaykh begins to say the things that the pen cannot write, that the imagination cannot invent, the things that cannot rise to the consciousness of the profane."[191] The text does not divulge this great secret, for fear, no doubt, that the book may fall into the hands of an orthodox adversary. But the "sacrament of the proper Name" gives us an intimation of what it is. This decisive moment of the "Quest for the Imām" is the awakening of consciousness to the secret of the motto: "He who knows himself knows his Lord."[192]

God?"). Cf. the initiatory names (*ism ṭarīqat*) composed of an Imām's name and of a substantive or adjective expressing a relation of personal devotion to the Imām; for example, in Iran (notably since the restoration of Ṣūfism at the end of the 18th century by Nūr 'Alī Shāh) the names composed with 'Alī (= *Excelsus*) Shāh (= *Rex*): Nūr 'Alī Shāh (*Lumen Excelsi Regis*), Mast 'Alī Shāh (Intoxicated with King 'Alī), Majẕūb 'Alī Shāh (Filled with ecstasy by King 'Alī), etc.

191 The Quest for the Imām is now at its end (of course we cannot interpret the revelation of the secret to mean that the new adept is given the secret "address" of the hidden Imām; we have already quoted more than one text showing that the relation to the Imām cannot be reduced to any local or physical proximity). To make it clear that he is speaking of an inward *Quest* and pilgrimage, the author presents its phases in terms of the *ta'wīl*, that is, the spiritual exegesis of the rites observed in their literal sense by the pilgrims to Mecca. The *ta'wīl* of these rites corresponds exactly to the spiritual metamorphosis of the adept: he is able to don the *iḥrām* which the pilgrims don to enter the sacred territory. He is able to accomplish the "circumambulations" round the Ka'aba, to perform the prescribed rites, and to recite the usual prayers; he completes his pilgrimage by reciting the *Āyat al-Kubrā*. Now all this accords with what we know of the Ismailian *ta'wīl* of the rites of pilgrimage; to undertake the pilgrimage to the Ka'aba is gradually to abandon the beliefs that one professed by custom and conformism and to advance from the degree of *Mustajīb* to that of the *Ḥujjat*. To don the *iḥram* is to break away from the practices and the society of those who cling to the letter (*ẓāhir*) of religion. The "circumambulations" signify haste to reach the Imām, etc. (cf. *Kalāmi Pīr*, p. 96 of the text). This Quest might be illustrated by the biographies of famous Ismailians, such as Nāṣir-e Khusraw (cf. our *Étude préliminaire*, pp. 28–33), or Ḥasan Ṣabbāh (founder of Alamūt, converted to Ismailism at the age of seventeen after a grave illness, at Ray, his birthplace). One might also point out the analogies with the ritual of initiation practiced in Ṣūfism: special ablutions, change of raiment, imposition of a new name, sharing in the mystical chalice (a custom mentioned in the *Futuwwat-Nāmah*, or manuals of "spiritual chivalry," e.g. that composed in Persian by 'Abdurrazzāq Kāshānī), attesting this coalescence of Ismailism and Sufism which, after the Mongol invasions, gave Iranian Sufism, or Shiite Sufism, its special stamp.

192 Here I have not the space to comment on the stages of initiation as described by the orthodox apologists in their irreducible hostility to Ismailism: nine stages from the "hurling of the javelin" and the "physiognomic trial" by the *Dā'ī* (*zarq wa tafarrus*) to the final stage in which the adept sheds his scales and molts (*insilākh*). We are not entitled, merely because it is only the malicious accounts by the adversaries of

Indeed, the phases of our little spiritual romance present successively all the themes which, generally speaking, our texts group around the concept of "spiritual birth" (*wilādat-e rūḥānī*). The *Kalāmi Pīr*, for example (one of the principal records of the reformed Ismailism of Alamūt to have come down to us), declares that "physical birth" takes place in the world of the *tanzīl* (the letter of the revealed Religion), while "spiritual birth" takes place in the world of the *ta'wīl*, that is to say, the world of inward or esoteric exegesis. And here our author, following the Ismailian predilection for exegesis of the New Testament whether authentic or "apocryphal," sets a quotation from the Gospel of St. John: "Except a man be born again, he cannot see the kingdom of God."[193] This transition from the *tanzīl* to the *ta'wīl* seen as a new birth depends essentially on "knowledge of the Imām," which thus becomes an absolute necessity;[194] this *transitus*, the *exodus* of this *exegesis*, *is* this knowledge itself. Simultaneously this knowledge of the Perfect Man (*Insān Kāmil*) depends essentially on knowledge of one's Self. "He who does not achieve the knowledge of the Imām of his time and the knowledge of himself will die in ignorance."[195] The "Imām of *his* time": this should be taken not in the sense of an inoffensive chronology but rather in the sense according to which, as we have seen, every adept is a "period" of his Imām, who for him is his Aeon. To attain to this knowledge is, therefore, to take one's place among the Angels of the highest degree, the *muqarrabān*, to achieve beatitude in the two universes, which is knowledge of oneself. The Persian text is explicit: "He who knows himself, knows *his* God," and *that* is the knowledge of the Imām.[196] We are now in a position to say that the figure of the Imām presented itself to Ismailian Gnosis, at the height of its spiritual maturity, as a symbol of the Self, in a sense implying that far from opposing itself to a personal God (an opposition to which some of our writers on comparative mysticism incline), the Self can manifest itself only through this personal Figure which is its *maẓhar*, its epiphanic Form. In the presence of this epiphanic Form the situation re-

---

Ismailism that have come down to us, to deny the value of this initiation. Ismailism can justify itself without laying claim to orthodoxy; see résumé in Browne, I, pp. 411–15, and the remarks of Bernard Lewis in *Bulletin of the School of Oriental Studies* (1938), p. 696.

193 *Kalāmi Pīr*, p. 114 of the text, and Gospel of St. John 3 :3; it is quoted almost literally.

194 Ibid., p. 114.

195 Ibid., pp. 72, 114–15. For the Duodeciman Shiites, the Imām of the time is the Twelfth Imām, the "hidden Imām," whose parousia will transfigure the world.

196 Ibid., p. 73; cf. n. 177 above, the distich of Nāṣir-e Khusraw.

mains essentially *dialogical*. But it does not occur at the level of the community; it presupposes an authentic individuation, rising to repeat itself at each successive degree, like an increasing integration and proportional to this individuation.

This situation and this exigency of the "self alone with itself" delineate what it means to the True Believer to say "*my* God"; the *Deus revelatus* does not belong to all but to each according to his capacity for vision; and what this vision mentally visualizes is a *real* divine individuation as theophany. This situation is brought out by an admirable text attributed to the Christian physician Qusṭā ibn Lūqā (Constantine, son of Luke, 10th century),[197] which Ismailism seems to have appropriated by channels that are still unclear. With admirable precision this text sums up everything that we have here attempted to bring out regarding the meaning and theophanic functions of the Ismailian hierarchies:[198]

> 'Amalāq the Greek questioned his master, Qusṭā ibn Lūqā: "Will you teach me to know my God (*ma'būdī*)," he asked him, "so that I may approach only Him and take refuge only in Him?" The Sage said to him: "Do you know him who causes you to know yourself (*nafsaka*, your *Anima*), you who were ignorant of yourself? Him who shows you the advantages and the injuries that flow

197 Qusṭā ben Lūqā, a native of Baalbek, was of Greek descent; he was a Melkite, i.e., Orthodox Christian. According to the dedications of his works, he must have been born about 820 A.D. and have lived from 70 to 80 years (cf. *Encyclopédie de l'Islam*, art. s.v.). Famed as a physician, he was no less expert in philosophy, astronomy, geometry, and music. His profound knowledge of Greek, Syriac, and Arabic place his activity as a translator on a par with that of Ḥunayn ibn Isḥāq. Islamic culture assimilated a considerable portion of classical science through his translations. As a philosopher he is famed chiefly for his little work on the difference between soul and spirit (the πνεῦμα as a subtle body). His originality is shown in his attitude toward the occult sciences; he admits all the data (enchantments, conjurations, etc.) but explains them as psychic realities. From this point of view he deserves the full attention of psychotherapists. It is this aspect of his work that would seem to account for his presence in Ismailian esotericism.

198 This extremely important text is cited at length in Idrīs, ch. XIX, p. 225. No more than I can explain the "appropriation" of Qusṭā by the Ismailians, can I account for the presence of 'Amalāq, his disciple; so far only Paul Kraus had referred to an Ismailian text containing a narrative that must be identical with our own (cf. his *Jābir ibn Ḥayyān*, II, n. 1 on pp. 47–48). Kraus also pointed out that two treatises from among Jābir's "CXII books" bear the title "Book of the Amalekites" and that there seems to be no good reason for this name; however, "the Amalekites play a considerable role in the legendary history of ancient Egypt," and a book of *jafr*, attributed to the Sixth Imām, Ja'far Ṣādiq, mentions the 'Amāliqa side by side with Daniel, Solomon, and the philosophers.

from it for your life, when you took no heed of them? Him who causes you, on condition that you conform to his law, to know what will make you forget fear if you are menaced by it? Him who delivers you from sadness, who produces in you something whose inner sweetness you savor and whose power you sense at the same time, something that makes you independent of everything that is not himself? If you know him," he added, "it can only be as a part of yourself. Then indeed you have found your God (*faqad wajadta rabba-ka*); then you are a True Believer." And 'Amalāq asked: "O Source of the light of the Mystery! What is there beyond *my* God, in order that I may be among those who have obtained all?" And the Sage said to him: "*Beyond him there is he who is to him what he himself is for thee, a One for a One* (*wāḥid li-wāḥid*), and so forth up to the Threshold of Him in whom are contained all the Ones who are situated below him, of Him who can be attained neither by any Sage of his epoch nor by the people of his time, Him whom all those of his Aeon (*dahr*) need. That is the Lord of the Lords of this time, a Defender with a rank in creation which permits him to ask help of his exalted Lord and to be heard by his invisible protector; his invisibility in turn hides him from him who is below him, his elevation conceals him in its height; and so forth up to the ultimate One, the Lord of the world of the beginning, the Holy Spirit, he who is the primordial Archangel and the First Existent, from whom issues the Beginning and in whom culminates the Accomplishment. As for what is beyond him, it is Mystery without name, grace without number.

"Meditate, O my brother, the positions of the Sages and the symbols configured by those who know. Be faithful to the promises and oaths that have been received from you. Maintain your obedience to the *ḥudūd*. Know your *ḥadd* in gnosis (*ḥadduka'l-'ilmī*), then you will know your beginning and your end (*mabda'uka wa muntahāka*), and you will know *your* Imām, and you will attain to the *tawḥīd* of your originator (*mubdi'uka*). May God help you and guide you! May he raise you through the degrees of Deliverance. Glory be to him for having gratified us with the knowledge of the *ḥudūd* by which the Adored One is epiphanized. May he confirm us in obedience to his Friends by whom being is epiphanized in the hierocosmos."

It seems to us that throughout these pages we have merely been commenting on this text, so remarkable for its density. We have spoken of the theophanic function of the Ismailian hierarchies as shown us by the correspondence between the *ḥudūd* and the celestial hierarchies, in view of the sense of "horizon" implicit in the word *ḥadd*. And it is precisely there that we find the connection between knowledge of Self and the knowledge of *thy* God: "A One for a One" (*kath'hena* = *wāḥid li-wāḥid*). And this means: *thy* God is the mysterious Figure that appears at *thy* "horizon," thy *ḥādd*, which is thy "limit" and also thy companion of initiation (as Salmān-Gabriel for the Prophet), the horizon of thy transconsciousness. *Thine* Angel is the Angel of this theophany of thine, which is in the measure of thy being. But, as Qusṭā ibn Lūqā reminds us, *thy* God is also *his* God, that is to say, thy *ḥadd* also has its own *ḥadd*. To raise thyself to this *ḥadd* is to perceive a new theophany at a new level. And *thy* companion of initiation raises himself to a still higher horizon when he raises thee to his own horizon, and when simultaneously thou too raisest to thy horizon the companion who follows thee. This is the profound meaning of the sentence attributed to the Imām al-Mu'izz: "The True Believer is a true Believer only when he has raised up a True Believer like unto himself."[199] A "One for a One"—this is the formula for what we must here call a kathenotheism which goes hand in hand with angelology and the *Imitatio angeli*: a turning upside down of all the mystical hierarchies from the bottom to the summits of the pleroma. Thus we see that the invisible unity at the summit of these summits is not the unity of an "All-powerful" in an immediate and equidistant relation with *all* the Ones: there are successive and repeated integrations

199 Strothmann, pp. 61, line 3; 114, line 11; cf. Idrīs, ch. XX, p. 236; deliverance comes to the souls through their adherence to the *ḥudūd*; they ascend through the knowledge of those which precede him. Then they rise in the company of their *ḥudūd* toward the ranks of the Imāms, with whom the ascension of the Noble Temple of the *Qā'im* is completed. This ascension and this raising-up toward the Sublime Temple of the Intelligence, the First Emanation (= Soul), are unceasing. This adherence is for each soul its *tawḥīd*; it is the knowledge of the spiritual world in which consists the attainment to existence in the true sense, *perfectio secunda*. This ascension from degree to degree of the esoteric "Heavens," promoted by the help that each *ḥadd* gives to the next following, reminds us of two curious passages published by M. T. d'Alverny in "Les Pérégrinations de l'âme dans l'autre monde d'après un anonyme de la fin du XIIe siècle," *Archives d'histoire doctrinale et littéraire du Moyen-Age*, 1940–1942, pl. pp. 268–69, though these figurative allusions do not permit us to establish a material filiation between the anonymous Avicennan and Ismailism; it should be noted, however, that both the indications *socii omnes* on the circle of Nature and *cetera turba* in the tenth sphere just below (ibid., p. 273) rather suggest the hierarchical distribution that we have noted above. With this ascension toward the Imām-Qā'im, the substitute for the Tenth Angel, one may also compare the interpretation given by the Ishrāqīyūn of the Koranic allusion to the "cleavage of the moon," as signifying the conjunction of the mystic with the Active Intelligence (since the Angel of the Sphere of the Moon is also called Ismael).

of *dyadic unities* or bi-unities. The idea that governs the gradation of these "horizons" is the axiom that we have found at the beginning of Ismailian theosophy: the *Deus absconditus* is not the personal, revealed God; and it is an attribute of this latter, the only God with whom a personal relation is experienced, to be "unique for every unique individual," that is to say, uniquely revealed and visible at each theophanic horizon. At the highest accessible horizon the figure of the Imām who is the primordial Epiphany conditions and epiphanizes these epiphanies, uni*fies* each One for each One.

Now we may understand the ideas of our authors on the hierarchy of their sodality. We have already mentioned some of them; the essential is the idea of homology repeated from degree to degree. We recall that all the *ḥudūd*, all the spiritual ranks, mark as many *qiyāmāt*, Resurrections; each of the "companions" rises, "resuscitates" to the spiritual Forms which he attains when they rise to his "horizon," that is, when he gains awareness of them. That is why each *ḥadd* is a Resurrector, a *Qā'im*, for his own *maḥdūd*—that is to say, for the *ḥadd*, or companion, immediately below him.[200] Each *ḥadd* is an Imām for him who is next below, and he is the *Imāmate* for him whose *maḥdūd* he is (by whom he is "contained," as the Temple of Light supported by the Imām).[201] The esoteric sense (*ta'wīl*) of death is this transfer from degree to degree, from metamorphosis to metamorphosis, each time amplifying the dimension of vision.[202] We now understand why for each *degree* adherence to the preceding *ḥadd* who raises it up toward him is its *tawhīd*—as Qusṭā ibn Lūqā also declares—its unification of the Unique (*its* God), homologous to the *tawḥīd* that the second Intelligence accomplishes toward the first Archangel. The Ismailian profession of monotheistic faith thus escapes the trap of monism as well as the unconscious dualism of orthodoxy by becoming a kind of "monadism." The Cycle of the "eight resurrections" (which consists in traversing the eight Thresholds of "Para-

200 Cf. the text of Idrīs, quoted in Ivanow, *The Rise of the Fatimides*, pp. 54–55 of the Arabic text.

201 Idrīs, ch. XVI, p. 210; here there is a long development, which I can only mention here, in which the work of the *ta'wīl* is compared to the elaboration of the *nāsūt* (subtle humanity) of the Imām (cf. section 4 above); just as the divinity of the Imām is epiphanized by the *nāsūt*, so the theosophic Verities (*ḥaqā'iq 'ilm al-dīn*) are gathered together in the Initiators, the Perfect assembled in the *ta'yīd* (the celestial congregation), just as *lāhūt* or divinity is concentrated in the Imām, and can be manifested only by the subtle teachings of the *ta'wīl*.

202 Ibid., p. 223.

dise"[203] to the Threshold of the Imām) is the "Quest for the Imām" within the sodality seen as the "spiritual career" of the Ismailian adept.[204]

This Quest which raises each adept, which metamorphoses him from resurrection to resurrection, from degree to degree of the Temple of Light which is the Imāmate, the *lāhūt* of the Imām, is itself the ascension of this Pillar of Light which has enabled us to recognize in Ismailian Gnosis one of the most characteristic motifs of Manichaean Gnosis. We find this motif once again in the no less characteristic aspect of what has been called the *theologoumenon* of the "members." Here again we are indebted to Abū Ya'qūb Sejestānī—in this instance, to his personal interpretation of a text from the Gospel. But—and this is a highly remarkable detail—the lesson known to our Ismailian theosopher brings to the text, which we read today as authentic, a change which accords strikingly with a certain lesson from the Sermon on the Mount as read by the Gnostic Carpocrates (second century). Where our Bibles read: "First be reconciled to thy brother, and then come and offer thy gift" (Matthew 5:24), our Gnostic's text reads: "If thou seest that thou art not at peace with *thyself*, go first and be reconciled *with thyself*."[205] Now here is the version that we read in Abū Ya'qūb Sejestānī of a passage from the Gospel according to St. Matthew (25:40 and 45):[206] when "the Lord shall gather the just and the wicked in the same

203 Idrīs, ch. XVI, p. 236; these eight "thresholds" are the "eight resurrections" (*qiyāmāt*) marked by the degrees of the esoteric hierarchy (ibid., p. 221).

204 Cf. also a text of Mu'ayyad Shīrāzī quoted by Idrīs, p. 238; it lies in the fundamental structure of the human being that, having achieved his subtle Form, he becomes an Angel (*al-insān lā budda lahu 'an yaṣīra Malakan*). This growth is comparable to that of the physical body. The Noble Form must resemble more and more his "celestial parents" if he is to return to his origin, and he acquires this resemblance by adherence to the *ḥudūd* which draw the soul higher and higher toward them. He who separates from his material body, fulfilling this condition, is metamorphosed into the form of the *ḥudūd*, or celestial entities: he recognizes them and they recognize him; he joins them, taking his place in their company and in their abode.

205 My attention was called to this fundamental variant, as well as to the questions that will be raised below in conclusion, by one of C. G. Jung's seminars, "Psychological Aspects of Nietzsche's *Zarathustra*," Part 7 (multigraphed, 1936).

206 *Kitāb-al-Yanābī'*, *yanbū'* 38, in which Abū Ya'qūb asks himself how one can accept the absurdity of an outcome that would be identical for the good and the wicked after their passage to the other world, the absurdity of an indefinite production of individuals, century after century, if the result were not, after death, a different status in their very being? Shall we suggest that there exists an Author of this world who seeks to acquire some gain or to avoid some harm by producing this world? The proposition is absurd if it is taken in the sense of utilitarian relations founded on the exteriority of the parts to each other, but its significance changes entirely if it is taken in the sense of the Gospel text as commented on by Abū Ya'qūb.

place, he will say unto the just: how well ye have wrought and acted toward me! I was an hungred and ye gave me meat. I was thirsty and ye gave me drink. . . . The just will reply to him: When wast thou hungry and thirsty, when wast thou captive, that we should have given thee food and drink, clothed thee and delivered thee? And the Lord will say to them: Ye speak the truth, but what ye have wrought *for yourselves* (*bi-anfusikum*, for your own "souls"), ye have done it for me."[207] But our Bibles do not read "what ye have done *for yourselves*" but "unto one of the least of these my brethren." The profound motivation underlying the variant bears witness to a striking continuity between Christian and Ismailian Gnosis.

Abū Ya'qūb's passage calls for two remarks. The first is that his exegesis of the Gospel text shows us in all clarity to what degree he was aware of the profound relation between the two concepts of the *Self* and the *Soul* designated by the one word *nafs*. "It is the Soul of the World," he says, "which converses here *with its souls*, the individual souls that it needs to attain to what its rank implies—which means that it needs the intelligible gifts which the individual souls acquire in this world through the intermediary of sensible things."[208] Now as we have several times pointed out, to know one's Self, one's "soul," one's "total being," is to know one's personal God, that is to say, one's Imām. Hence it follows that the Imām is the figure of this Self, of this Soul whose epiphany progresses by way of the souls that work and act for it and with whom it carries on a dialogue. The second remark is that we have here the Ismailian version of the Manichaean theologoumenon of the "members," just as we had above the Ismailian version of the motif of the Cross of Light and of the Pillar of Light. There we stressed that this representation was based on the homology between *each* and *All*, a homology which finds a striking expression in the fact, among others, that each *ḥadd* is thought of as a "period" of the Cycle, of the Aeon which *is* its Imām. Let us further recall the celestial City which from time immemorial the Imāms have built "out of their souls by means of their souls." Then, indeed, what

207 The quotation ends as follows: "Then he will say to the wicked: how wickedly ye have wrought toward me! I was an hungred and ye gave me no meat. I was thirsty and ye gave me no drink. . . . Then they will say unto him: Lord, when hast thou been so? And he will reply to them: Yes, ye speak true, but all ye have omitted to do *for yourselves*, it is as though ye had omitted to do it *for me*."

208 To this identification of Christ with the Soul of the World we may compare the phenomenological identity analyzed by Widengren, pp. 82–83, between Christ as "Great Mind" in the work of the Syriac mystic Stephen bar Sudhaili and the Iranian and Manichaean conceptions that have already been mentioned here.

each individual does "for his soul," what each "period" does *for itself*, is done for the celestial City, for the entire Cycle.

At the same time this homology forms the foundation of the only strict ethic, the ethic that makes a man responsible to himself. For if you must first reconcile yourself with yourself, this implies that the form of your love (for any of your brothers) is yourself, and "your love is equivalent to what you *are*" (Nietzsche). Hence you must first do right by yourself; all the rest merely follows from this. In other words: you are responsible, that is, you *answer for*, the vision that is given to you of your God; the form of your vision and your worship, like the form of your love, are equivalent to what you *are*. And it is precisely this priority of *being* over *doing* that forms the foundation of the reciprocity presupposed both in the Gospel lesson of our Gnostics and in the Manichaean theologoumenon of the "members." "What you have *done* for yourselves, you have done for me." Since *doing* is a form of *being*, this implies that each soul has the responsibility by *being* to *make to be* the very entity that it exemplifies and of which it is a "member." We have spoken of a homology between the *each* and the *All*. This Gnostic feeling, carried to the limit, finds a powerful expression in a passage of the *Pistis Sophia*: "Amen I say unto you (it is Christos Angelos who speaks), *every* man who will receive that mystery of the Ineffable and accomplish it in all its *types* and all its *figures* is a man in the world, but he towereth above all Angels. . . . He is a man in the world, but he is king in the Light. . . . Amen I say unto you, *that man is I and I am that man*."[209]

Here we have a supreme metamorphosis by a typological identification which, however, does not presuppose a confusion of persons. It is equivalent to the solemn declaration of the Imām in regard to Salmān. Each soul has the vocation to become Salmān. But to become Salmān is to have a theophanic vision of the Imām, to be the Witness of his transfigurations, to perceive the Person hidden beneath the Veil of the empirical figure. And for this one must realize toward the Imām the individuation of a relation to which the vision will be proportional. That is why the scenes of Transfigura-

209 Cf. *Pistis Sophia, A Gnostic Miscellany*, tr. G. R. S. Mead (London, 1947), pp. 191–92; cf. *3 Enoch*, 1, ed. H. Odeberg, p. 179: ἄγγελος = δαίμων = ψυχή. The identity in kind between the spirit of the human being and the angelical nature is the necessary presupposition for the metamorphosis of this human being into an angel or celestial being (e.g., that of Enoch into Metatron). The "garment of glory," the "luminous garment," represents the higher celestial nature, the angelical nature (the reader is invited to meditate on the meaning of the words: I was naked and ye did not clothe me). The difference between man and Angel is only one of degree of perfection.

tion perceived in the "alone to the alone" have all the importance of experimental psychospiritual facts, marking the highest mode of "consociation" with the Imām, the degree of "spiritual Epiphany" (*ẓuhūr-e ma'nawī*). We have mentioned one of these above: by imposing secrecy the Imām Ja'far Ṣādiq taught the validity of strictly personal experience. There is another tale concerning the Imām Muḥammad Bāqir, who was the father and predecessor of the Imām Ja'far. We should like to cite it in conclusion, for it condenses everything that we have attempted to analyze here concerning the connections between the theophanies and the metamorphoses of the soul, the interconnection between the "thou *seest*" and the "thou *art*," as signs of the individuation that accomplishes the "alone for the alone."

The story comes to us from a familiar of the Imām, Jābir ibn Zayd al-Ju'fī (who is not to be confused with Jābir ibn Ḥayyān).[210] Entering the Imām's house, he finds him in a state of meditation, his rosary in hand, reciting these verses: "Glory to Him before whom every Veil that I lifted discovered a closed Door to me. Every closed Door that I encountered discovered to me a Veil!" A transmission of thought occurs. Mentally addressing his Imām, the visitor thinks: "Yes, thou art a sublime being." And the Imām raises his head and says: "The Sublime is he who has constituted the sublime. He who knows is he who has constituted someone who knows, through what emanated from Him into me. I am the serf of God, to whom he revealed himself. Worship no one but God." (The Imām thus warns against any temptation to attach oneself to his person as to a divine *Incarnation*. But immediately there follows the theophany that transfigures.) Jābir thinks inwardly: "This man is the Veil. What then will be he whom he veils?" (The question is comparable to that which was later asked of the Imām Ja'far; and the answer will be the same spiritual event.) Having mentally heard this question as well, the Imām raises his head again:

> I saw an extraordinary splendor gleaming in him, a dazzling light that my eyes could scarcely sustain or my intelligence contain. And the Imām said: "Here is one of Thy Saints whom thou hast heaped with thy favors." And to me he said: "Should I show thee still more?" "No," I said, "that is my measure." [In this reply Jābir already shows an awareness of the *qualem capere potui*.] "O Jābir!" he said to me, "rejoice at the good tidings. God has

210 Cf. the relation developed throughout by Idrīs, text quoted in Ivanow, *The Rise of the Fatimides*, pp. 62–63 of the Arabic text.

purified thee too,[211] in order that His Shadow may descend on thee, and that *through thee* may be manifested His Threshold, the most noble *Ṣalṣal*." [*Ṣalṣal* is the Gnostic name for Salmān. This attestation of Jābir's "purification" by an allusion to the Five Companions of the Mantle, of whom Salmān is the "sixth," means that Jābir too is *adopted* among the "members of the Household," *Ahl al-Bayt*. The Shadow, that is, the divine Protection descending upon him, engenders Salmān in him, just as the Holy Spirit descended on Maryam who bore Jesus and upon Jesus on the *dies natalis* of his Baptism.] "O Jābir! Salmān is one of us, the members of the Household. His exterior (*ẓāhir*, his exoteric self as he appears to the noninitiate) typifies the exterior of a closed Door. His interior (*bāṭin*, esoteric self) is a light from the veil of the Merciful and Compassionate. When a veil hides thee from the eyes and thy person shines through the heart of his splendor of Light, thou seest how much of it thou art capable of assuming, and the creatures see what in thee is its receptacle: it is He who utters what He utters in thee, it is He who says what He says by thee. As for us, we are on the other side of the Veil. He is for us the Manifested One (*ẓāhir*). And so when thou assumest that part of it which is precisely the part that thou assumest *of us*, we are *by thee* what we are in relation to Him. Hasten then to discover the true relation between us and him; thou wilt find then what was hidden from thee."

These are abstruse words, concise and charged with meaning. The scene of transfiguration, the theophanic event, is followed by a lesson that shows its conditions and implications. Like Salmān, Jābir can become (or rather, becomes) the *Ḥujjat*, the mirror in which is revealed (*maẓhar*) the Imām. For this the Imām must be epiphanized to him, must become "manifest" (*ẓāhir*) to him in a vision which is not that of the senses. But *to have* this vision is to assume in oneself the light of the Imām, it is *to become* oneself the mirror in which he reveals himself. Thus the circle is closed. For what thou seest is the part that the measure of thy being can assume, *carry, conceive*.[212] The text gives us an almost literal equivalent of the *Talem eum vidi qualem capere potui*, for indeed we have here an archetypal situation. Then, too, the Imām becomes "through thee" what he is in relation to the *Deus absconditus*: he is the mirror that reveals (*maẓhar*) him, because God is *for* him and *through* him the Manifested One *for* and *through Salmān*, in the

211 Allusion to the *Āyat al-taṭhīr* (33:3), or verse of Purification, singling out the members of the Household, the Five Persons of the Mantle to whom the Angel Gabriel—or Salmān—is added as sixth; cf. nn. 44–47 and 161–166 above.

212 As is suggested by the use of the root *ḥml* in our text.

measure in which Salmān-Jābir, as he to whom the Imām manifests himself (*zāhir*), is thereby the place and form of his Manifestation (*mazhar*): he *is* his "coming into this world" (cf. section 5 above). In other words, the hidden godhead stands in the same relation to the Imām as the Imām to Salmān. And this is the epiphanic mediation of the eternal Imām. To achieve the capacity for this vision is the supreme metamorphosis: it is to become the pure mirror in which the epiphanies are accomplished. It is to be the "Salmān of the microcosm," to be at the end of the "Quest for the Imām" —and it is to keep his *personal* secret inviolable.

Here we have verification of the spiritual experience to which we were led by Imāmology as a metamorphosis of Angel Christology. What we might call its "Docetism" is theophany lived as a theopathy, and vice versa, which amounts to saying that every transfiguration is accomplished correlatively for the two terms, or that the figures are transfigured only for the soul which is itself transfigured. And that is why the event is accomplished on the level of the superhuman, of the Angel, in the solitude of the "One with his One."

This presence of the *totality* in the *each* is a fundamental category of kathenotheism: it modalizes another vision of which the Imām Muḥammad Bāqir is again the hero. Here the theophany occurs after a scene which closely repeats a scene from the Childhood Gospels. Only the name has changed: the child Imām is substituted for Jesus.[213] His master makes it his duty to teach him the letters of the alphabet, but the little Imām interrupts him, takes the initiative, and formulates questions which transpose the lesson to the plane of the philosophical (*jafr*) alphabet. The master is dumfounded; it is the child Imām who ceases to be the pupil and becomes the master. His preceptor loses consciousness and in this state has five times a vision of each of the Five Pre-eternal Persons composing the divine Pentad (typified on earth by the Five of the Mantle); *each* one expresses himself in the first person singular as though he were at once *alone* and *all* the others. This is one of the most significant records of primitive Ismailian experience.[214]

213 This direct exegesis, from the Gospel of Thomas (in James, ch. VI, pp. 50 and 51, ch. VII, p. 56) to the *Umm al-Kitāb*, suddenly proves to be charged with unsuspected meaning if we observe that in this Gospel the Apostle is called "Thomas the Ismaelite, the philosopher." The same episode is mentioned in the *Epistula Apostolorum*, ibid., p. 486. We intend to come back to it.

214 Cf. *Umm al-Kitāb*, ed. W. Ivanow, fol. 19b–22. The master ('Abdallāh Ṣabbāḥ) ceases to see the little Imām and instead sees the Prophet transfigured, his face haloed in

Our inquiry begins with theophanic visions, and in theophanic visions it culminates. The circle has closed. We have seen why it could not but exclude any idea of Incarnation such as that which has been professed for many years by the official Christology of the Church. It seemed to us that we should elucidate the reasons for this exclusion by comparing the diverse forms assumed by Christology with the anthropology that goes hand in hand with it. From this point of view Ismailian Imāmology has shown us certain traits it possesses in common with the Angel Christology of Christian Gnosticism. We have seen the outlines of an anthropology which is a phase of angelology and which, as such, permits us to understand the metamorphoses of the theophanic visions; it is under this aspect that we have here developed the theme of *Man and Transformation.*

In analyzing the pure spiritual event of these theophanies, we have seen how a correlation takes form between the mode of the theophanic person's *real apparition* and the mode of the *seeing soul's consociation,* which varies with this person himself. This consociation, as postulate of the spiritual event, is confirmed in the secret dialogue with Christos Angelos in the evening solitude of the Mount of Olives, as it is confirmed in the instances of transfiguring vision individually attained by the devotees of this or that Imām. In this same correlativity, phenomenology discerns a situation and a mode of being contrasting in the extreme with those which ultimately prevailed in the spiritual history of the Occident. Very briefly, the postulates and implications of Angel Christology and Imāmology considered as one of its extensions contrast sharply with the doctrine of homoousia formulated by the Councils. As we know, this technical term of Christian theology bears within it grave psychological and sociological consequences, the remote echoes of which have long evaded a criticism whose own postulates hardly predisposed it to an analysis of the positive data of the soul and the connections between them. To affirm homoousia, that is, the consubstantiality of the Logos as second person of the Trinity, with the "Father"—to affirm

tresses of light: "I am the pure Lord, transcending all attribute and all description." Successively, he sees 'Alī, then Fāṭima. Dressed in silk and gold brocade, a green veil on her hair, Fāṭima declares: "There is no God beside me, neither in divinity nor humanity, neither in the Heavens nor on earth, outside of me, who am Fāṭima-Creator (in the masculine: *Fāṭima-Fāṭir*), it is I who created the spirit of the True Believers." In the end there appear the Imām Ḥasan, then the Imām Ḥusayn, who declares: "I am Ḥusayn ibn 'Alī, I am Ḥasan ibn 'Alī, I am Fāṭima the Radiant (*Fāṭima Zahrā'*); I am 'Alī al-A'lā (*Excelsus excelsissimus*); I am Muḥammad the Elect."

the homoousia of the incarnate Logos, as true God and true man, with *our* actual and present humanity—is, in both cases, to postulate the definite concept of a divine "nature" and of a human "nature." To define their relation by the term *homoousios* (ὁμοούσιος) is precisely what Angel Christology and Imāmology refuse to do. *Christos Angelos* is not consubstantial with the *Deus absconditus*; he is, for example, the first of the Seven Protoktistes, or first-created Archangels, or the "magnificent Angel" of the *Shepherd of Hermas*. Similarly, neither the primordial Archangel nor the Imām as Epiphany of the creative Logos is consubstantial with the godhead "whom the boldness of thought cannot attain." Moreover, their Epiphany is accomplished only by transfiguring at the outset the soul in which and to which it "shows itself," i.e., in whom the potentiality of the angel has already flowered. This potentiality itself excludes what our anthropology posits and defines as "human nature," and thereby it deprives the idea of an incarnation within the frame of this anthropology of any possible meaning. Consubstantiality would presuppose that the potentiality of the Angel were fully realized; for an Angel Christology, homoousia has and can have only an eschatological meaning.

The repetition of a single device ("he who knows *himself* knows *his* God," that is to say, his Imām) and its confirmation at the homologous degrees of the corresponding hierarchies have led us to recognize in the Imām the symbol, or *personal* Figure, of the Self and in this symbol to see the source and organ of the soul's metamorphoses. It is here that we discern the extreme gravity of the consequences that follow from the decision in favor of homoousia, that is, of consubstantiality (one substance), or else in favor of the position with its numerous shadings by which a pluralist monotheism attempted to consolidate and save its intuitions. One cannot, on the pretext that an authentically religious utterance necessarily implies a challenge to the demands of rational thought, maintain that such a pluralist monotheism is deficient in "religious meaning." For the adversaries of homoousia were not preoccupied with satisfying the exigencies of rational thought, and in the eyes of philosophical rationalism, adversaries and defenders of homoousia are doubtless equal in regard to passion for the irrational. In any case their opposition marks a profound struggle in the history of Christian dogmas. Perhaps its traces are discernible even in iconography—in the contrast between the primitive type of adolescent Christos (Orphic type, the Young Shepherd, etc.) and the type of Christos Pantokrator, the "Omnipotent." To pass from one to the other the active Imagination must traverse the entire distance that separates the representation of the incarnate Logos, consubstantial with the Father, and that of the celestial Angel in his theophanic and soteriological function. The idea of the Pantokrator suits only the former. But then, as we have seen, a very different conception of the *Imitatio Christi* is decided upon. If the guiding vision is that translated by Qusṭā ibn Lūqā, "One for the One," perhaps the practical implications of an Angel Christology recur in certain Ismailian attitudes that we have analyzed. It is, for example, the *mission* of the *Dā'ī* who calls a single soul and not a multitude, a soul which is not to be convinced of a dogma but—far from it—in which there must be awakened the meaning of the *ta'wīl*, of the spiritual exegesis which frees it from ready-made facts and "leads it back" to its "horizon," its own *ḥadd*, its Imām. To the homoousic conception affirming as a fact of universal history that "God made himself man" is opposed the personal theophanic vision which no man can either communicate or demonstrate. That is why the Imām Ja'far, far from allowing his adept to go and "convince" the others, imposes secrecy upon him. And Mullā Ṣadrā admirably defines the Imāmate as an angelical and divine reality in man. Here the idea of the Imāmate comes close to the "inner Christ" of our mystics. But it is difficult to constitute any sort of a Church with this "inner Christ"; it is still more difficult for secular thought to take possession of it in order to substitute the idea of a "social Incarnation" for the religious idea. For it would seem that angelology and sociology must remain forever alien to one another.

And here, no doubt, is one of the characteristic implications of Gnostic anthropology. By arousing the human being to the vocation of a potential angel, it causes him to move in this world as a Stranger, a "prince of the other world" on his way back to his native home. Hence this extreme gentleness, this appreciation of the derisory character of any exercise of the will to power, of any appetite for kingship, or for conversion tending to bring about a monolithic Unity. The Gnostic lessons of the apocryphal Gospel texts which recur in the writings of our Ismailians have given us this teaching: The form of your vision and of your worship bear witness to what *you are, you answer for* the vision you have of your God. And what God *becomes* is revealed in the mode of relation attested in man's mode of understanding Him.

Here it is not our task to apprehend in terms of pure phenomenology the consequences, *a parte Dei*, of homoousia and incarnation. God has ceased to be the Eternal in Heaven. Incarnated, He is buried in the flesh until the time comes for Him to be buried in the grave. And this Incarnation was the full Revelation of the godhead. Hence there is no more mystery; the mystery has been proclaimed on the housetops, it has been "profaned." Still, in terms of pure phenomenology this signifies identification to the point of perfect coincidence between consciousness and transconsciousness, a coincidence that was to have incommensurable consequences for the spiritual history of our Occident.

The mystery of the Cross of Light was the mystery of *Christus impatibilis*, saving his own through the love born of their common origin; it was this love of the heavenly angel that acted as a magnetism upon "His" terrestrial soul, *His* "member," to make it reascend toward him, to recall it to their common angelicity (here a homoousia as eschatological anticipation). The form of love thus lived and meditated upon was wholly different from that meditated upon and "realized" in the divine Incarnation, in compassion with the sufferings of the God incarnate, with the death of the Redeemer who was "true God and true man." But consciousness would fully "realize" the event that had here taken place, and Nietzsche would cry out: "God is dead, he has died of his pity for men." That is to say, in the context of consciousness, God has died of this homoousia, of his consubstantiality, his identity with his Incarnation. But what *meaning* would Nietzsche's words have had for Gnostics who knew the true meaning of "the coming of God into this world," the meaning of the epiphanies of the "One for the One," the meaning of the Angel? In the opposition between epiphanic Figure and Incarnation, *maẓhar* and *ḥulūl*, we can perceive, both in Gnostic Christology and in Ismailian Imāmology, the same demand for Mystery and the same protest against the violence done to this mystery by a conception implying that the godhead can have suffered death. We are compelled to note that the facts of the problem are mutilated if we content ourselves with opposing the Christian idea of the divine Incarnation and the strict transcendence of orthodox Islamic monotheism. Between the two there is a middle term, and this is the entire meaning of Shiite Islam, eminently of Iranian Shiism, and most particularly of Ismailian Imāmology. It is impressive that we should find here certain traits characteristic of a Christianity that has vanished from the historical scene, for this modifies the meaning of our encounter as men of the West with an Orient that is, to be sure, very different from the "modern" Orient. We perceive a kind of protest against a form which has become constitutive of our consciousness, which dominates our Christian theology of history as well as the secularized philosophies of a post-Christian era. And this protest, coming from the part of spiritual Islam in which Imāmology assumed the features of an ancient Christology, *also* brings to our ears the voice of a vanished Christianity. It comes to us like a question, perhaps urgent and imperious, and at the same time it rises up as an answer, the answer of those who know the mystery of the Cross of Light and who reply to the "God is dead" with the protest uttered in the Koran verse: "No, they have not killed him, they have not crucified him! They have been caught in the trap of the assimilation (*tashbīh*) committed by themselves."

3

From the Gnosis of Antiquity to Ismaili Gnosis

I.

The title of this study indicates not only what it aims to include, but also what it excludes. The historical data do not allow us to establish a comparison between what may have been the relations between the gnostics of the West and Ismaili gnostics during the Middle Ages. Even today we are still very far from having access to the body of texts that would have to be analyzed in order to know Ismaili gnosis in the details of its structure and development. Yet one can imagine that in the many little gnostic circles of the Latin West—which have been especially studied by P. Alphandéry, and which were more or less related to the Cathars—there must have existed certain conditions that would have permitted a dialogue. Whether or not that occurred, no trace of it has remained.

On the other hand, what has left its trace are the contacts that occurred under conditions quite alien to any spiritual interpenetration. It was not in some scholarly retreat, such as that in Toledo where the translations of philosophic texts from Arabic to Latin were prepared, that the Crusaders heard of the Ismailis. Every chronicler of the Crusades, however, from William of Tyre onward, had something to say in their regard. But what was known of them—and what inflamed imaginations very rapidly spread about—finally resulted in that cheap adventure serial of the "Assassins," and in the popular meaning that word had already assumed in the fourteenth century. People saw their hand everywhere, even in murder attempts in the West. Moreover, some troubadours even claimed their rank, inasmuch as they were ready, out of love, to make the supreme sacrifice for their ladies. The designation became traditional, even before being exploited for sensational stories, and it has persisted among many Orientalists since the seventeenth century. Where a text reads "Ismailis," they have casually translated "Assassins," as though they were the same thing. In forgetting that an Ismaili community still existed, they unwittingly made themselves, across the ages, obliging agents for the stubborn propaganda of the Abbasids or for Saladin's fanatical hatred.

Our purpose here is not to go back over those historical vicissitudes[1] or that lack of scientific integrity. A crucial change has occurred in the past twenty years or so, completely transforming the conditions under which our predecessors worked—confronted, as they were, with reports coming from Sunni theologians or historians vehemently hostile to every form of Shiism. At last we have gained access to authentic and complete treatises of Ismaili doctrine. These books are what will concern us here, and whoever has reflected on them already knows that Ismaili spirituality has absolutely nothing to do with those "tales of assassins."

What such reflection does call for is rather that sort of tolerant and comprehensive comparison which did not—or could not—take place in the Middle Ages. The first condition for that, moreover, is to determine the typology of the Ismaili system of understanding, in order to connect it with its closest spiritual family. It is remarkable that at the very moment when, thanks to the discovery of the Coptic manuscripts at Nag Hammadi, we can hope to have access for the first time to an entire library of ancient gnosis, we are likewise put in a position to be able to study the most significant recurrence of gnosis in Islam. If, at last, the unfortunate difficulties of access to the texts that we have experienced in both those domains were to be removed, then an encounter delayed for several centuries would finally become possible.

Perhaps one day we shall even be able to demonstrate the secret thread linking one gnosis to the other. But for the moment we must limit ourselves to noting some traces and signs which are already enough to raise the problem. In any case, it is possible to bring out certain structural homologies, and it is these, above all, that will hold our attention here. Moreover, gnosis has never had the character of a closed dogmatic system. The speculative freedom to which the gnostics of the second century testify is such that each one of them sets for himself the task of contributing to the discovery of the events of the Pleroma and enriching their symbols: what Irenaeus, in a hostile remark, interprets as an instability or contradiction in

1 For an overview, cf. Bernard Lewis, *The Sources for the History of the Syrian Assassins*, pp. 475–89 in *Speculum*, vol. XXVII (October, 1952).

their doctrines is only another testimony to their vitality. There was an analogous proliferation in the first centuries of Shiism, which left heresiographers with the same perplexity and inability to surmise the thread tying together the doctrines they recorded. A corollary of this is that Shiite gnosis in general, and Ismaili gnosis in particular, cannot be conceived simply as a continuation of ancient gnosis. It follows a path that is purely its own, eliminating some themes while it assimilates and transforms other perfectly recognizable ones.

The fact remains, however, that here we are indeed in the presence of a gnosis—that is, of a teaching which does not aim at some pure theoretical knowledge, of a *mode* of understanding which is not a simple act of knowing. It is not a teaching for the masses, but an initiatory teaching passed on to each specially chosen disciple. It is an esoteric knowledge (*ʿilm al-Bāṭin*), a knowledge of the Truth (*ʿilm al-Ḥaqīqa*) that, as such, gives rise to a new birth, a metamorphosis, the salvation of the soul. "This spiritual birth (*wilāda rūḥānīya*) takes place in the world of *ta'wīl*, while physical birth takes place in the world of *tanzīl*."[2] External religion or the literal form (*tanzīl*) and spiritual exegesis (*ta'wīl*) are the two poles. Etymologically, *ta'wīl* means "to bring back or lead back to . . .," i.e., to bring the literal forms (*ẓāhir*, *sharīʿa*) back to the plane of spiritual Truth (*ḥaqīqa*). By this exegesis, Ismailism transforms the literal forms of the Koranic Revelation in the same way that the gnosis of antiquity worked with the given forms of Christianity: it performs a transformation of all these forms, events, and persons into symbols. In so doing, it realizes a transmutation of the soul, its resurrection (*qiyāma*)—and thereby bears the fundamental feature that relates it to the other forms of gnosis.

Our primary concern here will be to call attention to some traces of that relationship, in so far as some important works that have only recently become accessible allow us to do so. We do not propose to undertake a complete accounting of what has been learned from the publications of the last twenty years: in the face of the tasks that still remain, such a listing

2 *Kalāmi Pīr*, ed. W. Ivanow, p. 114 of the Persian text. On *ta'wīl* as a spiritual activity, cf. H. Corbin, *Avicenne et le Récit visionnaire*, tome 1 (*Bibliothèque Iranienne*, vol. 4), Tehran-Paris, 1954, pp. 32–40 [*Avicenna and the Visionary Recital*, tr. Willard Trask, New York, 1960; reprinted Spring Publications, Dallas, 1980.], and *Etude préliminaire pour le « Livre réunissant les deux sagesses » de Nâṣir-e Khosraw* (*Bibl. Iranienne*, vol. 3a), 1953, pp. 65–73. [Above all, see *En Islam iranien* . . ., Paris, Gallimard, 1972/1978, Index, s.v. *ta'wīl*.]

would appear quite inadequate, just as any premature attempt at systematization would be vainly ambitious. For we are only at the very first stages. A pamphlet published by the Ismaili Society of Bombay on the occasion of its tenth anniversary (February 16, 1956) indicates that until 1922, scarcely three or four authentic works were known. Since then, the texts published in Arabic and Persian (and on a very diverse range of topics) constitute some forty titles. Moreover the *Guide to Ismaili Literature* of W. Ivanow (1933; 2nd ed. [1963]), mentions 691 titles.

If we can measure something of our ignorance in that fashion, these are not the only obstacles to be eliminated if we are to allow the first results of this dialogue to unfold. It would seem that gnosis has always been a controversial problem. From time to time, for example, one encounters peremptory assertions, coming from the most diverse quarters, such as that "Christianity and gnosis are heterogeneous and irreconcilable quantities." It is to be feared that this sort of preconceived opinion may forever prevent any real understanding or valorization. What should be said instead, is that there is a heterogeneity between historical, official Christianity and gnostic Christianity comparable to that existing between orthodox Islam and the Islam of the mystics (*Ahl al-ʿIrfān*): it is only straightforward intellectual honesty to recognize that fact. But where one goes beyond the bounds of hermeneutics is in maintaining this opposition in force when the *meaning* of those terms is still undetermined—i.e., in affirming a contradiction between gnosis and Christianity as such, or between gnosis and Islam as such. Or rather, it is true that the Koran, in its material, literal form, does not establish a gnostic religion; but one of the tasks of Ismaili studies ought precisely to be the uncovering of homologies between the gnostic conceptions of Christianity and the Ismaili gnostic conception of Islam.

II.

The oldest treatise now accessible to us seems to be the *Umm al-Kitāb*. It appeared in the *khaṭṭābī* milieu, so named after Abū 'l-Khaṭṭāb, the too enthusiastic disciple of the Imam Jaʿfar al-Ṣādiq. (d. ca. 148/765). "The Ismaili religion (*madhhab-e ismāʿīlī*) is that which was founded by the (spiritual) children of Abū'l-Khaṭṭāb, who sacrificed their lives out of devotion to Ismāʿīl, the son of Jaʿfar al-Ṣādiq."[3] Whether this archaic

3 *Umm al-Kitāb*, ed. W. Ivanow (*Der Islam*, XXIII), pp. 52–3 of the manuscript.

Persian text is the original text or a translation from the Arabic, in either case it faithfully reflects the ideas which were circulating in the 2nd/8th century among those circles in which the themes of Shiite gnosis took form. What those themes took over from earlier Gnosticism (for example, with Hishām al-Jawālīqī, Mughīra, Shalmaghānī, etc.) remains to be uncovered in the summary accounts provided by the heresiographers. The *Umm al-Kitāb* has been called a "proto-Ismaili" work, which is true, on the condition that one recognizes that certain of its themes are no longer to be found in the great treatises of the Fatimid period, while others, on the other hand, are only the first hint of subsequent developments.

At present, it is still difficult to follow in detail the transition between this first treatise and the Ismaili scholasticism of the Fatimid period. It is known that the fourth/tenth century was a period of intense intellectual fermentation:[4] the creative controversy in which four great Iranian Ismaili figures were involved (cf. §X below) provides us with some important information. Moreover, the vitality of the research and creative ability at that time are indicated by the notable differences between works that are virtually contemporary. There is, for example, a great difference in the structure of the heavenly Pleroma as it is described by Nāṣir-e Khusraw, and the schema set up by Ḥamīd al-Dīn Kermānī, who makes it correspond to the ten-fold hierarchy of the philosophers (the *falāsifa*, al-Fārābī and Avicenna).

After the completion of the great schism following the death of Mustanṣir bi'llāh (1094), the two major branches of Ismailism followed their own paths. The "old *da*ʿ*wa*" (*da*ʿ*wa qadīma*, to use Shahrastānī's expression) continued the Fatimid tradition in Arabic up to our own day.[5] The "new *da*ʿ*wa*" (*da*ʿ*wa jadīda*), the reformed Ismailism of the tradition of Alamūt, saw its literature, in the Persian language, devastated under the Mongol onslaught. We are indebted to the labors of W. Ivanow for our knowledge of some of its major monuments. The extreme interest of this literature lies in

4 See our Introduction to the *Commentaire de la Qaṣîda ismaélienne d'Abû'l-Haitham Jorjânî* (*Bibl. Iranienne*, vol. 6), Tehran-Paris, 1956. Not only does this commentary allow us to make some fruitful comparisons with that of Nāṣir-e Khusraw, but one of his direct disciples (undoubtedly Muḥammad Sorkh of Nīshāpūr) also testifies to the efforts and research of his master.

5 Among the Ismaili literature of the Fatimid era, the work of Nāṣir-e Khusraw stands out as being completely in Persian. Also in Persian are the above-mentioned commentary (n. 4) and the Persian version of *Kashf al-Mahjūb* attributed to Abū Yaʿqūb Sejestānī (ed. H. Corbin, *Bibl. Iranienne*, vol. 1, 1949) [2nd ed., 1980].

its revival of the gnostic awareness of early Ismailism and in its emphasis on the aspect of a religion of personal salvation, a religion of Resurrection (*dīn-e qiyāmat* or *rastakhīz*). It profoundly influenced all of Iranian Sufism, under the guise of which it continued to survive. Whatever one may think of the origins of Shams-e Tabrīz (i.e., whether or not he was the son of a grand-master of Alamūt), it should be noted that his "mystical secret" recorded in the *Walad-Nāmah* of the son of Jalāl al-Dīn Rūmī has its exact equivalent in the commentary on the *Khuṭbat al-Bayān* which Ismaili tradition has attributed to Ḥasan Ṣabbāḥ.[6] Moreover, this commentary is likewise of major significance for the history of Ismaili spirituality and its connections with Sufism.

III.

Still another difficulty awaits us if we attempt to situate the speculative theosophy of Ismailism in the context of the development of philosophy in Islam. I have just alluded to the schematization of the heavenly Pleroma in Kermānī and to its homology with that of Avicenna. The *falāsifa*, in their own way, likewise bear witness to gnosis in Islam. In reality, philosophic understanding always remains a wisdom (*ḥikma*), a gnosis that should provide spiritual salvation through the illumination of the soul. That is precisely its ultimate meaning, so that it would be arbitrary to consider Ismailism in isolation from Avicennism or the "Oriental theosophy" (*Ishrāq*) of Suhrawardī—not to mention its affinities with the theosophy of Ibn ʿArabī. In alluding to those connections, however, we can scarcely do more than suggest a program of research.

The Avicennan theory of the Intelligences (*ʿuqūl*), or angelology, sets forth a succession of syzygies that correspond to the structure of some of the major Gnostic systems. From each Intelligence (*ʿaql*), *Noūs*, or Cherub there proceeds a Soul (*nafs*) that forms a couple with it. A brief *Risāla* (*Risāla fī'l-Malā'ika*) even gives us their respective names.[7] The name of the first of these Cherubs, *Wajh al-Quds*, corresponds exactly to that of the first hypostasis (the *Monogenēs*) in the *Excerpta* of Theodotus: the "Face of the

6 Compare *Walad-Nāmah*, ed. Homāyī, [Tehran, 1315 h.s.], p. 197 (concerning the *maqām-e maʿshūq*) and the text of Ḥasan-e Ṣabbāḥ cited in *Kalāmi Pīr*, p. 81 of the Persian text (concerning *martaba-ye maḥbūb-e Ḥaqq*).

7 See our book *Avicenne et le Récit visionnaire*, tome 1, pp. 71–2, where this passage of the *Risāla* is quoted in its entirety [cf. above, n. 2].

Father." The *Taṣawwurāt* of Naṣīr al-Dīn Ṭūsī preserves the same schema, although there it is complicated by the fact that not only the Intelligence, but also the Soul produces acts of contemplation that give rise to being.

In Ismailism, on the other hand, this syzygial structure is enriched by an aspect which could not figure in the Avicennan schema—i.e., by the correspondence and parallelism between the levels of the heavenly Pleroma (*al-ḥudūd al-ʿulwīya*) and those which constitute the esoteric hierarchy of the *daʿwa* (the "meso-cosm"), the different ranks of the Ismaili brotherhood (*al-ḥudūd al-suflīya*).[8] The *Nāṭiq* (the "Enunciating" prophet) is made to correspond to the First Intelligence (the first of the Cherubs in Avicenna), while his spiritual heir (*Waṣī*), the foundation (*Asās*) of the Imamate, corresponds to the Second Intelligence.[9] (The notion that an earthly person may represent or typify a heavenly hypostasis also occurs in medieval Latin gnosticism.)[10] The Second Intelligence could thus be regarded as the Soul of the world, forming, together with the First Intelligence, the primordial *dyad*. Or, following Avicenna, one could consider that both the First Soul and the Second Intelligence proceed from the First Intelligence at the same time. In either case, the problem arises of the relationship between the *ʿAql* and the *Nafs*, the Intelligence and the Soul: does the fact that desire is the natural principle of motion in the Soul imply some imperfection in Its being? Depending on one's decision, there will follow either the priority of the Prophet to the Imam, or that of the Imam, the Silent One (*Ṣāmit*), to the *Nāṭiq*. In general, the authors of the Fatimid period chose the first alternative; but the opposite continued to have its supporters. It appeared, for example, in Nuṣayrī texts, as well as in Jābir's alchemical speculations, in the order of precedence of the hypostases symbolized in the letters *ʿAyn* (ʿAlī), *Sīn* (Salmān), *Mīm* (Muḥammad).[11] In the tradition of Alamūt the precedence of the Imam is more and more strongly affirmed,[12] just as it is always either latent or openly avowed in Twelver Shiism (in which the

8 Cf. our *Etude préliminaire pour . . . Nâṣir-e Khosraw*, pp. 74–91 (on the symbolism of the worlds).

9 See the tables of concordance between the heavenly and earthly hierarchies (according to Hamīd Kermānī and Idrīs 'Imād al-Dīn) [above pp. 90–96].

10 Cf. Hans Söderberg, *La Religion des Cathares*, Uppsala, 1949, p. 13.

11 Cf. L. Massignon, *Salmân Pâk et les prémices spirituelles de l'Islam iranien*, Tours-Paris, 1934; H. Corbin, *Le Livre du Glorieux de Jâbir ibn Ḥayyân, Eranos Jahrbuch* XVIII, Zürich, 1950, pp. 61ff.

12 Cf. the little Persian treatise on Imamology: *Faṣl dar bayān-e shanākht-e Imām*, ed. W. Ivanow, Bombay, 1947.

priority of *nubuwwa* depends on first presupposing some portion of *walāya*, to which *nubuwwa* is then added). Thus the situation is at one and the same time dominated both by the "events" perceived in the Pleroma and by a prophetology that is brought to completion in an Imamology. In Ismailism, that Imamology is connected with a sort of Ebionite Christology (cf. §IX below).

Even later in Iran, in Shiite Avicennism, reflection on this eternal birth of the Avicennan Pleroma led to some remarkable reminiscences and comparisons. Sayyid Aḥmad ʿAlawī, one of the most brilliant students of Mīr Dāmād at Isfahan in the seventeenth century, made a connection between ancient Iranian Zervanism and the idea that already with the unfolding of the First Intelligence there emerges a shadowy dimension (its aspect of non-being, inasmuch as its being is not necessary in itself), a shadow that goes on growing and intensifying until the tenth and last Intelligence.[13] To be sure, this comparison does involve a profound modification of Zervanism, by delaying somewhat the moment at which the Zervanite schema makes its appearance (since Zervān here has become an angel in the Pleroma, rather than the absolute godhead). Moreover, this is the same transposition that one also finds in the cosmic dramaturgy of Ismailism, and the shift had already taken place in the doctrine of the Zervanites and the Gayomartians, as that was described by Shahrastānī (cf. §VII below). This transposition must be listed among those characteristics differentiating Ismaili gnosis from dualism in general. Here the crisis that gives birth to Darkness is conceived as situated within the Pleroma—but only so that the Darkness may be overcome and banished from It, as soon as it has emerged. That is why the Intelligence who will assume the role of the Demiurge in Ismaili gnosis has none of the disquieting traits of a Ialdabaoth, any more than the Angels governing the celestial spheres resemble hostile Archons. On the contrary, the notion of angelic *tarbiya* or pedagogy (already indicated in the *Miʿrāj-Nāmah* attributed to Avicenna)[14] shows the angels ready to come to the aid of the gnostic in order to help him to "escape," to return "home" and carry out his mystical *Miʿrāj*. Instead, the demonic force is on earth, where it manifests itself in the implacable battle carried on by the opponents of the Imam.

13 Cf. *Avicenne et le Récit visionnaire*, tome I, pp. 67–70, and *En Islam iranien . . .*, tome IV, pp. 9–54.

14 On the theme of the *Miʿrāj* and the *Miʿrāj-Nāmah* attributed to Avicenna, cf. *ibid.*, pp. 191–205.

This transposition, which shifts the Zervanite schema, as it was conceived by the Avicennans and the Ismailis, by one or more levels, allows us to establish a comparison differentiating the cosmogony of the *falāsifa* from the Ismaili cosmogony. First of all, this comparison should consider two dominant figures: that of the θεὸς ἄγνωστος (the "Unknowable God") and the Angel who assumes the function of the Demiurge.

For the *falāsifa*, the Necessary Being (*Wājib al-wujūd*) is the First Being (*al-Ḥaqq al-awwal*). He transcends the cosmos and the heavenly hierarchy, but it is permissible to attribute to Him certain predicates and relations that are not incompatible with His immutability. On the other hand, the "Originator" (*Mubdi*ʿ, προαρχή) of the Ismailis is absolutely unknowable, and nothing can be predicated of It: It is beyond both being and non-being, beyond yes and no. A dialectic of double negatives concludes with the primordial "Originated" being (*al-Mubda*ʿ *al-awwal*), the First Angel Who is in fact the basis of the divine Name, *Al-Lāh*.

The Tenth Intelligence, the Active Intelligence (ʿ*Aql fa*ʿʿ*āl*) of the *falāsifa*, has its homologue in Ismailism (in the schema of Kermānī). It was the predominant role of this Figure that kept pure Avicennism from being assimilated by orthodox Latin scholasticism, which retreated in the face of the fundamentally angelological perspective which that Figure presupposes.[15] From the mystical narratives of Avicenna to those of Suhrawardī, His personal relation with the gnostic and the function of His heavenly pedagogy become both more precise and more emphatic. He is the end of the pilgrimage to the mystical Sinai described in the story of the "Occidental Exile" (*al-ghurba al-gharbīya*).[16] In that same work appear several familiar themes of Manichean gnosis: the young man thrown into the bottom of a *well*, the *Stranger* who is reawakened to the awareness of his self by a *letter* sent to him by his heavenly family, the stages of the pilgrimage of return, etc.[17]

If there is a Figure that would call for a comparison between the spirituality of the East and West during the Middle Ages, it is surely this

15 Cf. *ibid.*, pp. 118ff.

16 See the Arabic text and Persian translation of the *Risālat al-ghurba al-gharbīya*, in *Oeuvres philosophiques et mystiques de Sohrawardî*, ed. H. Corbin (*Bibliothèque Iranienne*, vol. 2), Tehran-Paris, 1952 [2nd ed. 1977], pp. 274–97. [French translation in *L'Archange empourpré*, fifteen mystical treatises and tales translated from the Persian and Arabic by Henry Corbin, Paris, Fayard, 1976, pp. 265–89.]

17 Cf. Acta Thomae, 108–13 (The Hymn of the Soul) and *Kephalaia*, pp. 181–2.

Angel *paredros* or "guide" who reveals the meaning of the Song of Songs to certain Jewish mystics and who is invoked by certain of Dante's companions (Dino Compagni, for example) as the *Madonna Intelligenza*. The *falāsifa* identified this Figure with the Angel of revelation who is Gabriel, i.e., the Holy Spirit; in Suhrawardī, He is designated as the "Angel of humanity" (*rabb al-nawʿ al-insānī*). In Ismailism this Intelligence becomes the "spiritual Adam" (*Adam rūḥānī*), i.e., the celestial *Anthropos* well known in different schools of ancient gnosis. As such, He is the protagonist of a drama which has no equivalent in the cosmogony of the pure *falāsifa*, a drama which makes Him fall from the third to the tenth angelic rank, and which is the origin of all our mytho-history[18] (cf. §VII below).

However, there are still other points of contact between Ismailism and Suhrawardī's theosophy of *Ishrāq* that remain to be explained. There is the idea of the "*Imām*," in the form that it appears in the prologue to the *Kitāb Ḥikmat al-Ishrāq*. There is also the very project of an "Oriental theosophy" (*ḥikma ishrāqīya* or *mashriqīya*), as Suhrawardī himself conceived it. Returning to Avicenna's scheme (an abortive one, in his opinion), Suhrawardī sets up the idea of an "oriental knowledge," based upon the notion of an "Orient" which is not registered on our maps, but was well known to the gnostics.[19] Strangely enough, a comparable expression can be found in the writing of Alain de Lille.[20] Foreshadowing the scheme of the Byzantine philosopher Gemistos Plēthon, Suhrawardī wished to combine the teachings of Plato and Zoroaster. His project may appear less surprising if we relate it to the way in which Ismaili prophetology conceived of Zoroastrianism. Since the teaching of Zoroaster, the *ḥujjat* of the fourth *Nāṭiq*, had been corrupted by his successors (cf. §X below), the idea of restoring that teaching to its original purity had to come. That was the project of Shihāb al-Dīn Yaḥyā Suhrawardī, *shaykh al-Ishrāq*.

18 [Henry Corbin later substituted for this term the expression *hiéro-histoire*, "sacred history," due to certain possible misunderstandings of the term "myth"].

19 Cf. our *Prolégomènes I* and *II* to *Oeuvres philosophiques et mystiques de Sohrawardî* (vol. I: *Bibliotheca Islamica*, vol. 16, Istanbul 1945 [2nd ed. Tehran-Paris, 1976]; vol. II: *Bibliothèque Iranienne*, vol. 2, Tehran-Paris, 1952 [2nd ed., 1977]), [and *En Islam iranien* . . ., vol. 2].

20 "Sicut in mundo maiori firmamentum movetur ab Oriente in Occidentem et revertitur in Orientem, sic ratio in homine movetur a contemplatione Orientalium, id est caelestium . . . consequenter descendit ad Occidentalia, id est ad considerationem terrenorum . . . deinde revertetur ad Orientem, iterum considerando caelestia," *Patrologia lat.*, 210, 866. (I owe this reference to Mlle M. T. d'Alverny.) Alain de Lille (second half of the twelfth century) was a contemporary of Suhrawardī (d. 1191).

IV.

Here we can only recall in general terms certain themes common to all the schools of gnosis—those in which, given that broader affinity, the particular inspiration governing Ismaili gnosis reveals itself most clearly. First of all, there is the theme that we have just mentioned: that of the unknowable, impredicable, ineffable Divinity (τὸ ἄῤῥητον), the Abyss of Silence which is the origin of all the becoming of the worlds. Ismaili gnosis, rejecting any metaphor borrowed from the notion of "father," refers to It as the *Mubdiʿ*, the "Originator" (cf. προαρχή) eternally giving rise to the archangelic Pleroma (the *Dār al-Ibdāʿ* or *ʿĀlam al-Ṣafā'*, the "World of Purity"). The crisis occurring in this Pleroma, to which all the forms of gnosis ascribe the great acts of Creation and salvation, is likewise brought into play by Ismaili dramaturgy; but here it is with variations and nuances that evince the preoccupations of gnostics having to meditate, in particular, on the materials of Islamic revelation. The figure of the *Anthrōpos*, the Saved-Savior, and the relation between the heavenly *Christos* and his earthly manifestation, for example, have their homologues in the figure of the spiritual Adam (the *Adam rūḥānī*, the third Angel who became the tenth), and in His relation with the one who is His terrestrial counterpart, the Imam who leads back to Him all of His fellow souls, from one cycle to the next, until the final Imam who will bring to an end the Cycle of cycles, the Resurrector (*Qā'im al-Qiyāma*, in Persian *Khodāvand-e Rastakhīz*). Here, too, the motivating force of this dramaturgy is likewise the gnostic presentiment of the celestial origin and pre-existence of souls, as is clearly shown by Ismaili anthropology, which is ultimately only part of an angelology. Thus there also arises a classification of souls parallel to the classical division between pneumatic (*rūḥānī*, *ʿaqlānī*), psychic (*nafsānī*), and hylic (*jismānī*) ones.[21]

Now that these two terms, Ismaili gnosis and the gnosis of antiquity, have been identified, one can recognize that our aim of more deeply exploring their relations necessarily imposes a twofold task: discovering the indications of an actual transmission, and revealing the structural homologies and their meaning—this latter one being the particular task of the phenomenologist. Indeed, if the historian is not also aided by the phenomenologist in

21 Cf. in particular Nāṣir-e Khusraw, *Jâmiʿ al-Ḥikmatain*, ed. H. Corbin and M. Moʿīn (*Bibliothèque Iranienne*, vol. 3), 1953, chapter XI, pp. 135ff., and the introduction to the *Commentaire de la Qaṣīda* . . . (above, n. 4), pp. 83ff.

this case, given the scarcity of "archival documentation," he would most often have to limit himself to fruitless hypotheses. However, there are some facts that can put us on the trail of the actual contacts that must have taken place between Christian gnostics and those early Shiite circles whose fervor and enthusiasm helped form the beginnings of Ismailism.

We can start by distinguishing between what one could call, on the one hand, the encounters between *texts*, and on the other hand, contacts between *persons*. As for the former, these include, for example, passages showing how certain of the "apocryphal" Christian Scriptures which had originated in a gnostic setting were subsequently meditated and assimilated in the Ismaili milieu. Later on (§V), an example of Imamology will be taken up which was developed on the basis of an episode from the Gospels of Jesus' childhood, and any study concerning the relations between Ismaili gnosis and the gnosis of antiquity must pay particular attention to the occasional re-emergence and further development of the so-called "apocryphal" Scriptures. However, the encounter was not limited to those "apocrypha." It is also revealed in the form of certain variants modifying the canonical texts of the Gospels, variants which were known and cited verbatim by Ismaili authors; for the spirit which inspires those variants appears so authentically Gnostic that one must suppose that our theosophers had some knowledge (orally, if not in writing) of texts which we no longer possess. Moreover, in the fourth/tenth century the works of Abū Ḥātim Rāzī (*Aʿlām al-Nubuwwa*) and Abū Yaʿqūb Sejestānī (*Ithbāt al-Nubuwwāt*) demonstrate a first-hand knowledge not only of the Old and New Testament, but also of other religious sects (Zoroaster, Marcion, Mani, Mazdak, Bēhāfarīd, etc.).

A particularly striking example is the long quotation that Abū Yaʿqūb gives from the chapter of the Gospel according to St Matthew (25:35–46) announcing the last judgment of the nations by the Son of Man. A variant repeated twice there completely overturns the "social" perspective developed by the canonical text. Where the canonical text has: "Each time you did these things for the least of these my *brothers*, you did it for me," the version that Abū Yaʿqūb cites verbatim has: "The Lord will gather together the just and the wicked. . . . The just will say to Him: When were you hungry and thirsty, when were you in prison? . . . And the Lord will say to them: You speak rightly, but all that you have done *for yourselves* (or 'to your selves', 'to your own souls': *kullumā ṣanaʿtum bi-anfusikum*), that you have done for me (or 'to my self')." Moreover, Abū Yaʿqūb comments on this: "Here it is the Soul of the world (*Nafs kullīya*) who is conversing *with Its souls*, with the individual souls It needs in order to attain to everything Its rank includes; i.e., It needs the intelligible aptitudes that individual souls acquire in this world through the medium of sensible things."[22]

This variant has the remarkable peculiarity of substituting for the mention of 'brother' that of 'your self,' your own soul (*nafs*). Abū Yaʿqūb Sejestānī's exegesis shows that for an Ismaili theosopher the confirmation of this text occurred spontaneously. But so long as we are unable to identify the historical provenance and source of this variant—which is so important in that it centers the understanding of the Gospel text on the subjectivity of the individual person—we at least ought to identify the mental operation which led to this substitution and the motive which helped dictate this reading. In this respect, it appears to us that it might be possible to reconstruct the gnostic exegesis which supplied that motive, and at the same time to grasp at its source an intuition which was shared by Ismaili gnosis.

The Carpocratians give an exegesis of another passage in the same Gospel (Matthew 5:25ff. = Luke 12:58–59) which, if it is supplemented by the exegesis of that same passage in the *Pistis Sophia*, does seem to put us on the path toward a solution. There, the adversary from whom one must free oneself while one is still traveling along with him (i.e., during one's earthly life) is the "devil" who is supposed to take before the Judge (i.e., the Archon who is the Demiurge) all those souls who have left this world in an incomplete and impure state, so that they may be thrown into prison (i.e., the Hell of a new earthly body).[23] The *Pistis Sophia* indicates the profoundly subjective meaning of this "devil" when it identifies this adversary with the ἀντίμιμον πνεῦμα, that spirit which is the disfigured image of the soul, the source of all the evils within it: it is like a body which the hostile planetary archons have bound together with the soul, at the moment of its descent, when they made it drink from the water of the Cup of forgetfulness. This spirit is the "adversary" mentioned in the Gospel verse, the "other in me," the brother-enemy from whom the soul must free itself so that—having

22 *Kitāb al-Yanābīʿ*, *Yanbūʿ* 38 [ed. H. Corbin in *Trilogie ismaélienne, Bibliothèque Iranienne*, vol. 9, 1961]. Here we have shortened the quotation which Abū Yaʿqūb gives in full, and which ends with these words: "Everything which you failed to do *for yourselves*, it is as if you had failed to do it *for myself*."

23 Irenaeus, *Adv. Haer.* I, 25.4. Cf. G. R. S. Mead, *Fragments of a Faith Forgotten*, p. 232.

flung it back at the archons—it may appear, as pure Light, before the Judge who is the Virgin of Light.[24] So long as it dominates the soul, the soul cannot be at peace with itself, cannot rediscover the unity and wholeness of a being of Light. Conversely, to be at peace with oneself means precisely to overcome and eliminate this Shadow. From this perspective, a gnostic—whether he be Carpocratian or something else—could read and understand the immediately preceding verses (Matthew 5:23ff.) in the following manner: "First go and be reconciled *with yourself*,[25] and only then return and offer your gift at the altar." For, after all, no one can be at peace with his brothers (precisely in the sense of the Gospel text) who is not first of all at peace with himself. The priority of the subjective condition thereby becomes quite clear: your love is only worth what *you are*. Thus the modification that imposes this priority (and in just the way that Abū Yaʿqūb read it) simply derives experientially from this gnostic principle: What have you done *with yourself* and for yourself? The interpretive transition, the stages of which lead us in this way from the canonical text to the Gnostic text, corresponds exactly to the mental operation we can identify in the brief commentary given by Abū Yaʿqūb.

What Abū Yaʿqūb perceives in the text of Matthew 25:35–46 is a conversation between the Soul of the world and *Its souls*, the individual souls whom It needs to attain Its true rank. In Ismaili terms, this Soul of the world is our Demiurge, the spiritual Adam (*Adam rūḥānī*), the Third Angel who was the protagonist of the crisis in the Pleroma (cf. §VII below). He was the victim—the first, and without even knowing it—of an ἀντίμιμον πνεῦμα, the Iblīs-Ahriman concealed within himself, the Darkness that he would have to overcome and vanquish as soon as he came to recognize it, but which paralyzed his being so profoundly that from that first moment he fell back seven celestial ranks beneath his original level. The task of all his souls—i.e., of all those who, having come to earth, belong to his own Pleroma (cf. §VII and IX below)—is to help him to reconquer that

24 On this anthropology and posthumous destiny of the soul, see *Pistis Sophia*, chapters 111, 113 (containing the commentary on Matthew 5:25ff.), and 131.

25 This reading would also agree with another important variant that is given to us by the *Oxyrhyncus*: "Where there are two, they are not without God. But I say that where there is *only one*, I am with him." Cf. H. G. Evelyn White, *The Sayings of Jesus from Oxyrhyncus*, Cambridge, 1920, p. 36, and *Patrologia Orientalis*, IV, p. 155. This passage has been compared with a text from the *Gospel according to the Egyptians* and the *Second Letter of Clement*, chapter XII: "when the two (i.e., the masculine and the feminine) will become one."

distance. Hence that co-responsibility of the Soul of the world and *His souls*, which is here an Ismaili aspect of the "theologoumenon of the *members*" so characteristic of Manichaeism. Thus, what each soul does *for itself*, it also does for this Angel-Adam, the Ismaili figure of the Saved-Savior who, from one cycle to the next, reconquers His celestial rank (cf. §IX below) through the aid of *His souls* each overcoming its own Iblīs. This aid consists in each soul's eliminating, in its turn, its own ἀντίμιμον πνεῦμα, its Iblīs-Ahriman.[26] To free oneself from this Adversary is to rediscover oneself in the unity of one's being (the subjective side of the esoteric *tawḥīd*), to be free for "one's self"—i.e., for that form of Light which is joined to the disciple at the moment of his initiation, and which he must nurture and increase. For the solidarity which unites the *corpus mysticum*, the "Temple of Light" of the Imam, does not derive from the authority of a pre-existent social collectivity; it results from the establishment of a direct, personal connection of each disciple with the corresponding rank (the *ḥadd*) in the celestial Pleroma. Therefore, it was the most profound meaning of gnosis and Ismaili ethics that Abū Yaʿqūb recognized in the Gospel text: "What you have done for *your selves*. . . ." It is remarkable, moreover, that his reading of this passage corresponds so intimately to the way a gnostic of the second century would have read or understood a text of the Gospel.

Now, in addition to these encounters between *texts* (such as we can infer in bringing out their inner agreement), there are other testimonies, perhaps equally allusive but no less significant, pointing to certain contacts between *persons*. We cannot dwell here on the personality of Maymūn al-Qaddāḥ and that of his son ʿAbdullāh, nor on the meaning of their characterization as "Bardesanians"; nor can we make any judgment as to their exact role in the formation of Ismailism in its first stages. According to Ibn al-Nadīm, the author of the *Fihrist*, who wrote at the end of the fourth/tenth century and whose Shiite sympathies are well known, if there had "formerly" been a good number of Bardesanians in southern Mesopotamia, it seems that in his own time they no longer existed except in eastern Iran (Khorāsān) and in China (i.e., in Chinese central Asia).[27] Nevertheless, in the second/eighth century there must still have been a certain number of them in Mesopota-

26 Or in the philosophic terms indicated by Abū Yaʿqūb: in the soul's turning toward the sensible in order to "de-materialize" it into the intelligible and spiritual. This is the process of knowledge according to the *falāsifa* (al-Fārābī, Avicenna, etc.); it is precisely what unites the Active Intelligence and the souls It illuminates.

27 *Al-Fihrist li-Ibn al-Nadīm*, Cairo edition, p. 474.

mia, since one of the most notable friends and companions of the sixth Imam, Jaʿfar al-Ṣādiq, and of his immediate successors, was in contact with several of them. The figure of Hishām ibn al-Ḥakam deserves a thorough study.[28] A fervent disciple of the Imam Jaʿfar, a family friend of the Barmecids, in contact with all sorts of non-Muslim elements (Bardesanian gnostics, Manicheans, Nestorians, Jews), he was one of the first Shiite theologians and a supporter of the nascent Imamology. A good number of Shiite traditions refer to his authority. That someone so representative of the Shiite milieu could have had such "connections" and could even have served as an intermediary between them and the Imam should give some indication of the ways in which Gnostic ideas and influences were able to penetrate both Shiism and Sufism.[29]

One episode, among others, that stands out as particularly significant is an exegesis which Abū Shākir the Bardesanian (*Dayṣānī*) suggested to Hishām ibn al-Ḥakam: "'There is a verse of the Koran,' he said to him, 'which expresses a belief similar to the one we profess.' 'Which one?' 'The following: He who is a God in Heaven and a God on earth (43:84).'"[30] Hishām, being perplexed, referred this to the Imam, whose reply (as one might have expected) was inoffensively prudent.[31] As for the Bardesanian, he meant that the word "God" repeated twice in this verse should be understood each time as referring to a different "person." His intention was perfectly justifiable in terms of gnosis in general, since it seems to do nothing more than "lead back" the meaning of the Koranic verse to the established distinction between the Unknowable God and the δεύτερος θεός ("second God": the Anthropos, etc.); and this distinction corresponds precisely to that professed by Ismaili gnosis between the *Mubdiʿ* (προαρχή) and the primordial "Originated one," *al-Mubdaʿ al-awwal* or *Protoktistos*.

One would, indeed, expect to see the orthodox apologists attack at this point. And to be sure, the accusation against the Ismailis of professing the

28 Cf. the notice in Shahrastānī (*Milal*, Tehran, 1288, p. 87), who includes under the heading *Hishāmīya* both the school of Hishām ibn al-Ḥakam and that of Hishām ibn Sālim al-Jawālīqī.

29 Cf. W. Ivanow, *The Alleged Founder of Ismailism*, Bombay, 1946, pp. 97–8.

30 Cf. Kulīnī (or Kulaynī, according to the Iranian usage), *al-Uṣūl min al-Kāfī*, Tehran, 1334 h.s., vol. I, p. 128.

31 And for that matter, the Koranic verse, taken in its "exoteric" simplicity, does not offer any difficulty: Does not Abū Shākir himself bear the same name in Kufa and in Basra? But the Bardesanian was not fooled by this simplification; he remarked not without humour, that this reply was "an import from the Hejaz."

existence of "two Gods" does reappear with tiresome monotony. But if the orthodox vehemently attacked the notion of a supreme Divinity that is unknowable because It transcends every predicate and category, they seem to have been even more scandalized by the original dyad of the Pleroma: the pair formed by the first and second Intelligence (*ʿAql*), the primordial Originated being (*Mubdaʿ awwal*) and the First Emanation (*Inbiʿāth awwal*), *Noūs* and *Psychē*. Baghdādī, in referring to the *Kitāb al-Maḥṣūl* (of Muḥammad Nakhshabī), states that the *Bāṭinīya* (the "Esotericists") claim that since the First Intelligence gave rise to the Soul, the two of them together govern the world. Then he rather hardily identifies this doctrine with that of the Mazdeans or Magi (*Majūs*), according to whom Yazdān, having created Ahriman, governs the world together with him—Yazdān being the creator of all that is beautiful and good, while Ahriman is the creator of all that is bad and ugly.[32] Needless to say, in confusing Yazdān (Ōhrmazd) with Zervān, and in identifying the syzygy *ʿAql-Nafs* with the antithetical couple of Ōhrmazd and Ahriman, he compounded his errors. In fact, as we have already recalled and will have occasion to discuss again, one phase of the Ismaili cosmogony can be seen as homologous to a Zervanite schema; but that phase, in the Ismaili system, transposes the initial moment of conflict to such an extent that the dramaturgy of ancient Zervanism is essentially changed.

As for Daylamī, sensing the dangers that the esoteric *tawḥīd* could pose for the faith of the orthodox, he likewise denounces the "two Gods" who are the Intelligence and the Soul (*ʿAql* and *Nafs*, *Sābiq* and *Tālī*, *Qalam* and *Lawḥ*). Even more than that, it is the entire pleroma of *ʿUqūl* that he denounces as a multiplicity of Gods,[33] since their ontological status, although they are designated as "Angels" (*malāʾika, fereshtagān, Karūbīyūn* or Cherubim), is incomparably superior to that of the simple "messengers" of popular angelology. In fact, one could say that these degrees of the Pleroma (*ḥudūd, limites*, "horizons") assume a role as hypostases analogous to that of the divine Names in Ibn ʿArabī's theosophy—just as one could say that the Bardesanian who was Hishām ibn al-Ḥakam's confidant must have had a proper sense of their theological implications.

32 Cf. Baghdādī, *Kitāb al-farq bayn al-firaq*, ed. Muḥammad Badr, [Cairo, 1328/1910,] pp. 277–8 [= *Moslem Schisms and Sects*, part II, transl. by A. S. Halkin, reprint Philadelphia, 1978, p. 131].

33 Cf. Daylamī, *Die Geheimlehre der Batiniten*, ed. R. Strothmann (*Bibliotheca Islamica*, vol. 11), pp. 5–6 and 72–3.

V.

Given the present state of our knowledge, it is the structural homologies, even more than these passing contacts between persons, that can provide us with clear indications tracing a continuous path from the gnosis of antiquity to Ismaili gnosis. Such indications are to be found in the oldest work that has yet been made accessible to us, the treatise in Persian already mentioned above, entitled *Umm al-Kitāb*, which can be linked to the second/eighth century on the basis of one of its dominant motifs, the myth of Salmān.[34] While looking forward to a detailed study, we shall here point out some of its particularly significant themes.

1. The book is presented in the form of an initiatory discussion between the fifth Imam, Muḥammad Bāqir, and three of his intimate disciples or "beings of Light" (*rōshanīān*), as the Imam calls them. The prologue reports a story from the childhood of the holy Imam, when his teacher, ʿAbdullāh Ṣabbāḥ, was preparing to teach him the arithmological powers and symbolic meanings of the letters—i.e., the *jafr*, or philosophic alphabet (the role of which is no less important in Ismaili gnosis than for a Gnostic like Marcus Magus). However, with the first letter, *alif*, their roles are reversed: the poor teacher, whose learning is outstripped, becomes the pupil, and the young Imam becomes his initiator. This story repeats point by point one that is reported in the *Gospel of Thomas* and which is also known from the *Epistula Apostolorum*:[35] the young Imam has purely and simply been substituted for Jesus. This is a fact that helps to confirm the observation formulated in the previous section. Only here, it is not simply the gnostic version of a canonical Gospel that has been cited and given value by an Ismaili author; it is Imamology itself which, by taking over a narrative from those "apocryphal" scriptures so appreciated in gnostic and Manichean circles, reveals its affinity with a Christology to the point of actually supplanting it.

2. Another characteristic feature of this proto-Ismaili book is to be found in the predominance of groups of *five*, in what could be called the "pentad-

34 Cf. W. Ivanow, *The Alleged* . . ., p. 164.

35 Compare *Umm al-Kitāb*, pp. 13ff., the *Gospel of Thomas*, chapters VI and VII (M. R. James, *The Apocryphal New Testament*, pp. 51 and 56), the *Gospel of Pseudo-Matthew* XXXI (James, p. 77), and *Epistula Apostolorum* (James, p. 486). Irenaeus (*Adv. Haer.* I, 20, I) mentions this episode from the Gospels of Jesus' childhood as being a particular favorite among Gnostics of the Marcosian school. Moreover the *jafr* is nothing more than the arithmology which was already so amply developed by Mark the Magus; cf. *Divine Epiphany* . . ., above, p. 145.

ism" of its cosmology.[36] For all eternity, *Five* Lights, of *five* colors, exist in the Sea of Whiteness (*Baḥr al-bayḍā'*), the heavenly Palace of the Limit of Limits. These Lights are the "members" (*jawāriḥ*) and the epiphanies (*ẓuhūr*) of a single Person of Light (*shakhṣ-e nūrānī*); in human form, on the plane of terrestrial humanity (*basharīya*), they appear as Muḥammad, Ali, Fāṭima, Ḥasan and Ḥusayn—i.e., the "Five Persons of the Mantle" (*aṣḥāb al-kisā'*), whose theophanic role is also primordial in the gnosis of Twelver Shiism.[37] Beneath the Sea of Whiteness, nine domes (*qubba* or *dīwān*: "Heavens") are arranged in descending order, each with its distinctive color (chrysolite, fire, red, emerald, purple, sun, moon, lapis lazuli, water). In each of them, *five* Persons manifest in turn the Five Angel-archetypes of the Sea of Whiteness (first Gabriel, Michael, Seraphiel, Azrael, and Suriel; next *'Aql, Nafs, Jadd, Fatḥ, Khayāl*; etc.),[38] until this theophanic group reaches that microcosmic Earth which is the "Earth of the Heart" (*zamīn-e del*). There, *Five* Lights are conjoined in the thinking Spirit (*rūḥ nāṭiqa*) of the true believer, which is their "Sixth," their "uni-totality" or their Lord. At every level, including their microcosmic recurrence, these *Five* Lights can be recognized as another, distinctively Ismaili exemplification of the famous theologoumenon of the "members." (In Manichaeism, the *five* spiritual members or the Five Shekinas, Dwellings, or Manifestations of the King of the Paradise of Light, the *five* sons of the *Spiritus vivens*, the *five* Elements of Light who are the sons and armor of Ōhrmazd, the primordial Man, the *five* spiritual elements or virtues in the individual man—each of these groups of "Five" symbolically corresponds to all the others. In the gnosis of *Pistis Sophia*, cf. the First Imperative and the five sectors of Light, the great Envoy and his *five* auxiliaries. In the system of Basilides, cf. the *five* hypostases, etc.).[39] In the Islamic setting, moreover, the devotees of the

36 Cf. already the observations of L. Massignon, *Die Ursprünge und die Bedeutung des Gnostizismus im Islam* (*Eranos Jahrbuch*, 1937), pp. 63–5.

37 *Khaṣā'iṣ-e Fāṭimīya* [by Mullā Bāqir Kujūrī, Tehran, 1318 h.l.], pp. 84ff.; Ibn Abī Jumhūr, *Kitāb al-Mujlī*, [Tehran, 1324 h.l.] pp. 479ff. We must also mention all the Shiite commentaries on the Koranic verse 33:33 (the sanctification of the *Ahl al-Bayt*, the appearance of the Angel: "I am the 'sixth' of you five.").

38 For this pentad, see our *Étude préliminaire pour . . . Nâṣir-e Khosraw* (above, n. 2), pp. 91ff. If one preserves the equivalents of the archangelic triad mentioned there, the bond of theophanic subordination here would put the *'Aql* and *Nafs* in correspondence with Suriel (Uriel) and Azrael.

39 Cf. H.-C. Puech, *Le Manichéisme, son fondateur, sa doctrine*, Paris, 1949, pp. 75, 77ff., and notes 297 and 307; W. Bousset, *Hauptprobleme der Gnosis*, pp. 177ff., 231ff.

divine Pentad were designated by a special name: the *mukhammisa* (the "Pentadists").[40]

In addition, each one of these five Persons or "members" appears as comprehending within his own individuality all of the others. ʿAbdullāh Ṣabbāḥ, the teacher of the young Imam, overwhelmed by the incident just recalled, proceeds to contemplate in a state of ecstasy the successive epiphany of the five divine Persons. Each of them in turn, expressing himself in the first person singular, speaks as being in *unio mystica* with the others, each time as if he were simultaneously both himself, in his own personal individuality, and also all the others. Here the category that determines the perception of these theophanies functions as a sort of "kathenotheism."[41] This presence of the Whole in the individual is more particularly expressed in the terms through which Fāṭima informs the visionary of her being and prerogatives, terms which find another vivid illustration in the scene in which Gabriel, the Angel of Revelation, shows an Image of Paradise to those who are about to be exiled from the domes of Light: that Image is the person of Fāṭima.[42]

3. Another guiding theme which should be brought out here is the Seven Battles of Salmān against the Antagonist, Azaziel, and his cohorts. The apotheosis of Salmān "the Persian" or "the Pure" (Salmān Fārsī, Salmān Pāk) into an archangelic Figure indicates to us a characteristic aspect of proto-Ismaili gnosis,[43] while the very name of the Antagonist specifically reminds us of the one who, in the Books of Enoch, leads the revolt of the Angels assembled on Mount Hermon.[44] However, apart from the divine command directing the archangel Michael to bind and cast down the rebellious angels, and the sense of the horrible struggle that is revealed in a reflection of the archangel moved by compassion,[45] the stages of the conflict here follow their own scenario, quite different from the dramaturgy of

40 Kashshī, *Maʿrifat Akhbār al-Rijāl*, Bombay, 1817, p. 253.

41 Cf. *Divine Epiphany* . . ., above, p. 87; *Umm al-Kitāb*, pp. 39–43 of the manuscript.

42 *Ibid.*, p. 87, and *Umm al-Kitāb*, p. 211: Fatima is seated on a throne; her crown, sword, and earrings symbolize respectively Muhammad, her husband Ali, and the two infant Imams, Ḥasan and Ḥusayn. Compare Jaʿfar b. Manṣūr al-Yaman, *Kitāb al-Kashf*, ed. R. Strothmann (without his *imprimatur*), Oxford, 1952, pp. 35, 56–7; *Divine Epiphany* . . ., above, p. 87.

43 This is the feature which distinguishes the sect of the *Salmānīya*; cf. H. Corbin, *Le Livre du Glorieux de Jâbir ibn Ḥayyân*, (above, n. 11); L. Massignon, *Salmân Pâk* . . ., (above, n. 11), and *La Mubâhala de Médi·e et l'hyperdulie de Fâtima*, Paris, 1955.

44 Cf. I Enoch 6, translated by R. H. Charles, Oxford, 1912, p. 14, n. 2.

45 Enoch 68:11: "They have acted as though they were the Lord."

Enoch. It is important to note that this "prologue in Heaven" already contains the complete idea of that mytho-history[46] which will be developed later in the great treatises of Ismaili theosophy. Seven times, Azaziel responds to the twofold summons to acknowledge the "King Most High" and at the same time to worship Salmān—each time with the same defiance and denial, carrying along with him, in that negation, a group of his own kind. With each of these denials, he is stripped of one of those colored radiances which are the specific property and respective emblem of each dome of Light.

If one can say that Salmān here assumes the role of the archangel Michael of the Apocalypse (Revelation 12:7ff.), it must be added that he is more specifically like an archangel Michael who would be the "Son of God," such as He was represented in the faith of the Bogomils.[47] In fact, He is the great heavenly Prince (*dāwar*, p. 139 *et passim*) who at the same time both veils and unveils the supreme Divinity; he is both Its Doorway (*Bāb*) and Its Veil (*Ḥijāb*, p. 172). Thus it would not be appropriate to compare this δεύτερος θεός with Marcion's Demiurge, the "God of the Law" who is opposed to the good and unknown God. A relation of that sort could not correspond to Salmān's theophanic function. On the contrary, that theophanic role makes him the heavenly *Anthropos* ("O Salmān, You are my Doorway and my Book . . . You are my Right Hand . . . You are my Envoy and my Throne . . . You have my safeguard and you are my safeguard . . . My Spirit manifests Itself through your Veil . . . I am your Lord and you are the Lord of the believers. . . . You are the Lord of all the Heavens and all the Earths," p. 172). Thus he is not only like an archangel Michael who orders the Angels to worship Adam,[48] but he himself is the one before whom the Angels are ordered to prostrate themselves.[49] This event is described as the "prologue in Heaven" to a drama the echo of which reverberates on earth from Cycle to Cycle. There is at once an archetypal relation and a synchronism between Salmān's *seven* battles and the *seven* Cycles constituting a complete Cycle of prophecy. At the dawn of our own Cycle, Iblīs-

46 [Cf. n. 18 above].

47 Cf. H. Söderberg, *La Religion des Cathares* (above, n. 10), p. 78; H.-C. Puech and A. Vaillant, *Le Traité contre les Bogomiles de Cosmas la Prêtre*, Paris, 1945, p. 206.

48 According to the episode described in *Vita Adae et Evae* (= *The Books of Adam and Eve*, chapters XII–XVII in R. H. Charles, *Apocrypha and Pseudepigrapha of the Old Testament*, II, p. 137); the *Gospel of Bartholomew*, IV, 53ff. (M. R. James, *The Apocryphal New Testament*, p. 178).

49 *Umm al-Kitāb*, pp. 143ff.; Koran 7:10 [11].

Ahriman repeated, this time against the terrestrial Adam, Azaziel's defiance of Salmān, the heavenly Adam. Hence each one of the lesser cycles enclosed within the total Cycle feels the presence of Iblīs and his accursed crew.

It is important to emphasize once again that the author of the treatise *Umm al-Kitāb* was already well acquainted with this synchronism that is so characteristic of Ismaili prophetology (and which begins, in the later treatises, with a "prologue in Heaven" whose protagonist is the Third Angel: cf. §VII and IX below). He is perfectly aware of the underlying motive of this drama, which is expressed in terms that ultimately bring one face to face with the esoteric meaning of *tawḥīd*: Azaziel invokes against Salmān a God who is beyond all the Heavens, without mode or attribute or qualification, a God who does not manifest Himself to anyone or by anyone (p. 147). However, according to what the Imam Muḥammad Bāqir demonstrates in response to this (p. 149), to designate God, to say "huwa Allāh," can have no other positive content but the fivefold theophany that is recapitulated within the luminous Person of Salmān, the supreme theophany which was itself "Uncreated" (*nā-āfarīda, nā-makhlūq*, p. 252), yet which was the first to proclaim the affirmation of *tawḥīd*, by refusing to claim divinity for itself. That is precisely the secret of theophanies, the secret which is also their paradox.

Without theophany, God is only a pure indetermination which cannot be worshipped at all. But if theophany is necessary, it must be accomplished as an anthropomorphosis perceived by mental vision, on the archangelic level of Salmān, not on the plane of a material incarnation (cf. p. 172, quoted above). Moreover, if worship can be directed toward a theophanic person, it is because that person, by refusing divinity for himself, thereby renders himself transparent to the Divinity, Who nevertheless can only be worshipped through that theophany. Azaziel's resort is only the recourse of agnosticism (*taʿṭīl*) to a purely abstract Divinity, one deprived of every Veil that could make It show through. Here, by a striking paradox, the orthodox literalistic profession of faith reunites with the absolute negation of the atheist, because the literal monotheistic dogma, by rejecting the theophanic function, destroys the transparency of the Veil; it confuses the Veil with the Divinity that It manifests, in believing that it may predicate of God what is only appropriate to His Veil. The meaning and necessity of theophany is revealed to Ismaili gnosis by that "prologue in Heaven", the mystery of which was pondered by all the schools of gnosis. The Ismaili makes it the very secret of the esoteric *tawḥīd*: without these theophanic figures that the Imam opposes to Azaziel's claim, monotheism would perish in its own triumph, through the most subtle treason—that by which one imposes on oneself a denial of oneself. That, essentially, is the intuition which ultimately lies at the very origin of Shiite gnosis and its Imamology.

4. Finally, it is fitting to bring up an aspect which comes at the very conclusion of the treatise *Umm al-Kitāb* and which may perhaps allow us to rejoin the Book of Enoch once again. This conclusion is dominated by the microcosmic relationship already mentioned, i.e., by the ultimate identity of essence between the Savior and the souls whom He saves. Thus the beings of Light, the *rōshanīān* to whom the Imam is speaking, have the same Origin and are Its "members." At the end of this initiatory conversation, the disciples learn that each gnostic is in turn called upon to become this Salmān who takes upon himself the attributes of the archangel Michael and the heavenly *Anthrōpos*—because his *Rūḥ nāṭiqa* with its *five* lights, the "Angel of a thousand names," is none other than the "Salmān of the microcosm" (*Salmān-e ʿālam-e kūchak*, pp. 392–3). No doubt, this is for them a revelation as overwhelming as that moment when Enoch learns that "The Son of Man is *you*" (I Enoch 71:14).

VI.

As for the Divinity which remains hidden behind the veil of Its theophanies, no name or attribute or qualification can be given to It. The purely negative designations to which the gnostics have recourse have only one goal: to preserve this Divinity from any assimilation to a mode of created or originated being. The Unknowable God (θεὸς ἄγνωστος, in the Clementine Homilies), the Unnameable God (ἀκατανόμαστος θεός, Carpocrates), the Ineffable and the Abyss (Ἄῤῥητος, Βυθός, Valentinus), the Unengendered One (Ἓν ἀγέννητον, Basilides), the Supreme God and Pre-Principle (ἀνώτατος θεός, προαρχή)[50]—all of these designations have their equivalents in the Ismaili terminology: the Originator (*Mubdiʿ*), the Mystery of Mysteries (*Ghayb al-Ghuyūb*), "He Who cannot be reached by the boldness of thoughts" (*man lā tatajāsaru naḥwahu 'l-khawāṭir*),

50 Cf. W. Bousset, *Hauptprobleme der Gnosis*, [Göttingen, 1907,] p. 84.

etc.[51] One cannot attribute to Him either being or non-being; He *is* not, but *causes to be.* Even beyond the One, He is the "Unifier" (*muwaḥḥid*), Who unifies all the Ones, Who "monadises" all the monads. Thus the *tawḥīd* takes on the aspect of a monadology: at the same time that it separates this "Unifier" from all the Ones He unifies, it also affirms Him through them. The *tawḥīd* must avoid the twofold trap of *taʿṭīl* (agnosticism) and *tashbīh* ("assimilating" the Manifestation to That which is manifested). Hence there is the dialectic which is expressed in the two phases of a double negativity: the Originator is non-being and *not* non-being; He is not-in-place and *not* not-in-place; etc.[52] That dialectic corresponds to the twofold operation of *tanzīh*, which "removes" the Names and Attributes from the Supreme Divinity in order to refer them to the *ḥudūd* (both heavenly and earthly), and of *tajrīd* which immediately "isolates," sets apart, or re-projects the Divinity beyond these manifestations. In this way the theophanic function of beings is both grounded and safeguarded.

Ibn al-Walīd defines *tawḥīd* as "knowing the heavenly and earthly *ḥudūd* (the degrees or "limits") and recognizing that each of them is unique in its rank or degree, without being associated with any other. Thus the divine Names and Attributes refer to the angelic hypostases and their earthly exemplifications, and above all, to the First among them, Who is the Protoktistos (*Mubdaʿ awwal*), the Most Holy Angel (*al-Malak al-muqaddas*), the First Intelligence (*ʿAql awwal*). In fact, this is the Supreme Name (*ism aʿẓam*), and the very name of "God," *Al-Lāh*,[53] belongs to it, precisely because it is the Veil, maintained in its transparency through its being the founder of the very first *tawḥīd*, by refusing to claim divinity for itself and instead re-projecting it above and beyond itself—just as its homologue, Salmān, did in the treatise *Umm al-Kitāb*.

It is true that the Ismailis (Kermānī, for example) are the first to acknowledge what their dialectic of the divine attributes owes to that of the Muʿtazilites; but they are no less aware of the point at which their

51 For all that follows, cf. Ḥamīd al-Dīn Kermānī, *Rāḥat al-ʿaql*, [several editions] the entire second chapter; Idrīs ʿImād al-Dīn (the 19th Yemeni *dāʿī*, d. 872/1468), *Zahr al-Maʿānī*, chapters I–III (personal copy); Ibn al-Walīd (8th Yemeni *dāʿī*, d. 667/1268), *K. al-Mabda' wa'l-Maʿād* [ed. H. Corbin in *Trilogie ismaélienne*, *Bibliothèque* Iranienne vol. 9, 1961].

52 Cf. Abū Yaʿqūb Sejestānī, *Kashf al-Mahjūb* (above, n. 5), all of the first chapter.

53 Cf. R. Strothman, *Gnosis-Texte der Ismailiten*, p. 80 (*ism al-ilāhīya lā yaqaʿ illā ʿalā 'l-Mubdaʿ al-awwal*).

agreement ceases.[54] The Muʿtazilites end up allowing certain pre-eminent attributes to qualify the divine Essence. Moreover, even if they had continued to pursue their dialectic, the idea of theophanic mediation (by the Angel in the Pleroma, and the Imam on the earthly plane) could never have appeared on the basis of their premises alone. Ismaili Imamology has its roots in quite another source.

All of this theosophy unfolds in an affective tonality which it is important to recognize, since the signs that reveal it are precisely those that can help us to grasp the distinctively Ismaili formulation of the gnostic theme in question here: the contrast and the connection between the Unknowable God and the divine Figure Who is revealed at the farthest accessible horizon. One of these indications is the etymology which the Ismaili thinkers reserve for the divine name *Al-Lāh*, the name which in fact is applied to the First Intelligence, the Protoktistos. Deriving the noun *ilāh* from the root *w-l-h* (*ilāh* = *wilāh*), they see this name as referring to the profound emotion and sadness of the First Angel yearning to know his Originator (*Mubdiʿ*). Even better, taking the word *ulhānīya* ("divinity") as a sort of ideogram, they read it (by mentally introducing a *tashdīd*) as if it had been written *al-hānnīya* (an abstract noun formed from the *nomen agentis* of the first form of the root *h-n-n*): the state of someone who is sighing from sadness and melancholy. Moreover, it is not only the First Intelligence but the entire Pleroma (*jamīʿ ʿālam al-Ibdāʿ*) which, in feeling together with it this same ardent longing, also deserves the same title of "divinity" (*ulhānīya* = *al-hānnīya* = *ishtiyāq*, ["yearning"]). What is expressed in the name of the Divinity, Al-Lāh, is not some fulgurating omnipotence, but sadness and nostalgia.[55]

That is a striking feature and one in which the Ismaili soul characterizes its most intimate mode of perception. Perhaps, in light of that, the ephemeral success of the Fatimid theocracy would appear as a passing episode, as though that political success demanded a counterbalancing spiritual loss, which in turn could only be atoned for and overcome through political defeat. It is significant that the later treatises of the reformed

54 Cf. Nāṣir-e Khusraw, *Jāmiʿ al-Ḥikmatain* (above, n. 21), pp. 52–67, chapter concerning the discussion with the Muʿtazilites about *tawḥīd*.

55 Cf. R. Strothman, *Gnosis-Texte* . . ., p. 80 (a quotation from Kermānī); Jalāl al-Dīn Rūmī, *Mathnawī*, IV, 1169; Lane, *Arabic-English Lexicon*, I, p. 83 (but simply in the sense that *Ilāh* is the refuge for which one longs); and H. Corbin, *En Islam iranien* . . ., Vol. III, pp. 9–149.

Ismaili tradition of Alamūt rediscover and lend new meaning to these themes from the pre-Fatimid period, and that in Iran Ismailism has survived by rediscovering the way of Sufism.[56] Moreover, the works of the *Mustaʿlī* tradition, those which were written by the Dāʿīs of Yemen subsequent to the Fatimids and which summarize or expand on the treatises written during the Fatimid period, still retain their full "gnostic" religious and philosophic significance, independently of any temporal political references. It does indeed seem that the authentic Shiite conception of the Imamate, in addition to its eschatological dimension, also implies the "invisibility" of the Imam in this world, i.e., his purely spiritual mode of being. Practically speaking, for the *Mustaʿlī* branch of the Ismailis, as well as for a good portion of the Nizaris, the Imamate has returned to *ghayba*, just as it has for the Twelver Shiites.

VII.

Our mental habits would incline us to judge the meaning and effectiveness of spiritual doctrines by presupposing that their authors had as their task—if not as their conscious concern—"making history," and as if we could only judge them by reference to the "meaning of history." However, the complex dramaturgies of gnosis in general, and particularly of Ismailism, evidently call into question the very "meaning" and direction of what we call history. At the same time, the unique character of those dramaturgies puts us on guard against the most serious of the misunderstandings which we could fall into if we were to presuppose, without a more critical examination, that the modes of perception were identical on either side. What we perceive as an *event* in history may have been perceived—and may be perceived at this very moment—as occurring on the level of a mythohistory[57] and as having its significance only in relation to a *meta-history*. In such a case, in other words, one cannot invoke the "meaning of history" without renouncing it at the same instant, since here it is in fact *transhistorical*. Consequently, also, the thematic structure of events as such is quite different: the fact of the Incarnation at the center of history, for example, is one thing, and the fact of theophanies perceived at the present moment on the horizon of the Pleroma or the intermediate world is quite another. This

56 Cf. above, n. 6.
57 [Cf. n. 18 above].

is one of the most characteristic ways in which gnosis can invite us to meditate on the confrontation of Orient and Occident.

The mytho-history of Ismailism begins with a "prologue in Heaven," one version of which, from the treatise *Umm al-Kitāb*, has already been mentioned here [§V-3]. The presentation of this drama varies according to the structure of the Pleroma; that structure reached its definitive form with the work of Ḥamīd Kermānī, where there arises an "isomorphism" between the heavenly Pleroma (*Dār al-Ibdā'*) of Ismailism and the Pleroma of the ten Intelligences described by the *falāsifa* (al-Fārābī, Avicenna). The primordial "Originated One," the Archangel Protoktistos (*al-Mubda' al-awwal*), in its turn gives origin to the First Emanation (*Inbi'āth awwal*), which is sometimes designated as the Second Intelligence and sometimes as the Universal Soul (*Nafs kullīya*). From this dyad of the first two Intelligences, *Noūs* and *Psychē*, proceeds a third Intelligence (*'aql thālith*), which is the Second Emanation (*Inbi'āth thānī*). This is the one who is designated as the "spiritual Adam" (*Adam rūḥānī*), the protagonist of this drama which had Salmān as its hero in the presentation in the book *Umm al-Kitāb*. What constitutes the underlying motivation of this drama, as we have noted in relation to that treatise, is expressed in its reference to the esoteric *tawḥīd*. The First Intelligence initiates that *tawḥīd* by recognizing the Unique, or rather the Unifier of its being (or its self, *dhāt*), Who is beyond all categories and all predicates. Its own *negativity*, which it takes on in this way, is in fact its *ab-negation* (because it refuses divinity for itself), and it thereby becomes the Veil, the horizon or limit (*ḥadd*) by which the Divine shines through and appears to the following Intelligence (its *tālī*).

Thus from level to level, from each limit (*ḥadd*) to that which it limits (its *maḥdūd*) and which is in turn the limit or horizon for the one following it, this *tawḥīd* maintains the entire Pleroma in an ascending movement: each *ḥadd* ascribes the Divine to that "limit" which precedes it and which is the Veil through which the Divine appears to it; and this higher *ḥadd* in turn refers the Divine to the next "limit" or degree preceding itself. But then "it happened" that in a vertiginous stupor the spiritual Adam—the Third Angel, whose innermost being concealed the Azaziel-Iblīs (the other protagonist of this drama in the *Umm al-Kitāb*)—brought this movement to a halt. Like Azaziel, he agreed to recognize the *Mubdi'* (the θεὸς ἄγνωστος), but he refused to recognize the pre-eminent theophanic role of the Angel who preceded him (his *Sābiq*). Thus he was the first among all the beings to commit the twofold error which is at once that of the atheist and the orthodox believer: either he must leave the Divine in pure indetermination (*taʿṭīl*), or else he must make It determinate. But since he failed to recognize the theophanic function of the Angel who preceded him, he inevitably had to fall into *tashbīh*—and ultimately, by setting up his own predicates as being those of the Unique and Supreme Divinity, he had to raise himself up into a sort of Ialdabaoth. The myth that in this way relates the crisis in the Pleroma to the contradiction undermining the monotheism of official, exoteric religion is remarkably profound. However, this spiritual Adam-Angel is not Azaziel, even though he unknowingly harbored this Azaziel-Iblīs within himself. The doubt that he feels is precisely the rising to consciousness and the exteriorization of the Darkness which had remained hidden within him, and which from then on he can conquer and hurl back outside himself. In a way, he is like an archangel Michael who gains his own victory over himself, i.e., over the antagonist who had been latent within his own being. This is the "Zervanite movement" in the Ismaili cosmogony.

Yet this immobilization of the Angel-Adam did bring about a delay or "retard" (*takhalluf*): a distance is thereby opened up within the Pleroma, a distance which is numbered by the *seven* Cherubim or divine Words, the seven other Intelligences who follow Him (each of them being the "Imam" of an entire pleroma). Their number corresponds to that of the *seven* periods marking out the Cycle of Prophecy (a synchronism analogous to that of the *seven* battles of *Salmān*). This *cyclical time* is eternity "retarded" by the stupor of the Third Angel; its periods are the rhythmic "pulsations" marking the reconquest of this distance and retardation. Brought back to consciousness with the help of the other Intelligences (like the Aeons together interceding for Sophia in the Valentinian gnosis), this heavenly Adam stabilizes himself at a level which is no longer the third, but the tenth (corresponding to that of the Active Intellect in the schema of the *falāsifa*), the measure of his "retard." He has thrown his own Darkness outside himself: on earth, it will form the posterity of Iblīs-Ahriman, while those who follow him in his repentance will be his own descendants, the posterity of the heavenly Adam. It is so that he may come to their aid that he is installed as the demiurge of our world. And reciprocally, it is with their aid that, from Cycle to Cycle—each time that an Imam-Resurrector (*Qā'im al-Qiyāma*) will lead back to the Pleroma the "Temple of Light" formed by all the souls of Light belonging to the initiates of his Cycle—the Angel-Anthropos will be lifted up one more level toward his original rank.[58]

Even outlined in its most general features, this "prologue in Heaven" allows us to establish several points. If, during a "time" which is the very origin of time, this Angel who must subsequently assume the function of the demiurge does give in to the vertigo of a Ialdabaoth, he has nothing else in common with that figure. He is not at all the Demiurge of that name (who is neither good nor bad, and somewhat disturbing), but rather a being of Light who is compassionate toward his own beings, whom he saves after having delivered himself. He is pre-eminently the Ismaili figure of the Saved-Savior.

Of course, this unique nature of the Ismaili demiurge holds true *a fortiori* for Salmān, the hero of the treatise *Umm al-Kitāb*. There, Iblīs-Azaziel was also a member of the Pleroma, but a personage entirely different from that of Salmān; while here we have an Iblīs at first hidden within the Angel-Adam, who then had to tear him out of himself. But in both cases, the event takes place *within* the Pleroma: here, too, gnostic emanatism tends to reabsorb the dualism of Manichaeism and Zoroastrianism.[59] The spiritual Adam is not like Gayomart, who is attacked from without by Ahriman and killed by him; it is within Adam's own will that Iblīs-Ahriman emerges in actuality—but far from succumbing to him, he triumphs over him for good. Nor is the heavenly Adam a primordial Man who is overwhelmed by Matter: rather, the Darkness was in him, but he expelled it from himself. And finally, that opacity in his being was brought about by his pretension of producing a *tawḥīd* which was in fact that orthodox monotheism which claims to know the Unknowable. *That*, then, is Iblīs. And perhaps it was also out of the determination to overcome that nostalgic yearning for the Unknowable, forgetting that the Divine (*ulhānīya*, §VI above) *is* precisely "nostalgia."

Because this crisis arises inside the Pleroma, within a being of Light, and is not instigated from outside by a pre-existing contrary power of Darkness, we can understand how the orthodox apologists, although they were mistaken, could have perceived a Zervanism here (even without knowing

58 Our brief summary of this "drama in Heaven" is based primarily on the books of Idrīs ʿImād al-Dīn (chapter IX) and Ibn al-Walīd cited in n. 51 above. For more details, see our two studies, *Cyclical Time . . .* and *Divine Epiphany . . .*, above.

59 Cf. W. Bousset, *Hauptprobleme . . .*, pp. 106ff., 130ff., 208–9.

that name). One need only refer to the section that Shahrastānī devotes to the Zervanites and the Gayomartians to observe how close they are to the schematic structure of Ismaili cosmogony. In both instances, it is definitely a single being who gives birth to the two contrary powers, but it is no longer the original Absolute Divinity. Zervān has become one of the beings of Light, an angel of the Pleroma: he corresponds to the Third Angel of the Ismaili Pleroma. In both cases, the other Angels intervene to help lead to victory the battle against Darkness. In Ismailism, the outcome is a victory of the Angel over himself, the expulsion of the Iblīs-Ahriman. To be sure, Iblīs' essential substance (the negativity of the deniers, the antagonists, and the *aḍdād*) is also intermingled in the creation that the Demiurge produces to aid his fellow-souls. But this intermingling is by no means the sign of an agreed-upon *condominium*: in no way is it a legitimation of Ahriman's rule for some definite number of millennia.[60] Despite these differences, it remains true in both cases that the cosmic dramaturgy has its origin beginning with the splitting apart of a being that was originally single and unique. It is the emergence of a *doubt* that is expressed as the appearance of *Darkness*, a Darkness which *is* distance, separation, *retard*: Zervān the Unlimited *turns aside* into a "time of long domination"; Eternity, "retarded" by the Third Angel's doubt, *turns aside* into a "cyclical time" which is the time of the Redemption of the world.

The conception of this *retard* allows us to bring out other structural homologies. For example, the dramaturgy of *Pistis Sophia* (chapters 58–66) recognizes two stages: the *Sōter* frees Sophia from chaos, from the clutches of the Archons and her own germs of matter, and delivers her to a place which is beneath the thirteenth Aeon: it is only during His heavenly ascension that Christos brings her into the thirteenth Aeon.[61] Or again, in Valentinian gnosis: the divine hero liberates a Sophia held captive in the lower world; the second and final stage is only completed at the end of the "historical" process of Redemption.[62] According to the Ismaili schema, this "distanciation" is exemplified by the *retard* (*takhalluf*) of the Third Angel, who "falls back" to the tenth rank. The intervening distance of seven levels measures

60 Cf. our *Cyclical Time* . . ., above, pp. 20ff, 41ff.

61 Cf. W. Bousset, *Hauptprobleme* . . ., p. 272. (But we cannot see why this should be considered a compilation, as though the myth of the deliverance of Sophia by the Sōter had been artificially related to Jesus, whereas it is really an essential connection.)

62 *Ibid.*, p. 270.

out the "pulsations" of the seven periods of the Cycle of Prophecy, the turning aside from the eternal time of the Pleroma into the historical time of the Redemption. But this latter time is not our linear, boundless, and evolving time. It is cyclical and "involuted": it leads back and is itself led back to its origin. Because it is a Cycle of cycles, it is a liturgical time in each of whose periods (at each "festival," as the *Ikhwān al-Ṣafā'* put it) the same protagonists reappear: these periods mark the successive stages of Salvation.

The connection of the *Sōter*, Christos Angelos, with the human Jesus corresponds to the connection of the Tenth Angel with the Imam. In describing the composition of the person of the Imam, Imamology reproduces, in its own way, a Docetic Christology. While the humanity (*nāsūt*) of the Imam is the outcome of a whole cosmic alchemy, His divinity (*lāhūt*) is explained in terms that indicate an explicit recurrence of the Manichean theme of the "Pillar of Light" (*'amūd al-Nūr*) or Pillar of Glory.[63]

The "distanciation" produced in the Pleroma *is* the birth of a historical time whose "meaning" or end is precisely to free the gnostic from History. That is how the *synchronism* is established between the events in the Pleroma and a prophetology accompanied by an Imamology. This is one of the original aspects of Ismaili gnosis. While it integrates into its vision a schema of prophetic succession analogous to that of Ebionism and Manichaeism, it also indicates a difference: here that succession has not yet come to an end. The *Verus Propheta* will only gain His repose with the coming of the last Imam, the Resurrector (cf. §IX below). Yet, just as the heavenly ascension of the earthly Christos marks Sophia's entry into the thirteenth Aeon, so likewise the ascension of each Imam with all of his "Temple of Light" at the end of a Cycle marks the progressive elevation of the Angel-Adam as he returns toward his original rank.

VIII.

The twofold allusion that has just been made to the theme of Sophia and to prophetology raises the question of the presence of a figure homologous to

63 Cf. the chapter on "Imamology and Docetism," in our *Divine Epiphany* . . ., above, pp. 103–17; and compare Bousset, *Hauptprobleme* . . ., p. 270: the earthly Jesus receives the pneumatic or spiritual element of his being from Sophia, the psychic element from the Demiurge, and his "apparitional Body" results from an alchemy that took place in the higher worlds.

Sophia in Shiite gnosis in general. In a certain sense, the figure of the Third Angel, the Saved-Savior, combines the roles of both Sophia and the Sōter. There is more, however. About the person of Fatima, the dearly beloved daughter of the Prophet and the one who gives rise to the line of the holy Imams, are clustered the themes of what could be called a Shiite Sophiology. There is a paradox here: the contrast between the exaltation of the figure of Fatima and the abject status which has generally been the lot of the Feminine in the Islamic world. Here, a part of the necessary research would belong to analytical psychology. The treatise *Umm al-Kitāb* already suggests an interpretation of that situation. When the angel Gabriel had shown to those who were about to be exiled from the domes of Light an image of Paradise, which was the very person of Fatima encompassing the divine Pentad, Iblīs-Ahriman rushed to assume the form of a woman (and had his followers take on that form) so as to deceive the gnostics and lead astray their desire to return to Paradise.[64] Thus, the earthly Feminine appears as being in contradiction to the heavenly Feminine. It is at this latter level that the person of Fatima is exalted. She is the *majmū ʿ al-nūrayn*, the "confluence of the two Lights" (of prophethood and the Imamate, *nubuwwa* and *walāya*): that is why she is at the center of prophetology and Imamology in Ismaili gnosis. The *luminous* aspect of the Feminine is indicated by the power with which it is invested and the masculine attributes which are bestowed upon it, thereby compensating for the situation in which it is maintained by a patriarchal world on the social plane. Fatima the Radiant is extolled as Fatima-*Fāṭir*, Fatima-"*Creator*" (in the masculine), in the sense of "initiator," one endowed with the primordial theophanic function (cf. n. 42 above). It may be observed that the Valentinian Gnostics likewise called upon Sophia in the masculine, as κύριος ["Lord].[65] This appellation is a prevalent feature of the *Nuṣayrī* texts.[66] One may connect with it certain aspects, as they were contemplated in Sufism, of the Prophet's own designation of his daughter as "mother of her father" (*umm abīhā*).[67]

Fatima the Radiant (*Fāṭima al-Zahrā'*) appears as an archetype exemplified in numerous recurrences, which are carefully noted by the typology

64 *Umm al-Kitāb*, pp. 212–13; cf. the references given above, n. 42.
65 Irenaeus, *Adversus Haer.* I, 5, 3; *Umm al-Kitāb*, pp. 40 and 60.
66 *Tabarānī*, *Festkalender*, ed. R. Strothmann, [in: *Der Islam* 27, 1944–46,] index s.v.; cf. the beautiful *qaṣīda* of Ibrāhīm Ṭūsī (d. ca. 750/1350), translated by L. Massignon in *Der gnostische Kult der Fatima im schiitischen Islam* (*Eranos-Jahrbuch*, 1938), pp. 167ff.
67 Cf. *En Islam iranien* . . ., t. III, pp. 9–149.

of Ismaili *ta'wīl*. Generally speaking, the feminine figures who exemplify this archetype are, like Fatima herself above all, so many typifications of gnosis (*ʿilm al-bāṭin, ʿilm al-ḥaqīqa*), of the initiation into this gnosis, and of the Life which this gnosis breathes into the "dead," i.e., into those who are unknowing and unconscious.[68] Thus, her esoteric rank is above all that of the *Ḥujja*, the "Proof" or Witness of the Imam, indeed even a substitute for the Imam who, being in possession of the *ta'wīl*, is the source of that Life which resurrects the dead. This dyad (of Imam and Ḥujja) is already apparent on the plane of the Pleroma, where the Third Angel, the Spiritual Adam (*Adam rūḥānī*) forms a syzygy with an eternal Eve who is referred to as the "leaven of the initial creation" (*al-khamīra al-ibdāʿīya*). She is at once the nostalgia of the heavenly Adam and his return to his Paradise: she is the one who, from cycle to cycle gives birth to all of his fellow-souls in the angelic state.[69] On the earthly plane, we find Eve, as Adam's wife, typifying the esoteric content of the *sharīʿa*; she is the one who knows its meanings contained within the symbols, and that is why Adam cannot fulfill the *sharīʿa* of this cycle without her.[70] This Adam–Eve mystey reappears in all the periods: just as the Kaaba is the symbol of the Ḥujja, so is Noah's ark (*safīna*); only those who take their place there will find salvation. It is only through the Ḥujja that one may be conjoined with the Imam. The "Supreme Mary" (*Maryam al-Kubrā*), who in turn exemplifies the heavenly Eve, was Jesus' Ḥujja, because it was she who opened the doors of gnosis which had been closed, by being the first to appeal to ʿĪsā, the master of the new *sharīʿa*. Similarly, the "Supreme Fatima" (*Fāṭima al-Kubrā*) was the Ḥujja of the first Imam during the period of the "sixth Adam"[71] (i.e., Muhammad: for this reminiscence of Ebionism, cf. §IX below).

This syzygy allows us to interpret some surprising indications which tend to suggest that, in certain cases, this feminine Ḥujja refers to a masculine initiate. That is the case, for example, in the work of Qāḍī Nuʿmān: Jesus' virgin birth refers to his initiatory birth. During a time of occultation of the Imam, Jesus was called to his mission by an initiate who had received, for

68 Jaʿfar ibn Manṣūr al-Yaman, *Kashf*, p. 98.
69 Idrīs ʿImād al-Dīn, *Zahr al-Maʿānī*, chapter X; *Cyclical Time* . . . above, pp. 41ff.
70 Naṣīr al-Dīn Ṭūsī, *Taṣawwurāt*, [cf. *Cyclical Time* . . ., above, p. 42, n. 49], p. 50 of the Persian text; *Cyclical Time* . . ., above, pp. 46ff.
71 Jaʿfar ibn Manṣūr al-Yaman, *Kashf*, pp. 97–98; on the arithmological value of the number 290, the "cipher" of Maryam's reappearance in Fatima, cf. L. Massignon, *La Mubâhala* . . ., (above, n. 43), pp. 28ff.

that purpose, the vocation of his Angel (his heavenly *ḥadd, ḥadduhu al-ʿālī*): this is the meaning of his spiritual birth "without a father."[72] This interpretation is likewise applied to other cases, but it does not by any means lead us to a pure and simple elimination of the Feminine. For this much remains: either the Feminine appears under the guise of certain masculine designations, or else the Masculine presents itself under a feminine aspect. In either case, what is involved is a symbol of *totality*, a recurrence that is at least implicit of the symbol of the androgyne (the *mas femineus* of the alchemists, the *männliche Jungfrau* of Jacob Boehme): what is envisaged here is the Feminine in its creative spiritual function. This is how one should understand the feminine aspect under which the Imam is likewise perceived when he is designated as the "spiritual mother" (*mādar-e nafsānī*) of his initiates.[73] As the possessor of *ta'wīl*, he brings about their spiritual birth (*wilāda rūḥānīya*) and thereby exemplifies the heavenly Eve of the *Adam rūḥānī*.

This has an important implication for prophetology. It has more than once been noted that Ebionite prophetology had its continuation in Islamic prophetology in general. However, this prolongation is to be observed a great deal more authentically in the prophetology and Imamology of Ismaili Shiism. As we may recall, there is a twofold lineage here: that of the Enunciating Prophets (*Nuṭaqā'*) who proclaim the religious Laws, and that of the Imams (in groups of seven), which originates in each period with the spiritual heir (*Waṣī*) of the *Nāṭiq*. Each *Nāṭiq* forms a sort of syzygy with his *Waṣī* (Adam-Seth, Noah-Shem, Abraham-Ismael, Moses-Aaron, Jesus-Shamʿūn, Muhammad-Ali), thereby typifying the dyad of the First and Second Intelligence (*Noūs* and *Psychē*). Now because the Imam corresponds to the feminine principle, in being the source of the spiritual birth of the initiates, one might be tempted to compare this schema to the twofold lineage of Ebionite prophetology, with its masculine prophecy founded by Adam and the feminine prophecy begun by Eve. Unfortunately, as we know, in Ebionism this feminine line represents false prophecy, the demoniac element. Thus the comparison becomes a differentiation at this point,

72 Qāḍī Nuʿmān, *Asās al-Ta'wīl, Qiṣṣat ʿĪsā* [ed. Aref Tamer, Beirut, 1960, pp. 299ff.]. Here we may recall in passing the very personal exegesis of Eugene Aroux, for whom the "Ladies" in Dante's work signify the initiates of Albigensian Templarism.

73 Nāṣir-e Khusraw, *Jāmiʿ al-Ḥikmatain*, p. 242; *Wajh-e Dīn*, [ed. Gholam-Reza Aavani, Tehran, 1977, pp. 322ff.].

because Ismaili Imamology does not at all agree with that disparagement.[74] On the contrary, although it is true that the authors of the Fatimid period generally opted for the precedence of the *Nāṭiq* over the Imam, nevertheless, there is a constantly reappearing tendency in all Shiite sects, sometimes secret and sometimes explicit, to affirm and establish the priority of the Imam—i.e., the precedence of *walāya* over *nubuwwa*. Fatima is precisely the "confluence" of those two Lights.

IX.

With this reservation in mind, one can but acknowledge certain remarkable homologies between Ebionite prophetology and Ismaili prophetology. Having dealt with those similarities at length elsewhere,[75] I shall only mention here a few essential themes. These are, above all, the idea of the True Prophet and the myth of Adam. Admittedly one does encounter the idea of a succession of prophets in the Koranic text and in the *ḥadīth*, but the number of prophets who are named and the order in which they are mentioned involve quite a few variants. In fact, it is only in Ismaili gnosis that the notion of a succession implying a recurrence, as well as a specific periodization, are explicitly formulated. We have already mentioned earlier that the Cycle of Prophecy is marked off by seven periods or partial cycles (*adwār*) brought to a close by the final Imam, the *Qā'im al-Qiyāma* or Resurrector. The seven *Nāṭiqs* correspond to the "seven pillars of Wisdom" or the "hebdomad of the Mystery" as they are depicted by Ebionite prophetology—i.e., as reappearances of a *Christus aeternus* or Adam-Christus whose first form of epiphany was the initial man (cf. the text cited at n. 71 above, where Muhammad, the *Nāṭiq* of the sixth cycle, is designated as the "sixth Adam"). Yet it is with the lineage of the Imams, even more than in the line of prophets, that the theme of the True Prophet "hastening toward his place of repose" is brought into play. Undoubtedly it is natural that reflection should more easily recall the line of Imams of this current period than those of the earlier cycles (as reconstructed with the help of Biblical and extra-Biblical materials).

74 It admits, for example, certain reasons for Aaron's priority over Moses. On the other side, cf. O. Cullmann, *Die neuentdeckten Qumrantexte und das Judenchristentum der Pseudo-klementinen* (Beiheft 21 of the *Zeitschrift f.d. Neutest. Wiss.*), pp. 39 and 41, which insists on the fact that the Essenes, for their part, rejected that Ebionite radicalism which included Aaron's priesthood in the line of false prophecy.

75 Cf. *Divine Epiphany* . . ., above, §§1 and 2.

To the idea of the *Christus aeternus* there corresponds the idea of an Imam who remains unique and eternal through the persons of his theophanies. To the sinlessness of Adam (ἀναμάρτητος), who was the first of them, there corresponds the "immunity" which preserves the Most-Pure Imams from any sin or blemish (*maʿṣūm*). To the idea of Christ as the recapitulation (ἀνακεφαλαίωσις) of his predecessors and as the one in whom the True Prophet finds the place of his repose, there corresponds the idea that all the partial *Qā'ims* are "recapitulated" in the last one among them, the *Qā'im* of the *Qiyāmat al-Qiyāmāt*, whose "Temple of Light" is the *majmaʿ* or coalescence of all of the others. Jaʿfar ibn Manṣūr, in his *Kitāb al-Kashf*,[76] mentions that according to the testimony of Jābir al-Juʿfī, the *rāwī* of the fifth Imam Muḥammad Bāqir, this Imam reported that his own ancestor, the first Imam ʿAlī ibn Abī Ṭālib, proclaimed one day from the pulpit of Kūfa: "'I am the Christ (*al-Masīḥ*) who heals the blind and the lepers, who creates the birds[77] and disperses the storm-clouds (i.e., he is the "second Christ," *al-Masīḥ al-thānī*, as Jaʿfar ibn Manṣūr remarks). I am he and he is I (*anā huwa wa huwa anā*). . . . In truth, Christ is the *Qā'im bi-'l-Ḥaqq*, he is the king of this world and of the other world . . . ʿĪsā ibn Maryam is part of me and I am part of *him* (*huwa minnī wa anā minhu*).[78] He is the supreme Word of God (*Kalimat Allāh al-kubrā*). He is the Witness testifying to the mysteries, and I am That of which he testifies.' This is what the Commander of the Faithful said. In truth, the *amr Allāh*[79] is continuous (*muttaṣil*) from the first of God's Prophets and Envoys, from the first of the Imams of His religion until the last of them. Whoever obeys the last of them, it is as though he obeyed the first of them, because of this continuity of the *amr Allāh* as it passes from the first one to his immediate successor and so on down to the last." This statement, among many others, best illustrates the aspect of Ismaili Imamology which we are emphasizing here.

The idea of Adam's sinlessness has as its consequence a distinct affinity between Ebionite and Ismaili Adamology—however distant both may be from the Biblical conception and the Pauline typology.[80] The entire Ismaili

76 Cf. *Kashf*, pp. 8–9.

77 An allusion to the Koran 5:110.

78 These are exactly the terms in which the Prophet expresses himself with regard to Ali, his *Waṣī*: cf. *Safīnat Biḥār al-Anwār*, II, 192; *Kalāmi Pīr*, pp. 79 and 84 of the text.

79 Concerning the *Amr Allāh* (or *amr ilāhī*) = *inyan elohi* (*res divina*), cf. H. J. Schoeps, *Aus frühchristlicher Zeit*, Tübingen, 1950, pp. 205ff.

80 For what follows, cf. *Divine Epiphany* . . ., above, §2 (*Ebionite Adamology and Ismaili Adamology*); Idrīs ʿImād al-Dīn, *Zahr al-Maʿānī*, chapter XII; Naṣīr al-Dīn Ṭūsī, *Taṣawwurāt*, XVI.

dramaturgy of the departure from Paradise corresponds to that interpretation which attributes the entry of evil into our world not to the fall of heavenly Angels, but rather to the fall of the children of Seth, gathered together on Mount Hermon, who up to then had led the "life of Angels." The Koranic verse 2:28[30] ("When your Lord said to the Angels: 'I am going to establish a representative on earth . . .'") is here interpreted as a conversation between the last Imam of the cycle of epiphany (*dawr al-kashf*) which preceded our present cycle of occultation (*dawr al-satr*) and his disciples. The signs of the impending catastrophe induced the last Imam of that cycle to provide for the re-establishment of the Law and the discipline of the arcane, i.e., the concealment in an exoteric form of those Truths which would henceforth be accessible only through the veil of symbols. Then the events unfolded: the investiture of the young Adam (by his father, the Imam Hunayd); the order given to the "Angels" (i.e., to the *ḥudūd*, the "earthly angels") to bear witness to their obedience to him; and the refusal of Iblīs, personified then by Ḥārith ibn Murra, who represents the Darkness of that negation and denial which the Angel-Adam had cast out of himself during the "prologue in Heaven." All of this drama proceeds from one central intuition: it is not the "partial Adam," the founder of our cycle, who is responsible for the poverty and suffering of our world. The causes of evil and of death are far earlier than the present cycle of our history. The sin of "our" Adam, or rather his error, was to give in to Iblīs' suggestions out of generosity toward his fellow-souls: he wished to claim for them that knowledge of the Resurrection which had still been possessed by the people of the *dawr al-kashf*. But his request was a transgression, since it infringed on the mission which would fall to the lot of the *Qā'im*. And yet Adam's repentance, which was accepted, purged him of that error. . . .

X.

It is appropriate to connect the Ismaili conception of the cycles of Prophecy, in the way in which we have just very briefly alluded to it, with the conception that Ismailism succeeded in forming of other religions: i.e., what was the extent of its capacity to take them into account, and of its effort to integrate them and give them meaning within the cycle of its mythohistory.[81] Moreover, since the relation of gnosis to Iranian religions, and in

81 [Cf. n. 18 above.]

particular to Zoroastrianism, was and still is on our agenda, it is worth while mentioning briefly here some sources showing the meaning Ismaili theosophy gave to Zoroaster and to Zoroastrianism. It should be clearly understood that what is at question is not whether Ismailism is a reappearance of Zoroastrianism: that would be to agree with the apologists of orthodoxy (such as Baghdādī), and our preceding remarks should have shown the one-sidedness of that thesis. On the other hand, Ismailism's integration of Zoroastrian prophecy within the complete Cycle of Prophecy demonstrates both the ecumenism of Ismaili theosophy and the resources which its complex hierarchies provided for constructing a satisfactory schema of history.

We owe our information concerning this subject to a controversy which marked the fourth/tenth century and which involved four great Iranian Ismaili figures. Muḥammad Nasafī (or Nakhshabī, d. 331/942) wrote a book, the *Kitāb al-Maḥṣūl*, in reply to which Abū Ḥātim Rāzī wrote a corrective work entitled *Kitāb al-Iṣlāḥ* (several chapters of which have a valuable complement in his *Kitāb Aʿlām al-Nubuwwa*). Abū Yaʿqūb Sejestānī replied in favor of M. Nasafī, his friend, with a new book, the *Kitāb al-Nuṣra*. In turn, Ḥamīd Kermānī attempted a learned arbitration in his *Kitāb al-Riyāḍ*. We will not be able to study this important episode in the history of Ismaili thought in depth and detail until a manuscript of the *Kitāb al-Maḥṣūl* is rediscovered. On the other hand, however, thanks to Abū Ḥātim Rāzī, we can already form some idea of what was debated concerning the case of the Zoroastrians.

In no way did it involve challenging their status as Ahl al-Kitāb or refuting their claims on that point.[82] Rather, what was in question was the thesis of M. Nasafī, who connected the Zoroastrians with the religion of the third *Nāṭiq* (i.e., Abraham) and connected with that origin certain of their religious prescriptions, such as taking the sun for their *qibla* or wearing as their distinctive and symbolic sign the *zunnār* (i.e., the *kosti*). Abū Ḥātim Rāzī's own position is as subtle as it is instructive. His book *Aʿlām al-Nubuwwa* is marked by a firsthand knowledge of the Old and New Testament, as well as of other sects. There we find, for example, Daniel's vision interpreted as referring to the succession of the four great religions (Mazdaism, Judaism, Christianity, and Islam).[83] The positive valuation of

82 Contrary to what one might suppose from the too brief allusion of W. Ivanow in *Studies in Early Persian Ismailism*, 2nd ed., p. 117.

Zoroastrianism that is already indicated by this hermeneutic is further confirmed by the *Kitāb al-Iṣlāḥ*. The latter work stresses on several occasions the story which has the first Imam intervening to prevent Omar from killing the Mazdeans: "They have a Book and a Prophet, even though they have altered their Book."[84] The author observes that if the Imam does not declare that their religious code originates with Abraham, neither do the Mazdeans themselves make any such claim. They affirm that they have a Prophet (*Nabī*) and a Book; that is all. Now in addition, the rank of *Nabī* is explicitly given to Zoroaster in several statements attributed to the sixth Imam and to the Prophet himself. It was for that reason that the Prophet allowed the Zoroastrians to fulfill their obligations by means of the *jizya*, while he refused to allow this for the Arab idolaters.[85]

What Abū Ḥātim does take exception to is the thesis of M. Nakhshabī connecting the Mazdeans with the cycle of Abraham.[86] What he knows from a reliable source, having learned it from his predecessors, is that Zoroaster (Zarhusht) was one of the *Lāḥiqs*, i.e., one of the *Ḥujjas*, belonging to the cycle of the 4th *Nāṭiq*, who was Moses. One of the deputies (*khulafā'*) of the Imam, during an interreguum or period of occultation of the Imam of that time, gave Zoroaster the investiture; this was also the case with David. There are quite a number of symbols of all that which the initiate is able to decipher: there is, for example, the fact that the Mazdeans practice the deep bow (*rukū'*), which corresponds to the rank of the *Ḥujja*, and not the full prostration (*sujūd*) corresponding to the rank of the Imam. And if the Magi mention that their *Nabī* wrote for them a book of *twelve* thousand volumes (*jald*), that is likewise an allusion to the fact that he was one of the *twelve Hujjas* who were each sent out into one of the twelve *jazīras*. Finally, our author is likewise able to give an esoteric meaning to the *zunnār* (i.e., the *kosti*), the sacred cord that the Zoroastrians wear around their waist (Abū Ḥātim stresses that this is actually one of Zoroaster's prescriptions, not Abraham's): the four knots (*'aqd*: knot or "pact") refer respectively to the fourth, fifth, sixth, and seventh *Nāṭiq*—this last being the *Qā'im*, the *ṣāḥib al-dawr* or "master of the Cycle" who recapitulates it in its entirety.[87]

83 Cf. *A'lām al-nubuwwa* [ed. Salah al-Sawy, Tehran, 1977, p. 52f.]; cf. the hexaemeron of the *'ālam-e dīn* in Nāṣir-e Khusraw, *Jāmi'* . . ., p. 165.

84 For what follows, cf. *Kitāb al-Iṣlāḥ*, pp. 43–5 (personal copy).

85 *Ibid.*; cf. the *ḥadīths* grouped together in *Safīna* II, 527. The position taken by Nāṣir-e Khusraw in *Wajh-e Dīn*, pp. [333ff.] is therefore completely atypical.

86 Likewise for the *Kalāmi Pīr* (p. 65), Zoroaster was a *Ḥujja* of the Imam, who appeared at the end of Abraham's period.

What Abū Ḥātim knows very well is that after the Zoroastrians' *Nabī* had set up the laws of their belief for them, the Magi altered those rules and made substitutions in them, just as the Jews had done after Moses and the Christians after Jesus. This was the work of the Antagonist, who is never absent from any period of Prophecy. Their wise *Nabī* had taught them, for example, that the totality of being encompasses two principles (*aṣl*): the *mubdaʿ* and the *makhlūq*, i.e., the eternally originated (*dār al-ibdāʿ*) and the creatural world. But they changed this doctrine so as to set up a *Mubdiʿ* and a *Khāliq* as eternal antagonists. In other words, Abū Ḥātim quite clearly recognizes that there is on the one hand the syzygial duality of the invisible heavenly Pleroma (*dār al-Ibdāʿ*) and the visible world, corresponding to the pair *mēnok-gētīk* in the Pahlavi texts—and on the other hand, there is the dualism of the two principles Ōhrmazd and Ahriman. Now if one observes in an Ismaili of the tenth century the awareness of this difference, along with the positive valuation [of Zoroaster] it makes possible, that will provide a context for viewing Suhrawardi's effort, in the twelfth century, at founding his doctrine of *Ishrāq* on a revivification of the wisdom of ancient Persia, as he understood it.

This positive valorization which relieves Zoroaster of the responsibility for the dualism of the Magi postulates in addition a larger historical construction the elements of which are outlined in the *Kitāb Aʿlam al-Nubuwwa*. The upshot of this story is that the alteration of the doctrine of Zoroaster (Zarhusht) was the work of a certain Zāratos,[88] whose master was a disciple of Pythagoras who had come to Persia.[89] This involves a curious mixture of traditions, which should be studied in the overall context of the legends of Zoroaster. Abū Ḥātim mentions traditions which have Zoroaster living in the time of Jamshīd, and which identify Jamshīd with Solomon the son of David. Thus one can glimpse the twofold trace of traditions which on the one side connect Zoroaster's activity to the Semitic religious world, while on the other side they relate him to the legend of Pythagoras. But it seems that

87 *Kitāb al-Iṣlāḥ* [above, n. 84]; it is remarkable that Abū Ḥātim already knew a symbolism of the four knots of the *kosti*, while in our own day an Orientalist, Junker, interpreted them in turn as the symbol of a Zervanite tetrad: cf. *Cyclical Time* . . ., above, p. 28.

88 *Ibid.*, pp. 118ff.

89 *Ibid.*, pp. 118 and 129. Shahrastānī, at the end of his notice on Pythagoras, likewise mentions this disciple; unfortunately, the identification of these proper names would require further research. Cf. also Cumont and Bidez, *Mages hellénisés*, I, pp. 36ff., 103ff.; II, pp. 37 and 48.

a certain splitting of his person has occurred, either as a reflection or as a consequence of the variations of this prophet's name in Greek (Ζωροάστρης and Ζαράδυς or Ζάρατος). In fact, Abū Ḥātim does distinguish between a Zoroaster (Zarhusht) who is the founder of the Magi, and a Zāratos who was the corrupter of his doctrine. Here, indeed, the legendary theme contains its aspect of truth, since it expresses all that distance which in reality separates Zoroaster the original Iranian prophet from the figure of Zoroaster as the Chaldean Magus.

As for the insertion of Zoroaster in the esoteric hierarchy of the *da'wa* as the *Ḥujja* of the fourth *Nāṭiq*, that follows from an archetypal image which orders historical time according to the modality of a liturgical time, since it involves a Cycle. The entry of particular personages into that cyclical time is governed by the ritual form of a cosmic liturgy, according to the function that they assume there. Here there are no pre-existent material facts in an immediate state already situated by themselves. Instead, it is the mode of perception which is *situative*, which orders and controls the structures and relations according to the significance perceived—which here, for example, *situates* Zoroaster's appearance during the course of the fourth cycle. In the same manner, Mazdean prophetology *situates* Zarathustra's appearance on earth during the transition from the second to the third triad of millennia (at the time of Ahriman's invasion of the world), because it perceives in him the reappearance of the primordial Man. Likewise, when still another tradition *situates* him six millennia before Plato, that is because it perceives Plato as *Zarathustra redivivus*, the Savior who is to conclude the Aiōn.[90] The mode of perception is itself part of the "fact," whose meaning can only emerge thanks to a structure of which this mode of perception is itself a constitutive element.

For this reason, too, there are other figures which our theosophers cannot so easily succeed in integrating. The case of the Sabeans, of whom it was said that they had once been Christians, both typifies and allows one to classify what cannot be put into the other categories. The Sabeans likewise derived from a *Lāḥiq* or *Ḥujja* whose doctrine, like that of Zoroaster, was unfortunately corrupted by an agent of the eternal Antagonist. Similarly, Mazdak, Mani, and Bardesanes (Dayṣān) each acted, in their cycles, as adversaries of the *Lawāḥiq*, in the same way that the First Antagonist acted

90 Cf. H. S. Nyberg, *Die Religionen des alten Iran* [(Deutsch von H. H. Schaeder), Leipzig, 1938,] pp. 29–30.

towards the one who was the foundation of the Imamate. Thus Abū Ḥātim rigorously distinguishes their case from that of Zoroaster.[91] And Abū Yaʿqūb Sejestānī explains that Mazdak and Bēhāfarīd added their own prescriptions to those of Abraham (since for Abū Yaʿqūb, as for his friend M. Nasafī, Zoroaster's religion was the religion of Abraham), in the same way that Mani, Bardesanes, and Marcion added their ideas to those of Jesus, while believing that they were carrying out the work of renovators. In short, the first of these were, in relation to the Zoroastrians, what the misguided Sabeans were in relation to the Christians.

Clearly it would have been difficult to expect the occurrence of an open rehabilitation or revalorization of the names of these figures, whose doctrines are most often reduced to more or less accurately condensed formulas. The problem that the existence of their sects posed for our theosophers was quite different from the case of the Zoroastrians as *Ahl al-Kitāb*. However, they did appeal to them enough for Hishām ibn al-Ḥakam to establish those "relations" which we have recalled earlier here (§IV). All the more significant, then, is the reactivation of those archetypal themes which took place freely, so to speak, under the cover of anonymity. Let us conclude with this example: Abū Yaʿqūb Sejestānī analyses in detail the symbolic concordance between the four branches of the Christian Cross and the four words making up the *shahāda*. Then he contemplates the mystery of the Night of Destiny (*laylat al-Qadr*), whose mystical light transfigures all things, when suddenly there appears before his mental vision the image—perfectly recognizable to us—of the "Cross of Light" of the Acts of John and of Manichaeism.[92]

Our aim here was only to assemble certain indications and to bring together certain themes, not at all to sketch a systematization which would necessarily be premature, given the present state of our knowledge. Yet one can already foresee what larger scope will be given to a whole segment of the science of religions on that day—let us hope it will be soon—when we will at last be able to study those Coptic gnostic texts, already discovered some 10 years ago, in conjunction with the texts that Ismaili collections still hold in reserve. Gnosis was not born in Islam in the Middle Ages, any more than it is a simple Christian heresy of the first centuries of our era; rather, it is something that existed long before Christianity. There was a gnosis in

91 *Aʿlām*, pp. [69ff.].
92 *Kitāb al-Yanābīʿ*, *Yanbūʿ* 31; cf. *Divine Epiphany* . . ., above, pp. 101–2.

Christianity; there has been one, and perhaps there still is, in Islam—and perhaps it may yet provide for an unforeseeable spiritual encounter between Orient and Occident. For gnosis itself, in all its manifold forms and variants, also deserves to be called a *Weltreligion*.

Subject Index

A

B

C

D

M

N

Q

R

S

T

U

V

W

X

Y

Z

Index of Authors and Titles

A

B

C

D

E

F

G

H

I

J